S. Chandrasekhar: Man of Science

Subrahmanyan Chandrasekhar (1910–95) discovered the Chandrasekhar limit at the age of nineteen, paving the way for the discovery of neutron stars and black holes. He was awarded the Padma Vibhushan in 1968 and the Nobel Prize in Physics in 1983.

Radhika Ramnath is a software professional based in Delhi whose career has spanned working with both government and multinational research organizations. She is the daughter of Chandrasekhar's youngest brother, and so had the opportunity to know him closely as well as hear him lecture on numerous occasions.

Chandrasekhara Iyer
m
Parvati

- **C.S. Ayyar (Babuji)** *m* **Sitalakshmi (Amma)**
- **C.V. Raman**
- **C. Ramaswamy** (Ramudu / Kunjappa)

Children of C.S. Ayyar and Sitalakshmi:

- **Rajalakhmi (Rajakka)** *m* **A.S. Ganesan** — Sriram, Sadasiv, Bagavant, Vasanti* (m V.H. Ram*), Uma*, Sekhar
- **Balaparvati (Chinakka)** *m* **P. Visvanathan** — Shanta, Kamala, Krishnan, Chander*, Vimala, Susheela, Seetha
- **Chandrasekhar (Anna / Ayya)** *m* **Lalitha***
- **Visvanathan (Chinanna)** *m* **Rajalakshmi** — Prem, Indira, Shiv*, Padmini
- **Balakrishnan* (Balanna) m Shyamala** — Malathi* (*m* Ramanthan*), Revathy
- **Ramnath** *m* **Shant** — Radhika*
- **Sundari** *m* **Ramaswamy** — Nalini*, Shyam
- **Savitri (Savitriakka)** *m* **Rajamani** — Sudha*, Rajini, Radha*
- **Vidya* (Vidyakka) m Shankar** — Shivakumar, Mahesh*, Sunder
- **Sarada (Saradakka)** *m* **Dorairajan** — Raghu, Ashok*, Harsha, Sumana, Bharath*

Note 1: Chandrasekhara Iyer and Parvati had four more children who haven't been listed here.

*Note 2: * denotes people who have contributed to this volume.*

S. Chandrasekhar

Man of Science

Edited by

RADHIKA RAMNATH

Foreword by

A.P.J. ABDUL KALAM

HarperCollins *Publishers* India

First published India by
HarperCollins *Publishers* in 2011
An imprint of HarperCollins Publishers
HarperCollins *Publishers* India, Cyber City, Building 10-A, Gurugram, Haryana-122002, India
www.harpercollins.co.in

1 2 3 4 5 6 7 8 9 10

P-ISBN: 9789350294406
E-ISBN: 9789350299593

Typeset in Cronos Pro 11/14

Printed and bound at
Manipal Technologies Limited, Manipal

*

HarperCollins *Publishers*, Macken House, 39/40 Mayor Street Upper, Dublin 1, D01 C9W8, Ireland

Contents

Editor's Note

19 October 2010 marks the centenary of noted astrophysicist and Nobel laureate Subrahmanyan Chandrasekhar. On this special occasion, this book attempts to re-introduce the common reader to Prof Chandrasekhar – the thinker, the scientist, and the man. The first part of this book is a collection of some of his more general essays and lectures, in which he lucidly and beautifully presents his views on several thought-provoking subjects, while the second part comprises a series of reminiscences by members of his family, including his wife Lalitha who celebrated her 100th birthday this year.

Chandra – the name he is known by throughout the scientific world – left India for Cambridge in 1930 at the age of nineteen, after graduating from Presidency College, Madras (now Chennai). On this voyage to England he discovered what later came to be known as the Chandrasekhar limit – considered to be one of the most significant discoveries in astrophysics in the twentieth century since it led to the discovery of neutron stars and black holes. He was awarded a Ph.D in 1933, after which he was elected a Fellow of Trinity College, Cambridge. In 1936, he returned to India and married Lalitha Doraiswamy, his fellow student from Presidency College. They went back to Cambridge, and almost immediately proceeded to Chicago, where he joined the faculty of the University of Chicago at the Yerkes Observatory; he remained with the University of Chicago till the end of his life.

In a career spanning over sixty years, Chandra's distinctive style of research resulted in a large number of papers and monographs, which have had a dramatic and lasting influence on several fields of astronomy and astrophysics. In the last years of his life, Chandra focussed on a study of Newton's *Principia*, reworking Newton's proofs using modern scientific methods. His book based on this work was published just shortly before his death in Chicago on 21 August 1995. He is survived by his wife Lalitha.

Among the many international prizes and honours bestowed on him are the National Medal of Science of the United States (1966), Padma Vibhushan (1968), Copley Prize of the Royal Society of London (1984) and the Nobel Prize in physics (1983).

The main themes covered in the selected essays and other writings in Part One of this book are his thoughts on the pursuit of science, creativity, his work, and his abiding closeness to India. He always illustrates his thoughts with examples from the lives and experiences of other great men, never from his own. As he states in his lecture 'The Pursuit of Science: Its Motivations', quoting Turgenev: 'We are speaking of other people, why bring in yourself?'

In this lecture, as well as in most of the others in which he talks about motivation and creativity, he draws deeply from the lives and works of giants in the fields of science, art and literature. In 'Newton and Michelangelo', he compares the minds and achievements of these geniuses – the scientist he considered to be the greatest ever, and the artist whose work had a huge impact on him. His deep respect and admiration for Newton also comes through clearly in his convocation address at Queen's University.

His continuing closeness and ties with India find expression in his 1968 Nehru Memorial lecture, his essay on 'Science in Pre- and Post-Independence India' as well as in 'Indira Gandhi: Some Recollections'.

The collection would not be complete without at least a brief exposure to some of his work. Though most of his work is too technical and complex for a lay reader, in his talk 'Know about Black Holes', his simple and masterly explanation of black holes ensures that anyone with a school-level knowledge of physics can understand the concept.

Part Two includes reminiscences by family members who knew Chandra personally and interacted with him at different stages of his life. These recollections focus on the person that Chandrasekhar was and the life that he led, more than the brilliant man of science that the world knows him to be. His wife Lalitha's reminiscences (written two years after he passed away) cover the sixty years of their lives together and the challenges they faced, while his brother Balakrishnan and sister Vidya start from the days of their shared childhood in Madras and traverse through the years that they lived apart. The interactions with his nephews and nieces bring out the person he was when he was already a celebrated scientist.

The writings and articles in this collection have been selected so as to cover the various aspects that made him the legend he is, and I hope we have been successful in that attempt.

Finally, I would like to add that for me, personally, it has been an honour to have been associated with bringing out this book on the occasion of my uncle's centenary and my aunt's 100th year.

New Delhi
November 2010

Radhika Ramnath

FOREWORD

IT IS INDEED A PRIVILEGE TO WRITE THE FOREWORD FOR THIS UNIQUE book on Professor Subrahmanyan Chandrasekhar, astrophysicist and Nobel laureate, in his centenary year. Chandrasekhar belonged to a family where discipline, achievement, focus and relationships were regarded all-important. Chandrasekhar was the nephew of Sir Chandrasekhara Venkata Raman, who won the Nobel Prize in physics in 1930. As a schoolboy, he would often go to the Marina Beach in Chennai, where he would reflect upon the vastness of the sea, and dream of growing up to be like Newton.

Chandrasekhar studied at Presidency College, Chennai, and then went to Trinity College, Cambridge, for his Ph.D. His sea voyage became history since his reflections on the ship's deck became the starting point for some very significant discoveries in astrophysics. Chandrasekhar is a good example of the teaching–research–teaching paradigm. In his own words, he taught a class of two students as diligently as a class of twenty, and that his 'entire class won the Nobel Prize'.

Radhika Ramnath, the editor of this book, is the daughter of Chandrasekhar's brother and my colleague, Dr Ramnath. The book is organized in two parts. The first part deals with Chandrasekhar's essays and writings which address everything from his views on science to society.

In his lecture on the pursuit of science, we find profound reflections on the lives and accomplishments of some of the great scientists of yore. The lecture dwells on the uniqueness of Kepler and the path he cleared for Newton. Citing examples, Chandrasekhar talks about scientists who could not enjoy the fruits of their labour fully, or did not receive the approval of contemporaries even after years of hard work.

Chandrasekhar eloquently states the importance of the unsung rigours of scientific work. 'The pursuit of science has often been compared to the scaling of mountains, high and not so high. But who amongst us can hope, even in imagination, to scale the Everest and reach its summit when the sky is blue and the air is still; and in the stillness of the air survey the entire Himalayan range in the dazzling white of the snow stretching to infinity. None of us can hope for a comparable vision of nature and of the universe around us. But there is nothing mean or lowly in standing in the valley below and awaiting the sun to rise over the Kanchenjunga.'

In the lecture on Newton and Michelangelo, Chandrasekhar explores whether there is any similarity between the motivations of scientists and artists in their respective creative quests. He confirms a single creative axis. 'When a supremely great mind is kindled, it leaves a blazing trail that remains a beacon for centuries.' I find these words of his quite appropriate for the occasion. His own gifted mind made a huge impact on the world of science, a blazing trail that has shone the path to very many researchers over the years and which will continue to do so for a long time to come.

In the article on astronomy and human culture, Chandrasekhar traces astronomy to antiquity and establishes its role in expanding the realm of human curiosity about the universe. The description of his interaction with Indira Gandhi offers an insight into the life of a leader saddled with development issues in a parliamentary democracy.

In the second part of the book, Chandrasekhar comes alive as a human being through the writings of his wife, brothers, nephews, nieces and other members of his wonderful family.

Lalitha Chandrasekhar, his wife, says that the 'steel of his determination won over the threat of Fate' and 'in this indomitable conflict, Fate had to accept defeat for a while.' She describes the way Chandrasekhar looked at his subject: 'I called the arrangements of all the details a formal garden; the errors were the weeds which had to be pulled out'. Chandrasekhar dedicated his passionate work on Newton's *Principia* to his wife.

We get a glimpse of the early experiences of the siblings, which nudged them towards an understanding of the need for discipline and made them realize why it was necessary to aspire for the stars. This upbringing has stood the whole family in good stead and enabled its members to strive for excellence in their fields of choice. Chandrasekhar, being the eldest son, was treated both as a role model and a responsible member of the family.

Even while away from home and engrossed in his intense research, Chandrasekhar maintained his connection with frequent telephone calls, letters and visits when possible. For every member of the family, particularly youngsters, he would send books that he would later discuss with them.

Chandrasekhar firmly believed that a scientist's life would be richer if it included, among the various influences, art and music. This culminated in 1975 in his lecture 'Shakespeare, Newton and Beethoven – Patterns of Creativity'.

The reminiscences of the family members clearly bring out how a person who dedicates himself to a cause that keeps him completely occupied in a different part of the world can stay connected to his roots, gratefully celebrate the memories of the past, reciprocate the love of the extended family, and continue to motivate the coming generations in unique ways.

This book will be an effective guide in the lives of the denizens of the modern, globalized world in which distances might have shrunk through electronic connectivity, but the need for bonding and togetherness is felt much more urgently. Such bonds could enrich families, countries and the world.

Chandra is celebrated in the country of his birth, the countries of his work, and throughout the world. The American astronomer Carl Sagan, who studied mathematics under Chandrasekhar at the University of Chicago, summed up the man and his science best: 'I discovered what true mathematical elegance is from Subrahmanyan Chandrasekhar.'

I hope the readers of this book benefit from the treasure of insights into the great man's life and thoughts, and that, having read this inspiring volume, they are truly motivated to pursue the 'consuming passion' of their lives.

APJ Abdul Kalam

Part I

Selected Lectures and Essays

one

The Pursuit of Science: Its Motivations[1]

I am grateful to President Ramaseshan for assigning to me the privilege of addressing you on this occasion celebrating the Golden Jubilee of this Academy. But for the tragedy which engulfed the country on October 31st of last year, this celebration should have taken place on November 7th, the 96th birthday of the Academy's illustrious founder and its President for its first 35 years. That this occasion is a moving one for my wife—a former student of Professor Raman—and myself must be obvious to you; and I shall not expand on it. That the occasion is also precious to me, on scientific grounds, derives not only from my having been a fellow of this Academy for all of its fifty years, but equally from the purposes to which this Academy is dedicated. Unlike other national academies, it has not sought, nor has it strived, to influence the public policies of the national government; nor has it followed the practice of awarding innumerable prizes, lectureships, and medals. The purpose of

1 Inaugural address at the Golden Jubilee Meeting of the Indian Academy of Sciences, Bangalore, 6 February 1985

this Academy, as enunciated by its founder, is to promote the pursuit of science in this country by providing journals and periodicals for the publication of scientific papers of the highest standards, and avoiding the necessity to seek foreign avenues.

During Professor Raman's lifetime, the Proceedings of the Academy, both series A and B, were published without lapse and without delay. Since 1970, when the affairs of the Academy passed on to his successors, this prime objective has so remained. By the efforts, principally of President Ramaseshan, the number of journals which are presently sponsored by the Academy has increased almost tenfold. And all these journals do indeed maintain the highest standards by strict refereeing. I cannot wish for the future of the Academy any better than to express confidently the hope that the steadily increasing standards of the past ten years will be sustained during the next fifty years.

* * *

I now turn with some apprehension to the subject of my address, 'The Pursuit of Science: Its Motivations'. This is a difficult subject if one is to avoid the common and the banal. The difficulty derives in large measure from the variety and the range of the motives of the individual scientists; they are varied and they are diverse: they are as varied as the tastes, the temperaments, and the attitudes of the scientists themselves. Besides, the motivations are subject to substantial changes during the lifetimes of the scientists. Indeed, it is difficult to discern a common denominator. What is it then, one can usefully say?

I shall skirt the problem and restrict myself to reflections—perhaps, disjointed—on the lives and the accomplishments of some of the great scientists of the past. And I shall, whenever possible, base my remarks on what they have themselves said or written. But reflecting on the motives and the attitudes of great men is beset with grave semantic difficulties of communication: the words and phrases that language allows in these contexts may suggest criticism or judgement. Therefore, let me make it clear from the outset that my remarks, at no place, are to be construed as having overtones or undertones of criticism or judgement. Indeed,

I have no rights to such criticism or judgement in the contexts I shall be speaking. I should also make it clear that during the course of my reflections that I shall present, thoughts derived from my own personal experience have been entirely absent. Since it may not be possible for me to emphasize these points at every stage, I shall begin with a quotation and a narration.

The quotation is from the concluding pages of Turgenev's *On the Eve* in which there is a statement by that silent but indomitable character Insarov: 'We are speaking of other people; why bring in yourself?'

My narration is of a conversation between Majorana and Fermi in the middle twenties when both of them were also in their middle twenties. (The conversation was reported to me by one who was present on the occasion.)

> **Majorana**: There are scientists who 'happen' only once in every 500 years, like Archimedes or Newton. And there are scientists who happen only once or twice in a century, like Einstein or Bohr.
> **Fermi**: But where do I come in, Majorana?
> **Majorana**: Be reasonable, Enrico! I am not talking about you or me. I am talking about Einstein and Bohr.

Since I shall be talking principally about scientists in the class of Einstein, Bohr, and Fermi, I should indeed be 'reasonable'.

One final reservation. The circumference of my comprehension does not extend beyond a very limited circle of the physical sciences. This is, of course, a most serious limitation when I am addressing myself to so general a theme; but I must abide by my limitation.

***

For a discussion of the motivations which impel one to pursue the goals of science, no example is better than that of Johannes Kepler. Kepler's uniqueness derives from the position he singly occupies at the great crossroads where science shed its enveloping dogmas and the pathway was prepared for Newton. Kepler, in his inquiries, asked questions that none before him, including Copernicus, had asked. Kepler's laws differ qualitatively from earlier assumptions about planetary orbits: the assertion that planetary orbits 'are ellipses' in no way resembles the kind of improvements that his predecessors had sought. In his analysis of the motions of the planets, Kepler was not preoccupied with geometrical questions; he asked, instead, questions such as 'what is the origin of planetary motions?', 'If the sun is at the centre of the solar system, as it is in the Copernican scheme, should not that fact be discernible in the motions and in the orbits of the planets themselves?'. These are questions in physics; not in some preconceived geometrical framework.

While Kepler's approach to the problem of planetary motions was radically different from that of anyone before him, his work is pre-eminent for the manner in which he extracted general laws from a careful examination of the observations. His examination was long and it was arduous: it took him twenty and more years of constant and persistent effort; but he never lost sight of his goal. For him, it was a search for the Holy Grail in a very literal sense.

Before I describe the manner of Kepler's search, I should like to say that I am in no sense a scholar of medieval astronomy. My knowledge of Kepler is in fact mostly derived from Arthur Koestler's *The Sleep-walkers: A History of Man's Changing Vision of the Universe*, some collateral reading, and some discussions with scholars who know very much more. Koestler's sensitive account of Kepler, his life and his achievements, includes numerous quotations from Kepler's own writings. My remarks are largely based on these quotations.

From the outset Kepler realized that a careful study of the orbit of Mars will provide the key to planetary motions because its orbit departs from a circle the most; and it had defeated Copernicus; and further that an analysis of the accurate observations of Tycho Brahe was an essential prerequisite. As Kepler wrote:

> Let all keep silence and hark to Tycho who has devoted thirty-five years to his observations.... For Tycho alone do I wait; he shall explain to me the order and arrangement of the orbits....

> Tycho possesses the best observations, and thus so-to-speak the material for the building of the new edifice....
>
> ...I believe it was an act of Divine Providence that I arrived just at the time when Longomontanus was occupied with Mars. For Mars alone enables us to penetrate the secrets of astronomy which otherwise would remain forever hidden from us...

Indeed, Kepler went to extraordinary lengths to acquire the observations of Tycho which he so badly needed. It is not an exaggeration to say that he committed larceny; for, as he confessed: 'I confess that when Tycho died, I quickly took advantage of the absence, or lack of circumspection, of the heirs, by taking the observations under my care, or perhaps usurping them....' And as he explained:

> The cause of this quarrel lies in the suspicious nature and bad manners of the Brahe family, but on the other hand also in my own passionate and mocking character. It must be admitted that Tengnagel had important reasons for suspecting me. I was in possession of the observations and refused to hand them over to the heirs....

With Tycho's observations thus acquired, the question which Kepler constantly asked himself was: If the sun is indeed the origin and the source of planetary motions, then, how does this fact manifest itself in the motions of the planets themselves? Noticing that Mars moved a little faster when it is nearest the sun than when it is farthest, and 'remembering Archimedes', he determined the area described by the radius vector joining the sun to the instantaneous position of Mars, as we follow it in its orbit. As Kepler wrote:

> Since I was aware that there exists an infinite number of points on the orbit and accordingly an infinite number of distances [from the sun], the idea occurred to me that the sum of these distances is contained in the *area* of the orbit. For I remembered that in the same manner Archimedes too divided the area of a circle into an infinite number of triangles.

This was the way Kepler discovered in July 1603 his law of areas. This is the second of his three great laws in Newton's enumeration that has been adopted ever since. The establishment of this result took Kepler some five years; for, already prior to the publication of his *Mysterium Cosmographicum* in 1596, Kepler had sought for such a law in connection with his association of the five regular solids with the existence of the six planets known in his time.

The law of areas determined the variation of the speed along its orbit; but it did not determine the shape of the orbit. A year before he had arrived at his final statement of the law of areas, he had in fact discarded circular orbits for the planets: and in October of 1602 he had written: 'The conclusion is quite simply that the planet's path is not a circle—it curves inward on both sides and outward again at opposite ends. Such a curve is called an oval. The orbit is not a circle, but an oval figure.'

Even after having concluded that the orbit of Mars is an 'oval', it took him an additional three years to establish that the orbit was in fact an ellipse. And when that was established he wrote:

> Why should I mince my words? The truth of Nature, which I had rejected and chased away, returned by stealth through the back door, disguising itself to be accepted. That is to say, I laid [the original equation] aside, and fell back on ellipses, believing that this was a quite different hypothesis, whereas the two, as I shall prove in the next chapter, are one and the same.... I thought and searched, until I went nearly mad, for a reason, why the planet preferred an elliptical orbit [to mine].... Ah, what a foolish bird I have been!

At long last in 1608 his monumental *Astronomia Nova* was published. As Koestler has written:

> It was a beautifully printed volume in folio, of which only a few copies survive. The Emperor [Rudolph] claimed the whole edition as his property and forbade Kepler to sell or give away any copy of it 'without our foreknowledge and consent'. But since his salary was in arrears, Kepler felt at liberty to do as he liked, and

> sold the whole edition to the printers. Thus the story of the *New Astronomy* begins and ends with acts of larceny, committed *ad majorem Dei gloriam*.

Ten more years were to elapse before Kepler discovered his third law: that the squares of the periods of revolution of any two planets is in the ratio of the cubes of their mean distances from the sun. The law is stated in his *Harmonice Mundi* completed in 1618. Here is how Kepler describes his discovery:

> On 8 March of this present year 1618, if precise dates are wanted, [the solution] turned up in my head. But I had an unlucky hand and when I tested it by computations I rejected it as false. In the end it came back again to me on 15 May, and in a new attack conquered the darkness of my mind; it agreed so perfectly with the data which my seventeen years of labour on Tycho's observations had yielded, that I thought at first I was dreaming.

Thus ended Kepler's long and arduous search for his holy grail.

In his first book, *Mysterium Cosmographicum*, Kepler exclaimed: 'Oh! that we could live to see the day when both sets of figures agree with each other.'

Twenty-two years later, he added the following footnote to this exclamation in a reprint edition of *Mysterium Cosmographicum* after he had discovered his third law and his poignant cry had been answered: 'We have lived to see this day after 22 years and rejoice in it, at least I did; I trust that Maestlin and many other men will share in my joy!'

***

In his novel, *The Redemption of Tycho Brahe*, Max Brod, the Czech writer who is known for his publishing, posthumously, the great works of Franz Kafka, portrays and contrasts the characters of Tycho Brahe and Kepler. While Brod's novel is historically, grossly inaccurate, yet the following imagined perception of Kepler by Tycho is an artist's idealization of what a scientist like Kepler might have been:

> Kepler now inspired him [Tycho] with a feeling of awe. The tranquility with which he applied himself to his labours and entirely ignored the warblings of flatterers was to Tycho almost superhuman. There was something incomprehensible in its absence of emotion, like a breath from a distant region of ice....

Is the tranquility and the absence of emotion which Brod attributes to his imagined Kepler, ever attained by a practising scientist?

May I digress a little at this point to say that Max Brod, when he wrote his novel, *The Redemption of Tycho,* was one of a small group in Prague that included Einstein and Franz Kafka. It has been said that Brod's portrayal of Kepler was influenced by his association with Einstein. Thus Walter Nemst is reported to have said to Einstein, 'You are this man Kepler.'

***

As I have stated, the most remarkable aspect of Kepler's pursuit of science is the constancy with which he applied himself to his chosen quest. To use a phrase of Shelley's, his 'was a character superior in singleness'. But does the example of Kepler provide any assurance of success for a similar constancy in others? I shall consider two examples.

First, the example of Michelson. His main preoccupation throughout his life was to measure the velocity of light with increasing precision. His interest came about almost by accident, when the Commander of the Naval Academy asked him (then an instructor at the Academy) to prepare some lecture demonstrations to illustrate Foucault's refinement of Cornu's determination of the velocity of light. That was in 1878; and it led to Michelson's first determination of the velocity of light in 1880. On the 7th of May 1931, two days before he died and fifty years later, he dictated the opening sentences of a paper that was posthumously published and which gave the results of his last measurement. Michelson's efforts resulted in an improvement in our knowledge of the velocity of light from 1 part in 3000 to 1 part in 30,000, i.e., by a factor 10. But by 1973 the accuracy had been improved to 1 part in 10^{10}, a measurement that made obsolete, beforehand, all future measurements. Were Michelson's efforts over 50 years then in vain? Leaving that question aside, one must record that during his long career, Michelson made great discoveries derived from his delight in 'light waves and their uses'. Thus, his development of interferometry leading to the first direct determination of the diameter of a star is wondrous. And who does not know the Michelson-Morley experiment which, through Einstein's formulation of the special and the general theory of relativity, changed and changed irrevocably our understanding of the nature of space and time? But it is a curious fact that Michelson himself was never happy with the outcome of his experiment. Indeed, it is recorded that when Einstein visited Michelson in April 1931, Mrs Michelson felt it necessary to warn Einstein, 'Please don't get him started on the ether.'

A second example is Eddington who devoted the last 16 years of his life to developing his 'fundamental theory'. Of this prodigious effort he said, a year before he died: 'At no time during the past 16 years have I felt any doubt about the correctness of my theory.'

Yet, his efforts have left no trace on subsequent developments.

Is it wise then to pursue science with a single objective and with a singleness of purpose?

***

While Kepler provides the supreme example of sustained scientific effort leading to great and fundamental discoveries, there are instances in which great thoughts have seemingly occurred spontaneously. Thus, Dirac has written that his work on Poisson brackets and on his relativistic wave equation of the electron were consequences of ideas '...which had just come out of the blue. I could not very well say just how it had occurred to me. And I felt that work of this kind was a rather "undeserved success".'

Dirac's recollection, that his ideas underlying his work on Poisson brackets and his relativistic wave equation of the electron came to him 'out of the blue', is an example of what is apparently not a unique phenomenon: Those who have made great discoveries seem to remember and cherish the occasions on which they made them. Thus, Einstein has recorded that:

> When in 1907 I was working on a comprehensive paper on the special theory of relativity ... there occurred to me the happiest thought of my life ... that 'for *an observer falling freely from the roof of a house there exists*—at least in his immediate surroundings—*no gravitational field.*'

This 'happy thought' was, of course, later enshrined in his principle of equivalence that is at the base of his general theory of relativity.

A recollection in a similar vein is that of Fermi. I had once the occasion to ask Fermi, in the context of Hadamard's perceptive 'Essay on the Psychology of Invention in the Mathematical Field' what the psychology of invention in the realm of physics might be. Fermi responded by narrating the occasion of his discovery of the effect of slow neutrons on induced radioactivity. This is what he said:

> I will tell you how I came to make the discovery which I suppose is the most important one I have made. We were working very hard on the neutron-induced radioactivity and the results we were obtaining made no sense. One day, as I came to the laboratory, it occurred to me that I should examine the effect of placing a piece of lead before the incident neutrons. Instead of my usual custom, I took great pains to have the piece of lead precisely machined. I was clearly dissatisfied with something; I tried every excuse to postpone putting the piece of lead in its place. When finally, with some reluctance, I was going to put it in place, I said to myself: 'No, I do not want this piece of lead here; what I want is a piece of paraffin.' It was just like that with no advance warning, no conscious prior reasoning. I immediately took some odd piece of paraffin and placed it where the piece of lead was to have been.

Perhaps the most moving statement in this general context is that of Heisenberg relating the moment when the laws of quantum mechanics came to a sharp focus in his mind. He has written:

> One evening I reached the point where I was ready to determine the individual terms in the energy table, or, as we put it today, in the energy matrix, by what would now be considered an extremely clumsy series of calculations. When the first terms seemed to accord with the energy principle, I became rather excited, and I began to make countless arithmetical errors. As a result, it was almost three o'clock in the morning before the final result of my computations lay before me. The energy principle had held for all terms, and I could no longer doubt the mathematical consistency and coherence of the kind of quantum mechanics to which my calculations pointed. At first, I was deeply alarmed. I had the feeling that, through the surface of atomic phenomena, I was looking at a strangely beautiful interior, and felt almost giddy at the thought that I now had to probe this wealth of mathematical structures nature had so generously spread out before me. I was far too excited to sleep, and so, as a new day dawned, I made for the southern tip of the island, where I had been longing to climb a rock jutting out into the sea. I now did so without too much trouble, and waited for the sun to rise.

There is no difficulty for any of us to share in Heisenberg's exhilaration of that supreme moment: we all know of the difficulties and paradoxes that beset the 'old' Bohr-Sommerfeld quantum-theory of the time; and we also know of Heisenberg's long puzzlement over these difficulties and paradoxes with Sommerfeld, Bohr, and Pauli. And he had already published at that time his paper with Kramers on the dispersion theory—a theory which in many ways was the precursor to the developments that were to follow.

But what is our reaction to Heisenberg's account of his ideas on the theory of elementary particles that he developed some thirty years later, after his tragic experiences during the war and his disappointments and frustrations of the post-war years? Mrs. Heisenberg, in her book on her husband, has written:

> One moonlight night we walked all over the Hainberg Mountain, and he was completely enthralled by the visions he had, trying to

> explain his newest discovery to me. He talked about the miracle of symmetry as the original archetype of creation, about harmony, about the beauty of simplicity, and its inner truth.

And she quotes from one of Heisenberg's letters to her sister at this time:

> In fact, the last few weeks were full of excitement for me. And perhaps I can best illustrate what I have experienced through the analogy that I have attempted, an as yet unknown ascent to the fundamental peak of atomic theory, with great efforts during the past five years. And now, with the peak directly ahead of me, the whole terrain of interrelationships in atomic theory is suddenly and clearly spread out before my eyes. That these interrelationships display, in all their mathematical abstraction, an incredible degree of simplicity, is a gift we can only accept humbly. Not even Plato could have believed them to be so beautiful. For these interrelationships cannot be invented; they have been there since the creation of the world.

You will notice the remarkable similarity in the language and in the phraseology of this description with the description of his discovery of the basic rules of quantum mechanics some thirty years earlier. But do we share in his second vision in the same way? In the earlier case, his ideas won immediate acceptance. In contrast, his ideas on particle physics were rejected and repudiated even by his long-time critic and friend Pauli. But it is moving to read what Mrs Heisenberg writes towards the end of her biography.

> With smiling certainty, he once said to me: 'I was lucky enough to look over the good Lord's shoulder while He was at work.' That was enough for him, more than enough! It gave him great joy, and the strength to meet the hostilities and misunderstandings he was subjected to in the world time and again with equanimity, and not be led astray.

***

A different aspect of the effect a great discovery can have on its author is provided by the autobiography entitled *The Traveler* by Hideki Yukawa. The book was written when Yukawa was past fifty. One would normally have expected that an autobiography entitled *The Traveler* by one whose life, at least as seen from the outside, had been rich and fruitful, would be an account of his entire life. But Yukawa's account of his 'travels' ends with the publication of his 1934 paper describing his great discovery with the sombre note: 'I do not want to write beyond this point, because those days when I studied relentlessly are nostalgic to me; and on the other hand, I am sad when I think how I have become increasingly preoccupied with matters other than study.'

***

While all of us can share in the joy of the discoveries of the great men of science, we may be puzzled by what those many, very many, less perceptive and less fortunate, are to cherish and remember. Are they, like Vladimir and Estragon, destined to wait for Godot as in Samuel Beckett's play; or, are they to console themselves with Milton's thought 'they also serve who stand and wait'?

***

I now turn to the role which approbation and approval play in one's pursuit of science. The example of Newton 'voyaging through strange seas of thought alone' is not one that any of us can follow.

I have referred to Eddington's lonely efforts in pursuing his fundamental theory. In spite of his expressed confidence in the correctness of his theory, Eddington must have been deeply frustrated by the neglect of his work by his contemporaries. This frustration is evident in his plaintive letter to Dingle written a few months before he died:

> I am continually trying to find out why people find the procedure obscure. But I would point out that even Einstein was considered obscure, and hundreds of people have thought it necessary to explain him. I cannot seriously believe that I ever attain the obscurity that Dirac does. But in the case of Einstein and Dirac people have thought it worthwhile to penetrate the obscurity. I believe they will understand me all right when they realize they have got to do so—and when it becomes the fashion 'to explain Eddington'.

The lack of approval by one's contemporaries can have tragic consequences when they are expressed in the form of sharp and violent criticisms. Thus, Ludwig Boltzmann, greatly depressed by the violence of the attacks directed against his ideas by Ostwald and Mach, committed suicide 'as a martyr to his ideas', as his grandson Flamm has written. And George Cantor, the originator of the modern theory of sets of points and of the orders of infinity, lost his mind because of the hatred and the animosity against him and his ideas by his teacher Leopold Kronecker, and was confined to a mental hospital during the last many years of his life.

* * *

A case very different from the ones I have considered so far is that of Rutherford.

Consider his record. In 1897 he analysed radioactive radiations into three types: α-particles, β-rays and γ-rays, a nomenclature that has survived to this day. In 1902 he formulated the laws of radioactive disintegration: the first time a physical law was formulated in terms of probability and not certainty: a forerunner of the probability interpretation of quantum mechanics that was to become universal some 25 years later. In 1905-1907 he formulated, together with Soddy, the laws of radioactive displacement and identified the α-particle as the nucleus of the helium atom; and, together with Boltwood, initiated the determination of the ages of rocks and minerals by their radioactivity. In 1909-1910, there were the experiments of Geiger and Marsden, the discovery of the large angle scattering of α-rays and Rutherford's formulation of his law of scattering and the nuclear model of the atom. Then in 1917 he effected the first laboratory transformation of atoms: that of nitrogen-14 into oxygen-17 and a proton by α-ray bombardment. In the twenties he was associated with the clarification of the relationship between the α-ray and the γ-ray spectra. And 1932—the *annus mirabilis* as R.H. Fowler called it—saw the discovery of the artificial disintegration of Li into two α-particles by Cockroft and Walton, of positrons in cosmic-ray showers by Blackett, and the neutron by Chadwick—all of them in Rutherford's Cavendish. In the following year, Rutherford, together with Oliphant, himself discovered hydrogen-3 and helium-3. Altogether, then, an accomplishment unparalleled in this century.

Rutherford's attitude to his own discoveries is illustrated by his response to a remark of one who was present at the moment of one of his great discoveries: 'Rutherford, you are always on the crest of the wave.' To which Rutherford responded: 'I made the wave, didn't I?' Somehow from Rutherford's vantage point everything he said seems right, even including his remark, 'I do not let my boys waste their time' when he was asked if he encouraged his students to study relativity!

Rutherford was a happy warrior if ever there was one.

***

So far, I have tried to illustrate some facets of the pursuit of science by drawing on incidents in the lives of some great men of science. I shall turn now to some more general matters.

I shall start with an example. It has been reported that when Michelson was asked towards the end of his life, why he had devoted such a large fraction of his time to the measurement of the velocity of light, he replied 'it was so much fun'. There is no denying that 'fun' does play a role in the pursuit of science. But the word 'fun' suggests a lack of seriousness. Indeed, the Oxford Dictionary gives to 'fun' the meaning 'drollery'. We can be certain that Michelson did not have that meaning in his mind when he described his life's main interest as 'fun'. If not, what precisely is the meaning we are to attach to 'fun' in the context in which Michelson used it? More generally, what is the role of pleasure and enjoyment?

While 'pleasure' and 'enjoyment' are often used to characterize one's efforts in science, failures, frustrations and disappointments are equally, if not more, the common ingredients of scientific experience. Overcoming difficulties, undoubtedly, contributes to one's final enjoyment of success. Is failure, then, a purely negative aspect of the pursuit of science?

A remark of Dirac's describing the rapid development of physics following the founding of the principles of quantum mechanics in the middle and the late twenties is apposite in this connection.

> It was a good description to say that it was a game, a very interesting game one could play. Whenever one solved one of the little problems, one could write a paper about it. It was very easy in those days for any second-rate physicist to do first-rate work. There has not been such a glorious time since then.

Consider in the context of these remarks, J.J. Thomson's assessment of Lord Rayleigh in his memorial address given in Westminster Abbey:

> There are some great men of science whose charm consists in having said the first word on a subject, in having introduced some new idea which has proved fruitful; there are others whose charm consists perhaps in having said the last word on the subject, and who have reduced the subject to logical consistency and clearness. I think by temperament Lord Rayleigh belonged to the second group.

This assessment of Rayleigh by J.J. Thomson has sometimes been described as double-edged. But could one not conclude, instead, that Rayleigh by temperament chose to address himself to difficult problems and was not content to play the kind of games that Dirac describes in his characterization of the 'glorious time' in physics as a time 'when second-rate physicists could do first-rate work'?

This last question concerning Rayleigh's temperament raises the further question: after a scientist has reached maturity, what are his criteria for his continued pursuit of science? To what extent are they personal? And to what extent are aesthetic criteria like the perception of order and pattern, form and substance, relevant? Are such personal criteria exclusive? Has a sense of obligation a role? I do not mean obligation with the common meaning of obligation to one's students, one's colleagues, and one's community. I mean, rather, obligation to science itself. And what, indeed, is the content of obligation in the pursuit of science *for* science?

Let me finally turn to a different aspect. G.H. Hardy concludes his *A Mathematician's Apology* with the following illuminating statement:

> The case for my life, then, or for that of anyone else who has been a mathematician in the same sense in which I have been one, is this: that I have added something to knowledge, and helped others to add more; and that these somethings have a value which differs in degree only, and not in kind, from that of the creations of the great mathematicians, or of any of the other artists, great or small, who have left some kind of memorial behind them.

Hardy's statement is made relative to mathematicians; but it is equally applicable to all scientists. I want to draw your attention particularly to Hardy's reference to one's wanting to leave behind some kind of a memorial, i.e., something that posterity may judge. To what extent, then, is the judgement of posterity (which one can never know) a conscious motivation in the pursuit of science?

* * *

The pursuit of science has often been compared to the scaling of mountains, high and not so high. But who amongst us can hope, even in imagination, to scale the Everest and reach its summit when the sky is blue and the air is still; and in the stillness of the air survey the entire Himalayan range in the dazzling white of the snow stretching to infinity. None of us can hope for a comparable vision of nature and of the universe around us. But there is nothing mean or lowly in standing in the valley below and awaiting the sun to rise over the Kanchenjunga.

two

Newton and Michelangelo[1]

I wish to compare Newton and Michelangelo in the larger context of whether there is any similarity in the motivations of scientists and artists in their respective creative quests. There are many pitfalls in addressing this question: the motivations of individual scientists and artists are diverse; they are strongly dependent on personal tastes and temperaments; and a consideration of this subject in the abstract and in general terms will rapidly degenerate into dilettantism. On this account, I shall restrict my consideration to an example from the most rarefied level of creativity: Newton in writing the *Principia* and Michelangelo in painting the ceiling of the Sistine Chapel.

The *Principia* and the frescoes, both in their realms are the supreme, unsurpassed expressions of human creativity. That their origins should be as similar as they are, is an astonishing and a revealing fact.

Neither Newton nor Michelangelo began their masterpieces with alacrity or enthusiasm: Newton had to be persuaded by Halley and

1 The original version of this lecture was given at the 44th meeting of Nobel Laureates in Lindau, on 28 June 1994, and was published in *Current Science*, 67, No 7, 10 October 1994, pp. 497–99

Michelangelo was forced by the imperious insistence of Pope Julius II. But once they started, their visions enlarged; and they both completed their great works in a time – about two years – that is hard even to imagine.

Let me contrast the cases of Newton and Michelangelo, alternately.

In 1666, while in his manor in Woolsthorpe during the plague years, Newton had his first thoughts on gravitation. As he recalled later in life:

> And the same year I began to think of gravity extending to the orb of the Moon, and having found out how to estimate the force with which [a] globe revolving within a sphere presses the surface of the sphere, from Kepler's Rule of the periodical times of the Planets being in a sesquialterate proportion of the distances from the centers of their Orbs, I deduced that the forces which keep the Planets in their orbs must [be] reciprocally as the squares of their distances from the centers about which they revolve: and thereby compared the force requisite to keep the Moon in her orb with the force of gravity at the surface of the earth, and found the answer pretty nearly. All this was in the plague years of 1665 and 1666, for in those days I was in the prime of my age for invention, and minded Mathematics and Philosophy more than at any time since.

And again in 1679, stimulated by some correspondence with Hooke, Newton showed that Kepler's law of areas was not specific to the inverse-square law of attraction but that it was valid for any law of centripetal attraction; and further that for a body revolving in an ellipse, the law of attraction directed to its focus is inversely as the square of the distance.

Nevertheless, he was reluctant to publish his results because of his uneasiness with the assumption:

$$\frac{a_{cc}(☾)}{g} = \left(\frac{\text{Radius of the earth}}{\text{Radius of the moon's orbit}}\right)^2$$

which implies that the earth attracts objects on its surface as if its entire mass is concentrated at the centre – an assumption most emphatically against 'common sense' (unless one had known of its truth already). Newton was to prove the theorem in question in 1685 which he had not suspected before the demonstration.

The real story of Newton's development of his theory of gravitation with the concomitant writing of the *Principia* begins with Halley's visit to Newton in Cambridge in August 1684 to inquire of Newton the character of an orbit that a particle would describe in a central inverse-square law of attraction. Newton's immediate response was that the orbit will be an ellipse and that he had established that result some years earlier. Halley, astonished at this prompt response, asked for a demonstration. Newton could not find his demonstration among his papers; and he promised to rework his proof and send it to Halley in due course. In trying to re-derive the result, Newton became sufficiently involved in the subject to give a course of lectures during the Michelmas term of 1684. He forwarded the substance of these lectures to Halley in November of the same year. Halley was so excited with what he received that he visited Newton again in November, and tried to persuade him that he should write out his lectures for publication.

After his visit to Newton in November, Halley reported to the Royal Society on 10 December 1684 that he had '...lately seen Mr. Newton at Cambridge, who had shown him a curious treatise *De Motu*, which was promised to be sent to the Society to be entered upon their Register'.

Halley had, thus, at long last persuaded Newton to write out the results of his investigations for publication; and the writing of what was to become the *Principia* began in earnest.

Indeed, Halley was described by Conduit as 'the Ulysses who produced this Achilles'.

***

Turning next to Michelangelo...

In March 1508, Pope Julius II called on Michelangelo to paint the ceiling of the Sistine Chapel which originally was blue with gold stars. Michelangelo accepted the commission even though he considered himself more a sculptor than a painter and preferred devoting his time to the monumental tomb of Julius II he had started in 1505.

Buonarroti loudly declined the Pope's call at first and it was only at the latter's repeated insistence that he finally set to work in May 1508. He carried on the task by himself, refusing even the help of labourers, while immersed in a thousand technical difficulties about which he writes in charming letters, still extant.

***

In the spring of 1685, Newton's attitude to writing the *Principia* changed when he proved, apparently after some initial difficulty, that the gravitational attraction of a spherical body on an external particle is the same as if its entire mass is concentrated at its centre. Newton had not expected this result; and it is not difficult to imagine that it must have goaded Newton to further effort. As Newton wrote to Halley on 26 June 1686: 'I never extended the duplicate proportion lower than to the superfices of the earth, and before a certain demonstration I found last year, have suspected it did not reach accurately enough down so low; and therefore in the doctrines of projectiles never used it nor considered the motions of heavens.'

It was probably in the early spring of 1685 that he was able to prove the required proposition. In an address given one hundred years ago, J.W. Glaisher, on the bicentenary of the publication of the *Principia* said,

> Newton proved this superb theorem – and we know from his own words that he had no expectation of so beautiful a result till it emerged from his mathematical investigation – that all the mechanism of the universe at once lay spread before him. When he discovered the theorems that form the first three sections of Book I, when he gave them in his lectures of 1684, he was unaware that the sun and earth exerted their attractions as if they were but points. How different must these propositions have seemed to Newton's eyes when he realized that these results, which he had believed to be only approximately true when applied to the solar system were really exact!

***

Before the imperious insistence of the Pope, Michelangelo was forced to give in. And not only did he accept, but after a time unsatisfied with the theme (of the twelve Apostles), he proposed to the Pope that it should be modified. Indeed, we have documentary evidence on the origin of the 'subject' of the vault written by Michelangelo himself to his friend Fattucci in January 1524, in which we read '...and having begun the said work it seemed to me it would work out but a poor thing and I told the Pope that by painting only the apostles there I thought the result would be poor. He asked me why and told him it was because they were poor too. Then he commissioned me anew that I should do what I wanted.' Only Michelangelo could have conceived that powerful synthesis, personal in the extreme, stamped both in form and thought with a single style – his own.

***

Newton's initial expectation of quickly completing the task of writing was thus frustrated. But under Halley's discreet but constant persuasion and quiet encouragement, *De Motu Corporum* evolved and broadened, swelling first in the early summer of 1685 to a pair of related books and then to a third book on the 'System of the World' until in its final version was ready for the printer in April 1687.

As Newton has recorded: 'I wrote in 17 or 18 months beginning in the end of December 1684 and sending it to the Royal Society in May 1686, excepting that about 10 or 12 of the propositions were composed before.'

As Rouse Ball has written: '...the first two books were really written in about six months, and the period of eighteen months which the whole composition is said to have occupied includes the time in which copies of them for the press were prepared, and much of the material for the third book collected.'

The manuscript for the first book was sent to press before 7 June 1686. In it, the three laws of motion (which every student of science can recite) are formulated with clear distinction between the notions of the inertial and gravitational mass and their equality; a logical and a coherent account of the dynamics of the motion of particles in general and under the influence of centripetal forces, in particular; the laws of gravitation; and the gravitational attraction of spherical and slightly oblate bodies and of circular rings.

In the third book, the propositions of Book I are applied to the principal phenomena of the solar system, the determination of the masses and distances of the planets and their satellites and an extended discussion of various perturbations affecting the orbit of the moon. The theory of tides is worked out in detail. The oblateness of the earth is shown to be caused by the earth's rotation; and it is quantitatively related to the difference in the polar and the equatorial values of gravity. Newton also investigates the motion of comets and shows that they belong to the solar system and explains how from three observations the orbit of a comet can be deduced.

This extraordinary range and variety of problems, almost all treated here for the first time, and written in magisterial style in less than two years, raises *Principia* to a level of intellectual achievement unparalleled in the history of science.

* * *

The preparation for the frescoes of the Sistine Chapel began in May 1508. The erection of the scaffolding was finished by July. In September, some assistants arrived from Florence and probably worked on the layout of the ceiling paintings, the architectural framework, the tracing of outlines on the rough mortar. The actual work of painting, carried out by Michelangelo himself, was started at the latest in January 1509. He began near the entrance, progressing towards the altar; the histories last in chronological order (the great flood, the sacrifice of Noah, and the drunkenness of Noah) were painted first. In September 1509, these three histories were finished, a year later two more, and again a year later all nine histories were complete, together with the surrounding figures of 'slaves' and 'seers', and also the four histories in the corner spandrels.

The nine episodes are ideally divided into three groups relating to the origins of Universe, of Man, of Evil. In the first group (*Division of Light from Darkness [1], Creation of the Sun and the Moon [2], Dividing the Waters from the Land and the Creation of the animals [3]*), God is the sole protagonist. He appears alone and solemn in the empty sky, and yet bursting with the energy which will erupt into a sudden, violent act of creation. In the second group, the figure of Man appears fragile and naked in contrast to the massive might of the figure of the Father. Adam, painfully awakened from the torpor of unconsciousness, is snatched into life as if by a magnetic force [4]; Eve responds to the sound of the divine command and assumes a prayerful attitude [5]. In the *Fall and the Expulsion* [6], the inescapable connection between sin and punishment is thrust upon us by the fusion of the two episodes into one, divided and nevertheless joined, by the fearsome apparition of the serpent. The high dramatic moment of Sin passes from the barren landscape into an eternal dimension. Mankind is the protagonist in the third grouping as the composition becomes crowded, not unlike a choral drama. We admire the calm serenity of the *Sacrifice of Noah* [7], as it contrasts with the dramatic agitation of the *Deluge* [8], that nameless cataclysm engulfing masses of humanity into terror and anguish. The cycle concludes with the *Drunkenness of Noah* [9], symbol of Man saved from danger but ineluctably slave to Sin.

The most tragic figure of the group is the prophet Jeremiah. The uncouthness of this man, whose existence appears to be almost entirely physical, makes a very strong impression. The thoughtful pose furthers the impression of an isolated and fettered bodily being in this man, in whose image, more than in any other from the ceiling, Michelangelo reveals his vision of himself.

On 14 August 1511, the eve of the feast of the Assumption of the Blessed Virgin, the frescoes of the ceiling were unveiled; then, until the end of September 1512, Michelangelo painted the 'Ancestry of Christ' in the lunettes; and on 31 October 1512, the first Mass was celebrated in the Sistine Chapel. The impression produced on Michelangelo's contemporaries by the monumental paintings was profound, and they have maintained their influence to the present day.

***

Let me conclude with this note. What I have tried to say during the past half an hour is simply this: When a supremely great creative mind is kindled, it leaves a blazing trail that remains a beacon for centuries.

three

Convocation Address[1]

First, may I congratulate everyone of you who will take your degree and wish you all the best in whatever vocation you may choose to follow.

Convocation addresses are commonly considered by graduating classes as a necessary boredom to endure. Perhaps, I shall be making matters worse by saying that my address this morning will consist of readings from Newton's great book, the *Principia*.

I should begin by explaining why I consider readings from the *Principia* as appropriate for the occasion. A few years ago by an accident of circumstance I came to studying the *Principia*. As my study progressed, I found that I was gradually recovering the same exhilaration and the same enthusiasm that I felt some sixty-five years ago when I first encountered 'Euclid's Elements'.

I hope that my readings from the *Principia* will remind you, to quote Longfellow, that 'the lives of great men can make our lives sublime'.

In the brief time allotted to me, I cannot even attempt to describe the magnificent and timeless edifice Newton erected in his *Principia*. The

1 Convocation address at the Queen's University, Kingston, Ontario, Canada, 1 June 1991

selections I shall choose, will I hope illustrate the perspicacity and the timelessness of Newton's exalted scientific vision.

In Book 1 of the *Principia*, Newton lays down the mathematical foundations of his universal law of gravitation in a magisterial sequence of 98 propositions with many accompanying corollaries, lemmas and scholia. And in Book III, he carefully delineates a chain of arguments that leads him to his law of gravitation. But first he enunciates four Rules of Reasoning.

RULES OF REASONING IN PHILOSOPHY

RULE I

We are to admit no more causes of natural things than such as are both true and sufficient to explain their appearances.

To this purpose the philosophers say that Nature does nothing in vain, and more is in vain when less will serve; for Nature is pleased with simplicity, and affects not the pomp of superfluous causes.

RULE II

Therefore to the same natural effects we must, as far as possible, assign the same causes.

As to respiration in a man and in a beast; the descent of stones in *Europe* and in *America*; the light of our culinary fire and of the sun; the reflection of light in the earth, and in the planets.

RULE III

The qualities of bodies, which admit neither intensification nor remission of degrees, and which are found to belong to all bodies within the reach of our experiments, are to be esteemed the universal qualities of all bodies whatsoever.

For since the qualities of bodies are only known to us by experiments, we are to hold for universal all such as universally agree with experiments; and such as are not liable to diminution can never be quite taken away. We are certainly not to relinquish the evidence of experiments for the sake of dreams and vain fictions of our own devising; nor are we to recede from the analogy of Nature, which is wont to be simple, and always consonant to itself.

Lastly, if it universally appears, by experiments and astronomical observations, that all bodies about the earth gravitate towards the earth, and that in proportion to the quantity of matter which they severally contain; that the moon likewise, according to the quantity of its matter, gravitates towards the earth; that, on the other hand, our sea gravitates towards the moon; and all the planets one towards another; and the comets in like manner towards the sun; we must, in consequence of this rule, universally allow that all bodies whatsoever are endowed with a principle of mutual gravitation.

RULE IV

In experimented philosophy we are to look upon propositions inferred by general induction from phenomena as accurately or very nearly true, notwithstanding any contrary hypotheses that may be imagined, till such time as other phenomena occur, by which they may either be made more accurate, or liable to exceptions.

This rule we must follow, that the argument of induction may not be evaded by hypotheses.

On these Rules of Reasoning, after some preliminary propositions, Newton grandly states his universal law of gravitation in:

PROPOSITION VII. THEOREM VII

That there is a power of gravity pertaining to all bodies, proportional to the several quantities of matter which they contain.

That all the planets gravitate one towards another, we have proved before; as well as that the force of gravity towards every one of them, considered apart, is inversely as the square of the distance of places from the centre of the planet. And thence (by Prop. LXIX, Book I, and its Corollaries) it follows, that the gravity tending towards all the planets is proportional to the matter which they contain.

Moreover, since all the parts of any planet A gravitate towards any other planet B; and the gravity of every part is to the gravity

> of the whole as the matter of the part to the matter of the whole; and (by Law III) to every action corresponds an equal reaction; therefore the planet B will, on the other hand, gravitate towards all the parts of the planet A; and its gravity towards any one part will be to the gravity towards the whole as the matter of the part to the matter of the whole. Q.E.D.

And Newton concludes his *Principia* with this moving statement:

> But hitherto I have not been able to discover the cause of those properties of gravity from phenomena, and I frame no hypotheses; for whatever is not deduced from the phenomena is to be called an hypothesis; and hypotheses, whether metaphysical or physical, whether of occult qualities or mechanical, have no place in experimental philosophy. In this philosophy particular propositions are inferred from the phenomena, and afterwards rendered general by induction. Thus it was that the impenetrability, the mobility, and the impulsive force of bodies, and the laws of motion and of gravitation, were discovered. And to us it is enough that gravity does really exist, and act according to the laws which we have explained, and abundantly serves to account for all the motions of the celestial bodies, and of our sea.

Even from these few selections, it should be clear to all of you that Newton 'was not of an age, but for all time'.

four

SCIENCE AND SCIENTIFIC ATTITUDES[1]

ONE OF THE MATTERS TO WHICH I HAVE DEVOTED SOME THOUGHT IN recent years concerns one's motivations in the pursuit of science, and some of my thoughts on the subject are included in the collection of my lectures, *Truth and Beauty: Aesthetics and Motivations in Science* (University of Chicago Press, 1987). In this essay, I wish to consider some related questions: (1) the aspect of nature that is in some sense the most incomprehensible; (2) the goals that one strives for in the pursuit of knowledge; and finally (3) the sources of one's satisfaction in such pursuits.

While these questions may seem disparate, it will appear in the discussion that follows that they are in fact related, even if only tangentially.

* * *

In the context of the first of the topics I have enunciated, I shall consider the following statement of Einstein: 'The most incomprehensible fact about Nature is that it is comprehensible.'

---

1 Published in *Nature*, 344, No. 6264, 22 March 1990), pp. 285–86

This expresses a profound truth and it is echoed in the writings of other great men of science. Thus, Eugene Wigner has written of the two miracles: 'the miracle of the existence of laws of Nature and the miracle of the capacity of the human mind to divine them'; and he has also written about 'the unreasonable effectiveness of mathematics in the understanding of Nature'. And Schrodinger considers that this latter capacity of the human mind to divine nature's laws may well be beyond human understanding.

Let me elaborate on these statements with two illustrative examples.

Geometrical curves, their beauty and their forms, held fascination for the Greeks; they are enshrined in their sculptures and their architecture. The straight line and the circle dominate Euclid; and the perfection of the circle was sacrosanct: it underlies Aristotle's conception of celestial bodies and it provides the basis for Greek astronomy from Eudoxus to Ptolemy. But the Greeks did not confine their studies to straight lines and circles only. They sought curves that would encompass the geometrical properties of straight lines and circles in a more beautiful and harmonious synthesis; and they discovered this harmony in the curves obtained as sections in a cone: the ellipse and the hyperbola. Their curiosity with respect to these curves was not motivated by any physical fact they discerned. And yet, in the second half of the third century BC, Apollonius of Perga wrote eight monumental volumes devoted to these curves. Apollonius is eloquent about their geometrical properties; he describes them as miraculous. But it did not occur to him, or to the other Greek mathematicians, that the curves, which they studied so earnestly for their intrinsic beauty, had any relevance to the real physical world.

Yet some eighteen centuries later, when Kepler was analysing the orbits of the planets on the Copernican system, he discovered that the very curves that the Greek mathematicians had studied for their intrinsic mathematical beauty were exactly those needed to represent the orbits of the planets (Fig. 1).

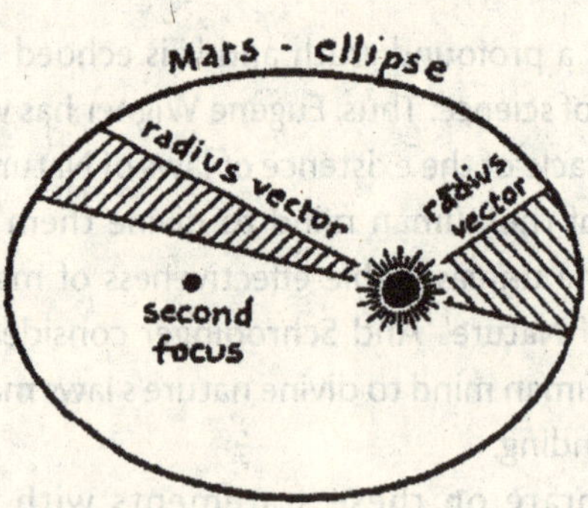

Fig. 1: *Kepler on his law of areas (the radius vector describes equal areas in equal intervals of time): 'Since I was aware that there exists an infinite number of points on the orbit and accordingly an infinite number of distances [from the Sun] the idea occurred to me that the sum of these distances is contained in the area of the orbit. For, I remembered that in the same manner Archimedes too divided the area of a circle into an infinite number of triangles.'*

Kepler on his law concerning the elliptical nature of the orbits of the planets: 'Why should I mince my words? The truth of Nature, which I had rejected and chased away, returned by stealth through the backdoor, disguising itself to be accepted ... I thought and searched, until I went nearly mad, for a reason, why the planet preferred an elliptical orbit...'

Commenting on this discovery of Kepler, Einstein has written:

> Our admiration for Kepler is transcended only by our admiration and reverence for the mysterious harmony of Nature in which we find ourselves. Already in antiquity, man had devised curves exhibiting the simplest forms of regularity. Among these, next to the straight line and the circle, the most important were the ellipse and the hyperbola. We see that the last two are embodied – at least very nearly so – in the orbits of heavenly bodies ... It seems that the human mind has first to construct forms, independently, before we can find them in things. Kepler's marvellous achievement is a particularly fine example of the fact that knowledge cannot spring from experience alone but only from a comparison of the inventions of the intellect with the facts of observation.

Let me repeat the crucial part of this remarkable statement: 'The human mind has first to construct forms, independently, before we can find them in things.'

I should like to illustrate this same aspect in Einstein's own development of his general theory of relativity, a theory that has been described as 'the supreme example of speculative thought'.

More than one hundred and thirty years ago in a celebrated lecture, Bernhard Riemann, analysing the foundations of geometry, came to the view that space is not a lot of points close together, but a lot of distances interlocked; and further, that these metrical properties of space are casually linked with its matter-content. He states: 'Therefore, either the reality on which our space is based must form a discrete manifold or else the reason for the metrical relationships must be sought for, externally, in the binding forces acting upon it.'

With this conception of the possible role of geometry in describing the physical world, Riemann developed a system of geometry more general than Euclid's, a system that has come to be known as Riemannian geometry.

Some sixty years later, Einstein was absorbed in trying to understand a miracle that underlies the Newtonian theory of gravitation and an inconsistency in it which he perceived. The miracle is that all bodies are equally accelerated in a gravitational field, as manifested by Galileo's well-known demonstration from the leaning tower at Pisa. It requires the inertial mass and weight to be identical – an enigmatic fact well established but not really understood before Einstein. And the inconsistency that Einstein perceived is that Newton postulated that the action of gravity at a distance is instantaneous, contrary to Einstein's own prohibition that no signal can be propagated with a velocity exceeding that of light. In resolving these paradoxes, Einstein found that Riemann's geometry provided him with a framework ideally suited for developing his general theory of relativity; not unlike Kepler, who found in the geometrical works of Apollonius the framework for his understanding of planetary motions.

And Einstein's theory, developed on what appeared to many of his contemporaries as a very frugal basis on which to found a physical theory, has revealed a richness of content that continues to baffle the imagination.

***

Accepting our 'inability' to understand the 'reasonableness' of Nature, what are we to understand by the common phrase 'The pursuit of knowledge' as it applies to science?

'Pursuit' has the common meaning of a chase in hunting; and, characteristic of our times, we are also familiar with the word in the combination 'pursuit-plane'. Is this association which the word 'pursuit' evokes intended? And if it is, are we to conclude that knowledge, like the fox in a chase, or the enemy plane in hot pursuit, is something whose existence we know of in advance and our pursuit is to aim for it. Of course, some aspects of what we include under knowledge are in this category. Thus, to unearth the fossil remains of creatures long past, or the relics of bygone civilizations, to scale the highest peaks, or to fathom the deepest oceans, are all endeavours of high human aspiration.

But one may still ask: is knowledge, then, something we seek to attain in the same spirit as the mountaineer who aspires to ascend the Everest 'because it is there'? If that is the case, what are we to understand when we are told that research is a quest after the unknown to chart territories whose existence we may not even be aware of when we started? Kepler did not know, when he began his long and arduous analysis of the centuries of accumulated observations on planetary motions, that buried in that mass of details were the simple laws he discovered. Neither did Newton know, before he saw the apple fall, that Kepler's laws could be understood so simply in terms of his laws of motion and of gravitation.

Perhaps I shall be accused of quibbling. For one may, in truth, say that in the pursuit of scientific knowledge – if I may be pardoned for that combination of words – while one does not aim for something which is material and concrete, one does aim for the enlargement of that order and that harmony which are the key signatures of nature. Indeed, for a scientist, the order, the harmony, the uniformity and the universality of the laws of nature are as real as the peak of the Everest is for the mountaineer. And so it is in the other branches of abstract knowledge.

But is that all there is to our quest for knowledge? Do we wish, for example, to quantify new knowledge by the extent to which others can share in it and still others can make use of it for human delight or for human welfare? And if that is our wish, what value do we attach to the refinement of one's own perception and to the enlargement of one's own vision? Is there no real content to Wordsworth's famous lines on Newton: 'The marble index of a mind for ever / Voyaging through strange seas of Thought, alone'?

Indeed, there is simple evidence that the very greatest artists, in their ennobled maturity, withdraw into themselves. Here, for example, is T.S. Eliot commenting on the late plays of Shakespeare:

> It seems to me to correspond to some laws of nature that the work of a man like Shakespeare, whose development in the course of his career was so amazing, that it should reach, as in *Hamlet*, the point at which it can touch the imagination and feeling of the maximum number of people to the greatest possible depth, and that, thereafter, like a comet which has approached the earth and continued away on its course, he should gradually recede from view until he tends to disappear into his private mystery.

What T.S. Eliot has said of Shakespeare applies equally to Beethoven. In his late compositions and especially in his late quartets, Beethoven was indeed 'Voyaging through strange seas of Thought, alone' – voyaging, in fact, to enlarge his own personal vision.

This attempt by the greatest minds to enlarge their personal vision is, I believe, manifest also in the remoteness and in the laminated and glacial style of Newton's *Principia*. The lasting value of the *Principia* lies as much in Newton's vision of the universe, as in the surpassing quality of his discoveries which it summarizes and organizes.

***

And finally I wish to consider the sources of one's satisfaction in scholarly endeavours.

Perhaps I should first eliminate, *ex cathedra*, that the rewards of scholarship consist of celebrity and of public honours. The supreme Magisters of Castalia, in Hermann Hesse's *The Glass Bead Game*, had learned to renounce them. I suppose that one does renounce them in the end – at least, one feels that one ought to transcend them. But the matter is not as simple as that. None of us are so immune to human sensibilities that we are not all, to some extent, sensitive to the approval of our colleagues whom we respect. And I am sure that all of us hope, each in his own way, that posterity will assign to us our due and humble places so long as we persevere at the limits of our capabilities.

But posterity can be harsh. Here, for example, is John Ruskin's criticism of the English painter Sir Joshua Reynolds:

> Why did not Sir Joshua – or could not – or would not Sir Joshua – paint Madonnas? ... Yet! While we acknowledge the discretion and simple heartedness of these men ... we have to remember ... that amiable discretion is not the highest virtue, nor to please the frivolous, the best success ... There is probably some strange weakness in the painter, and some final error in the age, when in thinking over the examples of their greatest work, for some type of culminating loveliness, or veracity, we remember no expression either of religion or heroism, and instead of reverently naming a *Madonna di San Sisto*, can only whisper modestly, 'Mrs. Pelham feeding chickens'.

If one recognizes that the rare moments of illumination one experiences during the course of one's life are the precious rewards, one is still troubled; for, one may ask: is he condemned to live only in the memory of his past moments of illumination? The answer, it seems to me, is that, if one is not to be so condemned, one must seek in one's enlarged and refined perception a source for quiet contemplation. In other words, 'Voyage through strange seas of Thought, alone.' But even this may not always be possible, as Hermann Hesse poignantly describes in his portraiture of Joseph Knecht in the *The Glass Bead Game*.

The Glass Bead Game is the wondrous tale of one who, in his youth, aspired to the ideals of Castalia and who, in time, rose to become the supreme Magister Ludi. But in the end, in deep doubts, he renounces his office, exiles himself from Castalia, only to be drowned accidentally in a Swiss lake.

Let me try to answer directly the question why one, fully aware of one's inherent and often insurmountable limitations, nevertheless devotes oneself to scholarship and to a life of constant endeavour, many failures and fewer successes? The answer is as T.S. Eliot has given in his 'Confidential Clerk': 'It is strange, isn't it, / That a man should have a consuming passion / To do something for which he lacks the capacity?'

five

Know About Black Holes[1]

I AM SURE THAT ALL OF YOU HAVE ENCOUNTERED THE TERM 'BLACK HOLES' in one context or another in the popular press or in popular scientific articles. I am afraid that the general impression you might have got from these popular articles is that black holes are mysterious objects resulting from speculative thought and further that these have mysterious and even malicious properties! Quite the opposite is what I should like to tell you. I would like to tell you how the concept of black holes is a very simple one and why we believe in their existence in large numbers in the astronomical universe.

Certainly to this audience I need not say that if you take a rocket and if you want to project it and have it escape the gravitational field of the earth, you must project it with a velocity in excess of a certain limit, and this limit is called the velocity of escape. Only when the velocity exceeds that limit, can the projected object escape from the gravitational field. A simple expression for this limit is written as:

---

1 Talk delivered at the Vikram Sarabhai Space Centre, Thiruvananthapuram, 30 October 1984, transcribed and published in the in-house journal *Countdown*

$$v^2 = \frac{2GM}{r}$$

where v is the velocity, G the constant of gravitation, M the mass of the earth, and r the radius of the earth.

Only when you project the rocket with a velocity greater than this value, will the rocket escape the earth's influence. Or you can put it in another way: If you project a particle with a velocity v from a body of mass M, only when the radius r of the body is greater than $(2GM/v^2)$ will the particle escape the gravitational influence of the body. If, however, r is less than this quantity, the particle projected with the velocity v will not escape. Consequently, you can ask the question: When would a particle projected with a velocity equal to that of light *not* escape from the body? Clearly, if r should be less than $2GM/c^2$, where c is the velocity of light, the particle would not escape. But we know that no particle on earth – no material particle in nature – can be projected with (or have) a speed equal to or in excess of the speed of light. Consequently, if light cannot escape from a body, nothing else can. That is what one says a black hole is.

A black hole is then an object on whose surface the force of gravity is such that even light will not escape from it. But this statement assumes that light is affected by gravity. That light is affected by gravity is a prediction of the general theory of relativity. Indeed, one of the predictions of the general theory was that if a light ray grazes the surface of the sun, it would be deflected by 1.75 seconds of arc. This is a very small effect. Nevertheless, the measurements by the British expeditions led by Eddington and Dawson in the early months of 1919 verified this. So we know that a light ray grazing the surface of the sun will be deflected by 1.75 seconds of an arc. Now, the sun has a radius of about 700,000 km and its mass is about 2×10^{33} gm. Suppose the sun was compressed by a factor 100, so that its radius is not 700,000 km but 7000 km. Then light will be deflected by 100 times the value. 100 times 1.75 seconds is close to three minutes. The smaller the fraction of the radius to which you squeeze the sun, the larger will be the deflection of light. It can be shown that if the sun could be compressed to a radius of 3.75 km then light will go round and round the sun like a satellite, instead of travelling in a straight line. If the mass of the sun is further compressed to a radius of 2.5 km, the force of gravity on it will be so large that even light will not escape from it. Then it cannot be self-luminescent; you can't see it and that is why you call it a black hole!

But, at this point you may say: If the sun with its present radius of 700,000 km and a mean density of 1.5 gm/cc (the density of water is 1 gm/cc) were compressed to a radius of only 2.5 km, its density would increase to something like 10^{14} gm/cc (i.e. 100 million million gm/cc)!

One's natural instinct would be to ask: Isn't that so high a density that it is impossible? It is not! Those densities are entirely within the realm of reality. For example, if you take an atom of gold or an atom of copper and you look at the nucleus, the entire mass of the nucleus is confined to a radius which is 10^{-13} cm and if you ask what the nuclear density is you will find that the density is of the same order as that of the compressed sun. So in reality there exist objects on the earth, viz., the nuclei of atoms, which have these densities. So to contemplate a density of 10^{13} or 10^{15} gm/cc is not in itself absurd. On the other hand, if you take an ordinary gas and say that you want to reach a density of 10^{13} or 10^{15} gm/cc, you must compress it in such a way that all the nuclei of the atoms are packed one on top of the other. To do this you have to get rid of all the electrons and bring the nuclei close together; but these nuclei have all the same type (positive) of charge and hence they repel each other; so you have to press them so close that you overcome the core-energy and in practice you may not be able to do that.

This is why normal matter does not have such high density. But during the natural course of evolution of stars it is possible for matter in a star to condense or collapse to such small dimensions that these densities are obtained. This conclusion is based on very, very simple arguments, both observational and theoretical. You may ask: why should a star like the sun which has a mean density of only 1.5 gm/cc during its evolution reach such high densities as 10^{13} gm/cc? The answer is that it is a structure which is supported by pressure. Where does the pressure come from? The pressure comes from the fact that radiation is flowing through it, and if a stage should come when radiation no longer flows through it, you would have a situation that the pressure cannot support the structure. It is like removing the foundation of a building; then it will collapse. So the nature of argument, which is very simple, is that if a time should come when the sun has exhausted its energy, the flow of radiation would cease and then it would collapse. At this point you may ask: will this happen? The answer is yes.

Let us take the case of the sun. Where does the energy come from? We know it comes from the burning of hydrogen into helium (i.e., fusion) and in the course of this, a certain fraction of the mass is liberated as energy. Therefore, if you know the luminosity, i.e., the rate at which the sun is radiating, you also know what fraction of the mass of the sun is converted into helium each second. If the entire mass of the sun were to be converted into helium you could calculate how long it would take for all the hydrogen to be burnt to form helium. Actually, of course, the sun is not completely composed of hydrogen. Further, the burning does not take place throughout the sun; it takes place only in the centre. But anyhow, you can set an upper limit to the life of the sun if you know its mass, its rate of radiation and the relationship between mass and energy; if you make that calculation you will find that the sun can exist – at the present rate of radiation (if at all it were composed wholly of hydrogen) – for 200 billion years, i.e. 2×10^{11} years. This is a very long time; indeed, it is rather comparable to the age of the universe itself. And we know that the sun has lived up to now for a period of that order of magnitude, and therefore might conclude that the sun would not lose a large part of its energy for a very long time.

However, if you take stars which are 10 times more massive than the sun, they radiate energy not with the luminosity of the sun, but with a luminosity which is sometimes hundred thousand and even million times more than that of the sun. Such stars are not terribly common; but for a substantial fraction of stars in the universe, the luminosities are hundred thousand to million times more, and consequently they would lose their energy not in 2×10^{11} years, but more like in a million years. But that is a very short time, astronomically speaking. So, consequently, there exist a large number of stars which must have exhausted their source of energy in times that are relatively short compared to the age of the universe.

And the fact that today we find in the universe stars with luminosities which are 1000, 10000, 100000 times that of the sun means that these stars must have been formed in relatively recent times, and therefore from most simple arithmetic you can conclude that the process of star formation is going on, and further that enormous numbers of massive stars must have exhausted their energy, and therefore must have been subjected to collapse. And this must have happened many, many times in the course of the evolution of the universe. The question therefore arises: What happens to these massive stars when they lose their energy? Now you notice that in all my arguments I have used explicitly the notion that the source of energy is related to the burning of hydrogen to helium.

The question as to what might happen to stars when they lose their energy was a question which was considered already in the middle of the 1920s, and in fact by Eddington himself. Why was the question considered at that early time? The reasons were two-fold. First, even if you don't know what the source of energy is, it is clear that sooner or later that source must be exhausted, and therefore sooner or later you must confront the problem as to what would happen to a star if it exhausted its source of energy. The second fact that made the problem interesting in the 1920s already is that one had discovered at that time, stars with very high density. These were the so-called white dwarfs and they had densities of hundred thousand or even million gm/cc. That was the first time that people found observational evidence for stars with high mean densities. And the question arose: Are these objects the end products of star evolution? Are these objects formed when every star exhausts its source of energy? Now, in order to answer these questions we must turn to theoretical considerations. If you take a star like our sun, even though the mean density is only 1.5 gm/cc, the mean temperature is 10–15 million degrees centigrade. At these temperatures, matter is highly ionized and the relation between the pressure and density is a standard one, namely that the pressure is proportional to the density. Suppose we take material from the sun which is a perfect gas at temperature of, let us say, 15 million degrees, and a mean density of say, 1.5 to 2 gm/cc. (At the centre of the sun the density is about 30–40 gm/cc with a temperature of 20 million degrees). Suppose we compress such a material.

How will the pressure change? You will find in the first instance that at a fixed temperature, as you increase the density the pressure would increase proportionally. But what happens at later times is that, when you compress the material sufficiently, the pressure increase is no longer proportional to the density, but begins to increase much more rapidly. In fact, the pressure begins to increase eventually in proportion to (5/3) power of the density. Moreover, the constant of proportionality is independent of the temperature! That is to say, if you take a gas at two different temperatures and you compress them sufficiently, eventually the relation between the pressure and the density for the two situations becomes exactly the same. If you did such a calculation you would find that, indeed, a star with a mass equal to that of the sun will have a mean radius 100 times smaller, and therefore a density which is of the order of a million gm/cc.

Now if this result had been true always, you would conclude that every star, when it loses its energy, must become a white dwarf with a mean density of the order of a million or 100 million gm/cc and that would be the end of the problem! But a new situation arose as a consequence of certain changes in the gas-laws in the framework of the quantum theory worked out independently by Dirac and Fermi. But the Fermi–Dirac law was derived for terrestrial experiments and could not explain things like electrical conductivity, thermal conductivity, and so on. In the laboratory, the electrons move with velocities which are small compared with the velocity of light. But when you take a mass equal to that of the sun, you find that electrons at its centre, where the temperatures are very high, move with one half the velocity of light. Half the velocity of light is still less than the velocity of light, but is still substantial, which means you must incorporate effects of special relativity to study the relation between pressure and density. Then it turns out that when the velocity of the electrons becomes comparable to the velocity of light, the index 5/3 changes in the limit to the value 4/3. That, you would say is a very small effect – from root of 5/3 to the root of 4/3. But the point is that the ultimate relation between pressure and density which a collapsed star would be expected to have is independent of temperature. It is a universal function which has a behaviour: root of 5/3 at low densities and root of 4/3 at high densities. When you put that into the theoretical calculations you find the rather remarkable result that equilibrium states for white dwarf matter do not exist for masses which are above a certain limit. This means that there is a limit to the maximum mass a white dwarf can have.

What the calculation shows is that if you take a star of mass greater than one and a half times the solar mass and if the process of collapse occurs, the process of collapse could not be arrested at a stage with mean densities of the order of million gm/cc. Or, to put it in another way, suppose I take a star less than this critical value – say one solar mass like the sun – then it will lose its source of energy and it will collapse, and the collapse will continue to a stage where the mean density becomes million gm/cc. At this point it will stop collapsing further and it will stay there indefinitely.

On the other hand, if you take a star with mass which is 2 to 3 times the solar mass, then it radiates energy at a much faster rate and it will evolve. It will exhaust its energy sooner, but as it collapses its contraction will not be arrested at a stage where the mean density is of the order of a million gm/cc. Then the question is: what will it do? If it cannot be arrested, it can do one of two things. It can eject all the excess mass and become a white dwarf. That does not seem to be reasonable because if you take a star of 5 solar masses, then it must eject 3.6 solar masses. If you take 10 solar masses, then it must eject 8.6 solar masses. It seems unreasonable that there is a law of nature which tells you that every star must, when it loses its energy, collapse in such a way that it must always eject the mass so that you have a residue less than 1.4 solar masses. In fact it is very unlikely to happen.

Consequently, such stars must collapse still further and the next question is: What is the next possible stage where the collapse could be arrested? It is, clearly, when the density becomes comparable to nuclear density. At this stage a transformation occurs: the neutrons which under normal laboratory conditions are radioactive, become a stable species. That is, in the environment of high densities, the protons capture the electrons which are there and become neutrons, which are now a stable species. The result is a neutron star. Of course we know now that neutron stars exist in nature. They are the so-called pulsating-stars or pulsars. So the fact that a massive star can collapse into a neutron star is a well-established fact.

Now the question arises: Can every star find a stable state of equilibrium as a neutron star? The answer is no. And the reason why neutron stars of every possible mass cannot exist comes from general relativity theory. This is something which I cannot explain to you in detail. But let me say that here we have to study in detail the stability of a star against radial oscillations. The result is that if you construct a stable neutron star, then depending on what its ratio of specific heats is, it will become unstable before it reaches some value, and therefore there exists a certain maximum mass for neutron stars. The actual calculation for this may appear complicated but the most general principles of relativity tell you that there must be a maximum mass for stable neutron stars, and when you compute it you find that it may be 2 or 2.5 times the solar mass.

Consequently, the picture of evolution is the following:

You take a star with mass less than one solar mass. It will become a white dwarf. You take a star with, say, three solar masses. Then it could collapse, and during the process of collapse it may shed enough matter (about one half solar mass) and you will be left with a core which is a stable neutron star – the so-called pulsar. When it fails to eject sufficient matter, no stable states are possible; it contracts and contracts and ultimately becomes a black hole!

The point which I have tried to explain today is that these considerations which are laid before you show that the concept of black holes is a very simple one. It does not require sophisticated calculations. Given that light is deflected by gravity – which is an experimentally demonstrated fact – the realization that given sufficiently high densities at sufficient compressions one must have a black hole, is clear.

The next question is: will, in the natural course of evolution of stars, black holes form? The answer is: Yes. The ingredients that had gone to show that there is a maximum limit to white dwarfs are very simple. This is a direct consequence of the equations of general relativity.

Let me just make one or two remarks here. Suppose you take a Newtonian star and assume that there is no pressure. Then it collapses. Then of course it will contract to a point, because gravitation will eventually overcome. On the other hand, supposing you have a slightest amount of pressure. Then the pressure will increase indefinitely and it will prevent further collapse. Or suppose you give it a slight rotation, then that will prevent collapse. But you can ask why it does not happen in general relativity. How is it that in the framework of general relativity, neither pressure nor rotation affects it? The reason is a very fundamental one. When you say that the pressure becomes high, it means that the constituent particles move with great speed and there is a lot of energy, and energy is mass – and therefore after a certain point the increase in pressure instead of counteracting gravity becomes gravity itself! The same thing with rotation. And therefore the reason why there exists a maximum mass for a neutron star follows from very simple considerations, and the fact that there are stars which must exhaust their source of energy is clear because we know that the source of energy is burning hydrogen to helium. We also know that there are stars that exhaust their energy in a million or 10 million years. So, consequently, the formation of a black hole is a direct consequence of the most elementary considerations.

I wish I had more time to tell you about black holes. What I wanted to tell you here is that contrary to the general impression you may have received from popular literature, the concept of black holes is a very simple one, and that their occurrence in nature follows from extremely general considerations – and that their existence in large numbers must be expected. The acceptance of this principle gives scope, and indeed has already given scope, to an enlargement of our view of the astronomical universe.

six

On Presenting the Bust of Ramanujan to the Royal Society[1]

Some years ago, I wrote with some hesitation to Sir Michael Atiyah, soon after he assumed the presidency of the Royal Society, whether he would be willing to accept on behalf of the Royal Society a gift of a bust of Ramanujan, my wife and I had in our possession. We were both honoured and pleased with Sir Michael's prompt response that he would be most willing to accept and added further that if the formal presentation were to be made during the tenure of his presidency, he would have Ramanujan's bust placed in his office as a companion to the one of Dirac's he already had there.

Ramanujan was elected a Fellow of the Society in 1918, he returned to India in 1919 and died within a year after his return, in 1920. The story of how a bust of one who had died in 1920 came to be made sixty years later is of some interest; and I hope that it is proper to tell that story on this occasion.

In his biographical notice for Ramanujan ('Proceedings of the Royal Society' [a], XCIX, pp. xiii–xxix), G.H. Hardy wrote:

1 Address delivered at the Royal Society, London, 11 May 1994

> It was his insight into algebraical formulae, transformation of infinite series, and so forth, that was most amazing. On this side most certainly I have never met his equal, and I can compare him only with Euler or Jacobi. He worked, far more than the majority of modern mathematicians, by induction from numerical examples: all his congruence properties of partitions for example were discovered in this way. But with his memory, his patience, and his power of calculation he combined a power of generalisation, a feeling for form, and a capacity for rapid modification of his hypotheses, that were often really startling, and made him, in his own peculiar field, without a rival in his day.

In his lectures on 'Ramanujan' at the Harvard Tercentenary Conference of Arts and Sciences in the fall of 1936, Hardy reassessed what he had written in 1921 as follows:

> I do not think now that this extremely strong language is extravagant. It is possible that the great days of formulae are finished, and that Ramanujan ought to have been born 100 years ago; but he was by far the greatest formalist of his time. There have been a good many more important, and I suppose one must say greater, mathematicians than Ramanujan during the last fifty years, but no one who could stand up to him on his own ground. Playing the game of which he knew the rules, he could give any mathematician in the world fifteen.

In more recent times, Ramanujan's reputation has been enhanced considerably. For example, the slight overtone of criticism implied in Hardy's remark 'the great days of formulae are finished' has been countered by 'the days of great formulae are not finished'. With respect to the fall and rise of Ramanujan's reputation, Bruce Berndt (the author of the five volumes of 'Ramanujan's Notebooks') has compared him to Johann Sebastian Bach, who remained largely unknown for years after his death in 1750. For Bach, the big turnaround came on 11 March 1829 with Felix Mendelssohn's performance of *St. Matthew's Passion.* For

Ramanujan, the roughly analogous event was George Andrews's discovery of the Lost Notebook in 1976.

And what is this 'Lost Notebook'.

G.N. Watson had worked on Ramanujan's papers for many years before World War II. When he died, Mrs Watson asked J.M. Whittaker (the son of E.T. Whittaker) to come and examine Watson's papers in his study. There, Whittaker recalled:

> ... papers covered the floor of a fair sized room to a depth of about a foot, all jumbled together, and were to be incinerated in a few days. One could only make lucky dips (into the rubble) and, as Watson never threw away anything, the result might be a sheet of mathematics but more probably a receipted bill or a draft of his income tax return for 1923. By an extraordinary stroke of luck one of my dips brought up the Ramanujan material.

This 'material', all 140 pages of it, was part of a batch of papers Dewsbury (the Director of Public Instruction at Madras during the early twenties) had sent to Hardy in 1923 and that had, somehow, wound up with Watson. After his 'lucky dip', Whittaker passed them on to Robert Rankin (Watson's successor in Birmingham), who in 1968 handed them to Trinity College.

And there it lay in the Trinity archives without anyone's knowledge till George Andrews rescued it. George Andrews, who had worked on problems related to 'mock theta functions' – the subject of Ramanujan's last letter to Hardy a few months before he died – came to Cambridge to explore if any related material was available in the Trinity archives. He was thrilled and excited by what he discovered in the 140 pages deposited in the archives by Rankin.

Richard Askey told me that he met Andrews coming down the great court in Trinity examining the papers he had on hand. And when Askey asked him whether he could have a look at the manuscript, Andrews said '5 pounds per glance'! And Andrews himself told me that when he presented a paper on the 'Lost Notebook' at a meeting of the American Mathematical Society, Dr Olga Taussky-Todd who was chairing the session, said, 'The discovery of the "Lost Notebook" is as sensational a discovery for the mathematicians as a complete draft of a tenth symphony of Beethoven would have been to the musicians.'

Let me continue with what Richard Askey has written in this connection:

> These pages [of the Lost Notebook] are not dated, but from internal evidence they were written late in Ramanujan's life, much of it in his last year. Two-thirds of the pages deal with basic hypergeometric series and most of this work is significantly deeper than Ramanujan's earlier work on the same subject. Try to imagine the quality of Ramanujan's mind, one which drove him to work unceasingly while deathly ill, and one great enough to grow deeper while his body became weaker. I stand in awe of his accomplishments; understanding is beyond me. We would admire any mathematician whose life's work was half of what Ramanujan found in the last year of his life while he was dying.
>
> Some of Ramanujan's work has one quality which is shared by very little other work. Most mathematics, including some very good work, is predictable. Much of the rest seems inevitable after it is understood, and it would eventually be discovered by someone else. Little of Ramanujan's work seems predictable at first glance, and after we understand it there is still a fairly large body of work about which it would be safe to predict that it would not be discovered by anyone who has lived in this century. Then there are some of the formulas Ramanujan found that no one understands or can prove. We will probably never understand how Ramanujan found them.

Let me conclude this part of my story with a quotation from Freeman Dyson:

> The wonderful thing about Ramanujan is that he discovered so much, and yet he left so much more in his garden for other people to discover. For forty-four years I have intermittently come back to Ramanujan's garden; and every time when I come back, I find fresh flowers blooming.

I now, turn to the other strand of the story: how the bust came to be made. It begins with a letter of Hardy's to me.

Hardy was to give a series of twelve lectures on subjects suggested by Ramanujan's life and work at the Harvard Tercentenary Conference of Arts and Sciences in the fall of 1936. In the spring of that year, Hardy told me that the only photograph of Ramanujan that was available at that time was the one of him in cap and gown, 'which makes him look ridiculous'. And he asked me whether I would try to secure, on my next visit to India, a better photograph which he might include with the published version of his lectures. It happened that I was in India that same year from July to October. I knew that Mrs Ramanujan was living somewhere in south India, and I tried to find where she was living, at first without success. On the day prior to my departure for England in October of 1936, I traced Mrs Ramanujan to a house in Triplicane, Madras. I went to her house and found her living in extremely modest circumstances. I asked her if she had any photograph of Ramanujan which I might give to Hardy. She told me that the only one she had was the one in his passport which he had secured in London early in 1919. 1 asked her for the passport and found that the photograph was sufficiently good (even after seventeen years) and that one could make a good negative and copies. It is this photograph which appears in Hardy's book *Ramanujan, Twelve Lectures on Subjects Suggested by His Life and Work* (Cambridge University Press, 1940). It is of interest to recall Hardy's reaction to the photograph: 'He looks rather ill [and no doubt was very ill], but he looks all over the genius that he was.'

The rest of the story as told by Richard Askey:

> The story of the thread from the 'Lost Notebook' to the bust is simple. Andrews has done a lot of very deep work trying to understand what Ramanujan discovered. Eventually, the *New York Times* heard about it and interviewed him. The *Hindu* followed with a more extensive interview, and also published an interview with Ramanujan's widow, Janaki Ammal. She lamented the fact that a statue of Ramanujan had never been made, although one had been promised. Andrews sent me copies of these interviews,

> and after a couple of months my subconscious finally got through to my conscious mind and it was clear that a bust should be made. Since Janaki Ammal was eighty, time was important,[1] so it was up to individuals rather than governments or societies, since institutions move slowly. My first reason for wanting a bust was simple: if Ramanujan's widow wanted one she should have it. That was the least we could do to show our appreciation of Ramanujan to someone who had been a great help to him. Later, I realized there was a second reason, which Janaki Ammal must have realized all along. She knew Ramanujan, and while she did not understand his mathematics, she knew that he was one of the few whose work will last. As long as people do mathematics, some of Ramanujan's work will be appreciated. In Ramanujan's case a more permanent memorial is appropriate: one which can be appreciated by those who do not understand his mathematics should be added to the memorial Ramanujan made for himself with his work.

From the desire to the accomplishment is a long way.

A likeness of Ramanujan had to be found. It was provided by the original of the photograph that is the frontispiece in Hardy's book on Ramanujan.

A sculptor was required who would accept the challenge of making a three-dimensional bust from a two-dimensional photograph. Askey found such a sculptor of distinction in Paul T. Granlund of Gustavus College, Saint Peter, Minnesota, USA.

A minimum of four busts had to be commissioned. Askey obtained enough funds by donations from the international community of mathematicians for one bust to be presented to Mrs Ramanujan (which it was in the fall of 1983). Askey acquired one; and my wife and I two.

That was how the bust that you see came to be made. And as Askey has said: 'While Granlund does not appreciate Ramanujan's mathematics as those of us who have studied it do, he studied Ramanujan's passport

1 Mrs Ramanujan died on 13 April 1994. She was ninety-four.

photo deeply, and the results show in the bust. He probably understands some things about Ramanujan that we do not.'

May I now present, the bust of Srinivasa Ramanujan to President Sir Michael Atiyah for his gracious acceptance on behalf of the Royal Society.

seven

Science in Pre- and Post-independence India

It is well known that the cultivation of modern science in India goes back to the introduction of Western education during the early decades of the nineteenth century. But the motives for the introduction of Western education by the original architects Lords Bentinck and Macaulay were not so worthy. In their Charter of 1813 they stated: 'Our aim should be to create a class of persons who would be Indian in blood and colour but English in tastes and opinions, in morals, and in intellect.'

The purpose, of course, was to provide clerks and assistants for the lower echelons of the growing bureaucracy of the British government. But it did not work quite that way. As a high official, Sir Richard Temple, wrote at a later time: 'Indians should therefore be exposed to an education of practical sciences which is a special preserve of Western Culture. These disciplines with their exact method will overwhelm the Indian mind and induce the requisite sense of inferiority.'

And in the Resolution of March 1835, it was provided: 'That the great object of the British Government ought to be the promotion of European literature and science: the available funds should be henceforth employed imparting to the Native population, knowledge of English Literature and Science through the medium of the English language.'

* * *

We should not, however, confuse the diabolical intention of the British government of the time with the remarkable individuals who came to India from Britain – along with the dross! One remembers men like Sir William Jones, an Indologist and a humanist who discovered India for himself through her art and literature; and in many ways was responsible for introducing to the West the rich heritage that was of India. He also made Indians more aware of their arts and literature, which they had largely forgotten through the political upheavals of the preceding centuries.

Slowly, however, Western science took root, aided by some of the British men of science who came and laboured in India. I may quote three examples: of Sir Mortimer Wheeler who by his research on ancient urban civilization of India restored Mohenjodaro as one of the great pre-Aryan civilizations; of the discovery of the cause of malaria by Sir Roland Ross; and of the vaccine for bubonic plague by Haffkine.

But the renaissance of indigenous scientists was simultaneous with and a part of the freedom struggle and the ferment in Indian society that followed. The renaissance included not only the great names of scientists such as J.C. Bose, C.V. Raman, P.C. Ray, S.N. Bose, Meghnad Saha, Srinivasa Ramanujan, and the engineer M. Visvesvaraya, but also individuals such as Mahendralal Sircar who established in Calcutta a private scientific laboratory (The Indian Association for the Cultivation of Science, which in 1928 was the laboratory in which Raman discovered the Raman effect) modelled after the Royal Institution in London; and Sir Ashutosh Mukerjee, a mathematician in his own right, and who, as a vice chancellor of the Calcutta University, created the first university in India with research and scholarship as its focus: it included among others P.C. Ray, C.V. Raman and M.N. Saha.

But all that I have said so far goes back to the pre-World War II years. Before leaving this period, I ought to say that there was hardly any governmental support for scholarship or research. All the research and scholarship there was, was confined to the universities.

***

With the end of the war, independence came – and with it, the premiership of Jawaharlal Nehru for some seventeen years. The essential ingredient of the Nehru era was Nehru's strong conviction that science was to be the key for the future prosperity of India. Indeed, already in 1938, a decade before independence, Nehru, in a statement to the Indian Scientific Congress meeting in Calcutta, stated:

> Science is the very texture of life. It is science alone that can solve the problems of hunger and poverty, of insanitation and illiteracy, of superstition and deadening customs and traditions, of vast resources running to waste, of a rich country inhabited by starving people ... Even more than the present, the future belongs to those who make friends with science.

And when he became prime minister, he was responsible for a Scientific Policy Resolution of 1958 as a major policy statement of the Government of India:

> The key for national prosperity apart from the spirit of the people, lies, in the modern age, in the effective combination of three factors: technology, raw materials, and capital, of which the first is perhaps the most important, since the creation and adoption of new scientific techniques can, in fact, make up for a deficiency in natural resources, and hence the demands of capital. But technology can only grow out of the study of science and its applications...
>
> Science has developed at an ever-increasing pace since the beginning of the century, so that the gap between the advanced and the backward countries has widened more and more. It is only

> by adopting the most vigorous measures and putting forward our utmost effort into the development of science that we can bridge the gap. It is an inherent obligation of a great country like India, with its tradition of scholarship and original thinking and its great cultural heritage, to participate fully in the march of science which is probably mankind's greatest enterprise today.

***

It is clearly impossible to relate even briefly all the initiatives that were taken during his and Indira Gandhi's premierships. But the two main areas in which Nehru associated himself were the development of the atomic energy program and, through it, space science; and the setting up of a chain of laboratories under a newly created Council of Scientific and Industrial Research. In both of these enterprises, he was associated with (and perhaps also motivated by) two able scientists of great vision: S.S. Bhatnagar and Homi Bhabha.

Bhatnagar was responsible for inaugurating some twenty or more national laboratories devoted to various aspects of science and technology. A few of the laboratories that come to my mind are the National Physical Laboratory, the National Chemical Laboratory, and the laboratories for the technologies of fuel, glass and leather, and electronics. I shall have more to say about the development of the atomic energy program later.

Another area of scientific activity initiated by Nehru, and which has grown significantly in the years since independence is defence research. In this area, he was largely influenced by his friendship and association with Lord Blackett, who was the president of the Royal Society during the years 1965–70. Blackett has given an interesting account of his association with Nehru and of the origins of defence research in India in his First Nehru Memorial Lecture in 1967.

***

Leaving these areas, let me turn to other aspects.

An important innovation in the field of higher education when Nehru was prime minister was the establishment of the Indian Institutes of Technology. Nehru's objective was as he stated: 'These centres of excellence, producing scientists and engineers of the highest calibre, have a special responsibility to provide leadership and innovation in evolving new patterns of development, in generating manpower and contribution to activities that will place India in the forefront of nations.' But Nehru's expectations were not fulfilled for reasons I will return to later.

Nehru also set up a Planning Commission, largely inspired by what he thought was the role of scientific temper in framing national policy. In setting up the Planning Commission, Nehru observed: 'The three fundamental requirements of India, if she is to develop industrially and otherwise, are: heavy engineering and machine-making industry, scientific research institutes and electrical power. These must be the foundations of planning.' He was the chairman of the commission during the entire period of his premiership; in this task he was ably assisted by another scientist of great merit and dedication, P.C. Mahalanobis.

***

It is not my intention to catalogue all the initiatives taken during the Nehru era: how we chose the part of science and technology; how we searched and found oil on land and offshore and exploited it; how we chose satellite space technology as the least expensive method of countrywide education and communication; how we constructed great dams; how we chose the way of nuclear energy; how we established factories; and how universal school education was introduced (with only partial success, it must be admitted). But in states like Kerala, which took advantage of the availability of education, literacy among men – and more importantly, among women – increased spectacularly with the consequent decrease in these states in infant mortality and even in the rate of population growth.

***

Let me leave generalities aside and describe briefly the advances that have been made in India in specific areas of research. I shall restrict myself only to those areas in the physical sciences in which I have some understanding.

First (and most importantly), the development of the atomic energy establishment. As I said before, the establishment of a viable and a far-sighted program of nuclear energy was due to the joint visions of Homi Bhabha and Jawaharlal Nehru. Their mutual understanding and confidence derived from a common background: both were at Cambridge and both had remained in Europe for many years before they returned to India; and they were both from the intellectual and aristocratic elite of India.

Since the initial idea of developing a program based on reactor physics was due to a memorandum which Bhabha wrote to Nehru, let me begin briefly with Bhabha's background.

When Bhabha returned to India with the outbreak of World War II in Europe, he was already a distinguished physicist with a considerable reputation both in Britain and in Western Europe. Even before the end of the war, Bhabha had initiated steps to found an Institute for Fundamental Research to embrace all the physical sciences with the aid of the munificence of the powerful Tata family (of which Bhabha was a member). Certainly, founding of the Tata Institute by Bhabha is one of the most significant events of post-independence India. It was with this background of accomplishment that Bhabha initiated the atomic energy program. Clearly, he could not have succeeded had it not been for the constant and enthusiastic support of Nehru. It is clearly not possible to go into all the details of what is now called the Bhabha Atomic Research Complex in Trombay. Let me only give a brief summary from one of the recent reports.

> Atomic Energy: The development and control, as well as use, of atomic energy for peaceful purposes are the prime objectives of India's atomic energy program. This program was a result of the vision that Bhabha had, as early as 1944, of the potentialities of

> atomic energy for power generation. And it was he who took the initiative to turn this vision into reality with emphasis on utilization of indigenous capabilities. The program primarily envisages the generation of electric power, and the development of nuclear applications for research, in agriculture, industry, medicine and other areas.
>
> India's overall long-term fuel-cycle strategy includes a first phase in which natural uranium-fuelled reactors would produce power and plutonium; a second phase in which plutonium-fuelled fast breeder reactors would produce power and more plutonium, as well as uranium-233, using thorium; and the third phase in which uranium-232 thorium breeder reactors would produce power.
>
> India is one of a handful of nations which has established her own capabilities over the entire gamut of nuclear cycles, right from exploration, mining, extraction, and conversion of nuclear materials, fuel fabrication, heavy water production, design and construction of reactors with all the subsystems and components, to reprocessing of spent fuel and waste management. Indian self-reliance has reached a stage where all the required activities can now be supported and sustained by the sound industrial infrastructure that has been created. This encompasses the feasibility studies, detailed project design, construction, installation, commissioning and operation of any plant in the entire nuclear cycle.

The next great initiative which was undertaken more fully during the premiership of Indira Gandhi was the Space Agency and particularly, the Indian Satellite Program. The person most responsible for the initiation of this program was Vikram Sarabhai. The main thrust of this program comprises satellites, launch vehicles, and associated ground equipment. Its main objective has always been to develop satellite-based communication for educational purposes, source survey, and weather forecasting. Of these, perhaps television services through satellite communication is the most important. At the present time, over ninety per cent of India's population has access to TV; and education by its means is perhaps the most important in the country's recent developments. Besides, telecommunication has been widely used for weather forecasting and disaster warnings.

***

Let me turn briefly to developments in pure science.

In mathematics, India has of course the good fortune of having Ramanujan as an example. To emulate him is of course, impossible; and to some extent, Indian mathematics was dormant in his shadow for two or three decades. But the building of the School of Mathematics of the Tata Institute changed all that: India has certainly one of the best schools of mathematics including many leading mathematicians.

In astronomy and astrophysics, the principal hurdle for modern research in the past had been the lack of proper observational tools. To a large extent this basic drawback no longer exists; the 234-centimetre Vainu Bappu telescope near Bangalore, with its modern auxiliary equipment, and three other medium aperture optical telescopes, provide the basic infrastructure for making advances in the field.

In the field of radio-astronomy, the country already possesses large instruments such as the Ooty synthesis radio-telescope and the Gauribidanur low-frequency array. More recently, the building of a giant meter-wave radio-telescope is already underway; and when completed in the 1990s, will be the largest telescope of its kind in the world.

And in physics, India has two or three very strong schools of condensed matter physics in Bangalore, Delhi, and Bombay. Comparable centres in cosmic-ray physics, plasma physics, geochemistry, and geophysics exist.

***

The mentioning of these developments in the area of pure science discloses an aspect of the Indian scene which is somewhat disconcerting.

Let me present the problem this way.

The number of Fellows of the Royal Society is by no means a satisfactory index of scientific progress; but it does provide some measure. By the end of the Second World War, there were living some eight Fellows of the Royal Society, and all of them were professors at a university: Calcutta,

Allahabad, Dacca, and Delhi. Today, there are some fifteen Fellows of the Royal Society. They are distributed among all the physical and biological sciences including agriculture. All of them have done their major scientific work in India. But none of them belong to any university. They are all members of one or another of the research institutes in Bombay, Delhi, Bangalore, or Calcutta. A conclusion one can draw from this disparity between pre- and post-independence India, is that the universities are no longer centres of learning. Research and scholarship, such as they are, are cultivated at the institutes.

* * *

I mentioned earlier that in building the various national laboratories and technological institutes in India, Nehru had expressed the hope that these institutes would provide able engineers and technicians for the building of India. But it has not worked out that way. First, the universities were greatly weakened by the scientists migrating to better-paid positions in the newly started research laboratories, creating a serious manpower problem for the growth of science and technology. One thought (and hoped) that the technological institutes would play their role instead, and indeed 'aid' for their building was provided by Western countries. These Institutes of Technology produced some of India's brightest engineers; but they promptly emigrated to Western countries, which (perhaps it is ungenerous to charge) conveniently changed their immigration laws to attract them. In some way it appeared to Indians that the Western countries were obtaining needed technological personnel with the relatively minuscule aid they provided for building these institutes. It is known, for example, that more than one-half the graduating classes of these Institutes of Technology sooner or later find permanent positions in the United States or Western Europe. The situation is not very different with doctors: the medical service in Britain would collapse if Indian and Pakistani doctors who staff their hospitals suddenly abandoned their positions. While the attraction of the higher standard of living is a lure for bright young scientists, engineers, and doctors from Third World countries, the source of the difficulty goes deeper: it lies in the lack of commensurate development of schools, colleges, and universities. That the universities, colleges, and their affiliated libraries have been neglected since independence is apparent to anyone who visits a university library after visiting one of the national laboratories. The question is insistent: why, since independence, men with the vision of Bhabha and Bhatnagar have not pressed equally for strengthening university schools and colleges.

***

So far, I have given a more or less objective account of the role that science has played in the administrative policies of India since independence; and what I have said may be familiar to many of you. I hope you will forgive me if I now turn to the narration of some incidents in which I myself played a part. But the centre stage belongs to Nehru and to Ramanujan. Besides, the story will in some ways be characteristic of the Indian scene during the earlier decades of this century.

Ramanujan is without question the greatest man of science that India has produced during this century. The tragic story of his early death and the brief years of his productive activity while in Cambridge, England, in association with G.H. Hardy, are well known. And Jawaharlal Nehru knew of him even before his famous address to the Indian Science Congress in 1938, from which I quoted at the outset. But Nehru's 'magnificent obsession with science', as someone has described it, went far deeper: he had a genuine appreciation for the intellectual aspects of the pursuit of science. Let me illustrate this fact.

It is well known that during the early 1930s, while languishing in a British prison, Nehru wrote weekly letters to his then teenage daughter, Indira, on India and world history. In one of them, referring to the origins of the Indian National Movement, he wrote: 'There was a cultural awakening also. Bengal produced one of our greatest countrymen of this age, the poet Rabindranath Tagore ... And among great Indian scientists I may name J.C. Bose, Ramanujan and Raman.'

May I turn to telling you how I came to know of Ramanujan myself and what it may reflect on the spirit among young men and women of India of those times.

It must have been a day in April 1920, when I was not quite ten years old, when my mother told me of an item in the newspaper of the day that a famous Indian mathematician, Ramanujan by name, had died the preceding day; and she told me further that Ramanujan had gone to England some years earlier, had collaborated with some famous English mathematicians, and that he had returned only very recently, and was well known internationally for what he had achieved. Though I had no idea at that time of what kind of a mathematician Ramanujan was, or indeed what scientific achievement meant, I can still recall the gladness I felt at the assurance that one brought up under circumstances similar to my own, could have achieved what I could not grasp. I am sure that others were equally gladdened. I hope that it is not hard for you to imagine what the example of Ramanujan could have provided for young men and women of those times, beginning to look at the world with increasingly different perceptions.

The fact that Ramanujan's early years were spent in a scientifically sterile atmosphere, that his life in India was not without hardships, that under the circumstances that appeared to most Indians as nothing short of miraculous, he had gone to Cambridge, supported by eminent mathematicians, and had returned to India with every assurance that he would be considered, in time, as one of the most original mathematicians of the century – these facts were enough – more than enough – for aspiring young Indian students to break their bonds of intellectual confinement and perhaps soar the way that Ramanujan had.

It may be argued, perhaps with some justice, that this was a sentimental attitude: Ramanujan represents so extreme a fluctuation from the norm that his being born an Indian must be considered to a large extent as accidental. But to the Indians of the time, Ramanujan was not unique in the way we think of him today. He was one of others who had, during that same period, achieved, in their judgement, comparably in science and in other areas of human activity. Gandhi, Motilal and Jawarhalal Nehru, Rabindranath Tagore, and a host of others, were in the forefront of the then fermenting Indian scene. The twenties and the thirties were a period when young Indians were inspired by the achievements and accomplishments of the men they saw amongst them.

I do not wish to leave the impression that Ramanujan's influence was only in this very generalized sense. I think it is fair to say that almost all the mathematicians who reached distinction during the three or four decades following Ramanujan were directly or indirectly inspired by his example.

***

Let me continue with the story of Ramanujan.

During the late forties after the war, Sir Alagappa Chettiar (as he was then) wrote to me inquiring if it might be useful for him to found a mathematical institute in Madras named after Ramanujan. I enthusiastically supported the idea; and when I returned to India briefly in 1951, the Ramanujan Institute had been founded a few months earlier. Its first director, T. Vijayaraghavan, was one of the most talented among Hardy's former students; he died at a comparatively early age in 1955. C.T. Rajagopal, a student of Ananda Rao, took over the directorship from him. Already at that time the financial status of the institute seemed shaky, since Alagappa Chettiar's fortune was melting away.

In April 1957, when Alagappa Chettiar died, the fate of the institute hung in the balance; Rajagopal wrote to me that the institute 'will cease to exist on the first of next month', whereupon I wrote to the prime minister (Jawaharlal Nehru) explaining the origin of the institute and the seriousness of its condition. Nehru's prompt answer was refreshing: 'Even if you had not put in your strong recommendation in favour of the Ramanujan Institute of Mathematics, I would not have liked anything to happen which put an end to it. Now that you have also written to me on this subject, I shall keep in touch with this matter and I think I can assure you that the institute will be carried on.' And it was; but haltingly and precariously, for the next twelve years.

And with this letter from Nehru, we have come full circle.

* * *

What is it one learns from the manner of the development of science in India since independence; and of the broader implications of the story I have narrated? The feelings of Jawaharlal Nehru on the night before he died may provide us a lesson.

On the morning he was found dead, by his bedside was a book of poems by Robert Frost opened on the page wherein we read:

> The woods are lovely, dark, and deep,
> But I have promises to keep,
> And miles to go before I sleep,
> And miles to go before I sleep.

eight

Astronomy in Science and in Human Culture[1]

It is hardly necessary for me to say how deeply sensitive I am to the honour of giving this second lecture in this series founded in the memory of the most illustrious name of independent modern India. As Pandit Jawaharlal Nehru has written, 'The roots of an Indian grow deep into the ancient soil; and though the future beckons, the past holds back.'

I hope I will be forgiven if I stray for a moment from the announced topic of my lecture to recall, how forty-one years ago, I was one of thousands of students who went to greet young Jawaharlal (as we used to call him at that time) on his arrival to address the National Congress meeting in Madras that year.

I recall also how the dominant feeling in all of us at that time was one of intense pride in the men amongst us and in what they inspired in us – Lokmanya Tilak, Mahatma Gandhi, Lala Lajpat Rai, Motilal Nehru, Jawaharlal Nehru, Sardar Patel, Sarojini Naidu, Rabindranath Tagore, Srinivasa Ramanujan – names that herald the giants that lived amongst us in that pre-dawn era.

---

1 Nehru Memorial Lecture, 1968

The topic I have chosen for this lecture, 'Astronomy in Science and in Human Culture,' is so large that I am afraid that what I can say on this occasion can at best be a collection of incoherent thoughts. In the first part of the lecture I shall make some general observations on ancient Hindu astronomy, particularly with reference to the way it relates Hindu culture to the other cultures of antiquity. I am not in any sense a student of these matters. My knowledge is solely derived from the writings of a distinguished historian of science, Professor Otto Neugebauer, who has kindly helped me in preparing this part of my lecture.

In the second part of the lecture, I shall say something about the particular role of astronomy in expanding the realm of man's curiosity about his environment.

One aspect of astronomy is certain: it is the only science for which we have a continuous record from ancient times to the present. As Abu l-Qasim Said ibn Ahmad wrote in 1068 in a book entitled *The Categories of Nations:* 'The category of nations which has cultivated the sciences form an elite and an essential part of the creation of Allah.' And he enumerated eight nations as belonging to this class: 'The Hindus, the Persians, the Chaldeans, the Hebrews, the Greeks, the Romans, the Egyptians, and the Arabs.'

Chronologically, the interactions between the leading civilizations of the ancient world are far more complex than this simple enumeration suggests. And a study of these interactions provides us with a most impressive testimony to man's abiding interest in the universe around him.

We know today that Babylonian astronomy reached a scientific level only a century or two before the beginning of Greek astronomy in the fourth century BC. The development of Hellenistic astronomy, after its early beginnings, to its last perfection by Ptolemy in AD 140 is largely unknown. Then, about three centuries later, Indian astronomy, manifestly influenced by Greek methods, emerges. This last fact raises the question as to the way in which this transmission of information from Greece to India took place. Its answer is made particularly difficult since it implies possible Persian intermediaries. Some centuries later, in the ninth century, Islamic astronomy appears influenced by Hindu as well as Hellenistic sources.

While Greek astronomy rapidly became dominant in the eastern part of the Muslim world from Egypt to Persia, the methods of Hindu astronomy persisted in western Europe even as late as the fifteenth century, as I shall indicate later.

As far as Babylonian astronomy is concerned, we know very little about its earlier phases. But it appears that a mathematical approach to the prediction of lunar and planetary theory was not developed before the fifth century BC: that is to say, barely prior to the corresponding stage of development of Greek astronomy. It is, however, generally agreed that the development of Babylonian astronomy took place independently of the Greeks.

An important distinction between the Babylonian and the Greek methods is this: Babylonian methods are strictly arithmetical in character and are not derived from a geometrical model of planetary motion; the Greek methods, on the other hand, have invariably had a geometric basis. This distinction enables us to identify their influence in Hindu astronomy, for example.

Let me make a few remarks on Greek astronomy as it is relevant to my further discussion.

The earliest Greek model that was devised to account for the appearance of planetary motion is that of Eudoxus in the middle of the fourth century BC. On this model, planetary motion was interpreted as a superposition of uniform rotations about certain inclined axes. In spite of many glaring inadequacies, this model had a profound impact on subsequent planetary theory. The culmination of Hellenistic astronomy is, of course, contained in Ptolemy's *Almagest* – perhaps the greatest book on astronomy ever written; and it remained unsurpassed and unsuperseded until the beginning of the modern age of astronomy with Kepler.

Ptolemy's modification of lunar theory is of special importance for the problem of the transmission of Greek astronomy to India. The essentially Greek origin of the *Surya Siddhanta* – which is the classical textbook of Hindu astronomy – cannot be doubted: it is manifested in the terminology, in the units used, and in the computational methods. But Hindu astronomy of the north does not appear to have been influenced by the Ptolemaic refinements of the lunar theory; and this appears to be true with planetary theory also. This fact is of importance; a study of Hindu astronomy will give us much needed information on the development of Greek astronomy from Hipparchus in 150 BC to Ptolemy in AD 150.

In early Hindu astronomy, as summarized by Varaha Mihira in the *Pancha Siddhantika*, we can distinguish two distinct methods of approach: the trigonometric methods best known through *Surya Siddhanta* and the arithmetical methods of Babylonian astronomy in the astronomy of the south. The Babylonian influence has come to light only in recent years; and I shall presently refer to its continued active presence in the Tamil tradition of the seventeenth and the eighteenth centuries.

I should perhaps state explicitly here that the fact that Hindu astronomy was deeply influenced by the West does not by any means exclude that it developed independent and original methods. It is known, for example, that in Hindu astronomy the chords of a circle (of radius R) were replaced by the more convenient trigonometric function Sin α = (R Sin a).

Before I conclude with some remarks on the simultaneous existence of two distinct astronomical traditions in India, I should like to illustrate my general remarks by two specific illustrations which are of some interest.

In 1825, Colonel John Warren of the East India Company stationed at Fort St. George, Madras, wrote a book of over 500 quarto pages entitled *Kala Sankalita* with a *Collection of Memoirs on the Various Methods According to Which the Southern Part of India Divided Time.* In this book, Warren described how he had found a calendar maker in Pondicherry who showed him how to compute a lunar eclipse by means of shells placed on the ground and from tables memorized as he stated 'by means of certain artificial words and phrases'. Warren narrates that even though his informer did not understand a word of the theories of Hindu astronomy, he was nevertheless endowed with a memory sufficient to arrange very distinctly his operations in his mind and on the ground. And Warren's informer illustrated his methods by computing for him the circumstances of the lunar eclipse of 31 May–1

June 1825 with an error of + 4 minutes for the beginning, - 23 minutes for the middle, and - 52 minutes for the end. But it is not the degree of accuracy of his result that concerns us here; it is rather the fact that a continuous tradition still survived in 1825, a tradition that can be traced back to the sixth century AD with Varaha Mihira, to the third century in the Roman Empire and to the Seleucid cuneiform tablets of the second and the third centuries.

A second instance I should like to mention is an example of the survival of Hindu astronomy in parts of the Western world that were remote from Hellenistic influences during the medieval times. A Latin manuscript has recently been published which contains chronological and astronomical computations for the year 1428 for the geographical latitude of Newminster, England. It used methods manifestly related to *Surya Siddhanta.* Obviously, one has to assume Islamic intermediaries for a contact of this kind between England of the fifteenth century and Hindu astronomy.

While *Surya Siddhanta* manifests Greek influence, Babylonian influence has recently been established in the post-Vedic and pre-*Surya Siddhanta* period. For example, in the astronomy of that period, the assumptions of a longest day of 18 *muhurtas* and a shortest day of 12 *muhurtas* were made. This ratio of 3:2 is hardly possible for India. But it is appropriate for Mesopotamia; and possible doubts about the Babylonian origin of this ratio were removed when the same ratio was actually found in Babylonian text. In addition, a whole group of other parallels between Babylonian and Indian astronomy have since been established. Thus, the most characteristic feature of Hindu time reckoning – the *tithis* – occurs in Babylonian lunar theory.

Clearly, all these facts must be taken into account in any rational attempt to evaluate the intellectual contacts between ancient India and the Western world. This problem of foreign contacts is by no means the only, or even the most, important fact that is to be ascertained. One must consider the Dravidic civilizations of the south on a par with the history, the language, and the literature of the Aryan component of Indian culture. It is, as Neugebauer has emphasized, this dualism of Tamil and

Sanskrit sources that will provide for us, eventually, a deeper insight into the structure of Indian astronomy.

In his book, *Rome Beyond Imperial Frontiers*, Sir Mortimer Wheeler comes to the conclusion that 'the far more extensive contacts with South India have been a blessing to the archaeologists' but he adds that 'these contacts had no influence on these cultures themselves'. Hindu astronomy provides an example to the contrary. Exactly as it is possible to distinguish between commercial contacts which India had through the Punjab or through the Malabar and Coromandel Coast, it is possible to distinguish the astronomy of the *Surya Siddhanta* on the one hand and the Tamil methods on the other. This distinction is indeed very marked. The *Surya Siddhanta* is clearly based on pre-Ptolemaic Greek methods while the Tamil methods, in their essentially arithmetical character, manifest the influence of Babylonian astronomy of the Seleucid–Parthian period.

One must not, of course, conclude that the Tamil methods were imported directly from Mesopotamia while the geometric methods came to the north via the Greeks, and through, possibly, Persian intermediaries. And as I stated earlier, the fact that the *Surya Siddhanta* appears not to have been influenced by the Ptolemaic refinements, provides an important key to the development of Hellenistic astronomy between the times of Hipparchus and Ptolemy.

A proper assessment of the role of Hindu science in the ancient world has yet to be made. The problem is made more difficult than is necessary by the tendency of the majority of publications of Indian scholars to claim priority for Hindu discoveries and to deny foreign influence, as well as the opposite tendency among some European scholars. These tendencies on both sides have been aggravated by the inadequate publication of the original documents: this is indeed a most pressing need. Since no astronomy at an advanced level can exist without actual computations of planetary and lunar ephimerides, it must be the first task of the historian of Hindu astronomy to search for such texts. Such texts are indeed preserved in great numbers, though actually written in very late periods. But the publication of this material is an urgent need in the exploration of oriental astronomy.

Let me conclude this somewhat incoherent account, bearing on the ancient culture of India, by emphasizing that its principal interest, lies not in the sharing or in the apportioning of credit to one nation or another but rather in the continuing thread of common understanding that has bound the elite nations of Abu l-Qasim Said ibn Ahmad, in man's constant quest to comprehend his environment.

The pursuit of astronomy at the more sophisticated level of modern science, since the time of Galileo and Kepler, is concerned with the same broad questions even though that fact is often obscured by the technical details of particular investigations.

Questions that may naturally occur to one, often appear to be meaningless in the context of current science. But with the progress of science, questions that appear as meaningless to one generation become meaningful to another. It is to this aspect of the development of astronomy in recent times that I should like to turn my attention now.

The first question that I shall consider concerns the assumption that is implicit in all science: Nature is governed by the same set of laws at all places and at all times, i.e., Nature's laws are universal. That the validity of this assumption must be raised and answered in the affirmative was the supreme inspiration which came to Newton as he saw the apple fall. Let me explain.

Galileo had formulated the elementary laws of mechanics governing the motions of bodies as they occur on the earth; and the laws he formulated were based on his studies of the motions of projectiles, of falling bodies, and of pendulums. And Galileo had, of course, confirmed the Copernican doctrine by observing the motions of the satellites of Jupiter with his telescope. But the question whether a set of laws could be formulated which governed equally the motions of all bodies, whether they be of stones thrown on the earth or of planets in their motions about the sun, did not occur to Galileo or his contemporaries. And it was the falling apple that triggered in Newton's mind the following crucial train of thought.

All over the earth objects are attracted towards the centre of the earth. How far does this tendency go? Can it reach as far as the moon? Galileo had already shown that a state of uniform motion is as natural as a state of rest and that deviations from uniform motion must imply force. If then the moon were relieved of all forces, it would leave its circular orbit about the earth and go off along the instantaneous tangent to the orbit. Consequently, so argued Newton, if the motion of the moon is due to the attraction of the earth, what the attraction really does is to draw the moon out of the tangent and into the orbit. As Newton knew the period and the distance of the moon, he could compute how much the moon falls away from the tangent in one second. Comparing this result with the speed of falling bodies, Newton found the ratio of the two speeds to be about 1 to 3600. And as the moon is sixty times farther from the centre of the earth than we are, Newton concluded that the attractive force due to the earth decreases as the square of the distance. The question then arose: If the earth can be the centre of such an attractive force, does a similar force reside in the sun, and is that force in turn responsible for the planets about the sun? Newton immediately saw that if one supposed that the sun had an attractive property similar to the earth, Kepler's laws of planetary motion become explicable at once. On these grounds, Newton formulated his law of gravitation with lofty grandeur. He stated: 'Every particle in the universe attracts every other particle in the universe with a force directly as the product of the masses of the two particles and inversely as the square of their distance apart.' Notice that Newton was not content in saying that the sun attracts the planets according to his law and that the earth also attracts the particles in its neighbourhood in a similar manner. Instead, with sweeping generality, he asserted that the property of gravitational attraction must be shared by all matter and that his law has universal validity.

During the eighteenth century, the ramifications of Newton's laws for all manner of details of planetary motions were investigated and explored. But whether the validity of Newton's laws could be extended beyond the solar system was considered doubtful by many. However, in 1803, William Herschel was able to announce from his study of close pairs of stars that in some instances the pairs represented real physical binaries revolving in orbits about each other. Herschel's observations further established that the apparent orbits were ellipses and that Kepler's second law of planetary motion, that equal areas are described in equal times, was also valid. The applicability of Newton's laws of gravitation to the distant stars was thus established. The question whether a uniform set of laws could be formulated for all matter in the universe became at last an established tenet of science. And the first great revolution in scientific thought had been accomplished.

Let me turn next to the second great revolution in the explicit context of astronomy that was accomplished during the middle of the last century.

During the eighteenth century, the idealist philosopher Bishop Berkeley claimed that the sun, the moon, and the stars are but so many sensations in our mind and that it would be meaningless to inquire, for example, as to the composition of the stars. And it was an oft-quoted statement of Auguste Compte, a positivist philosopher influential during the early part of the nineteenth century, that it is in the nature of things that we shall never know what the stars are made of. And yet that very question became meaningful and the centre of astronomical interest very soon afterwards. Let me tell this story very briefly.

You are familiar with Newton's demonstration of the character of white light by allowing sunlight to pass through a small round hole and letting the pencil of light so isolated fall on the face of a prism. The pencil of light was dispersed by the prism into its constituent rainbow colours. In 1802, it occurred to an English physicist, William Wollaston, to substitute the round hole, used by Newton and his successors to admit the light to be examined with the prism, with an elongated crevice (or slit as we would now say) l/20th of an inch in width. Wollaston noticed that the spectrum thus formed, of light 'purified' (as he stated) by the abolition of overlapping images, was traversed by seven dark lines. These Wollaston took to be the natural boundaries of the various colours. Satisfied with this quasi-explanation, he allowed the subject to drop. The subject was independently taken up in 1814 by the great Munich optician Fraunhofer. In the course of experiments on light, directed towards the perfecting of his achromatic lenses, Fraunhofer, by means of a slit and a telescope, made the surprising discovery that the solar spectrum is crossed not by seven lines but by thousands of obscure streaks. He counted some six hundred and carefully mapped over three hundred of them. Nor did Fraunhofer stop there. He applied the same system of examination to other stars; and he found that the spectra of these stars, while they differ in details from that of the sun, are similar to it in that they are also traversed by dark lines.

The explanation of these dark lines of Fraunhofer was sought widely and earnestly. But convincing evidence as to their true nature came only in the fall of 1859 when the great German physicist Kirchhoff formulated his laws of radiation. His laws in this context consist of two parts. The first part states that each substance emits radiations characteristic of itself and only of itself. And the second part states that if radiation from a higher temperature traverses a gas at a lower temperature, glowing with its own characteristic radiation, in the light which is transmitted the characteristic radiations of the glowing gas will appear as dark lines in a bright background. It is clear that in these two propositions we have the basis for a chemical analysis of the atmospheres of the sun and the stars. By comparisons with the spectral emissions produced by terrestrial substances, Kirchhoff was able to identify the presence of sodium, iron, magnesium, calcium, and a host of other elements in the atmosphere of the sun. The question which had been considered as meaningless only a few years earlier had acquired meaning. The modern age of astrophysics began with Kirchhoff and continues to the present. And we all know that one of the major contributions to our understanding of the spectra of stars and the physics of stellar atmospheres was made in our own times by Meghnad Saha.

Now I come to a question that man has always put to Nature: Was there a natural beginning to the universe around us? Or to put the question more directly: How did it all begin? All religions and all philosophical systems have felt the need and the urge to answer this question. Indeed, one may say that a theory of the universe, a theory of cosmology, underlies all religions and all myths. And one of the earliest cosmologies, formulated as such, occurs in the Babylonian epic *Enuma Elish* in the second millennium BC. The poem opens with a description of the universe as it was in the beginning:

When a sky above had not been mentioned'
And the name of firm ground below had not been thought of;
When only primeval Apsu, their begetter,
And Mummu and Ti'amat – she who gave birth to them all –
Were mingling their water in one;
When no bog had formed and no island could be found;
When no god whosoever had appeared;
Had been named by name, had been determined as to his lot –
Then were gods formed within them.

Whether the question of the origin of the universe can be answered on rational scientific grounds is not clear. It might be simplest to suppose that in all aspects the astronomical universe has always been. Or, alternatively, following Compte we might even say that it is in the nature of things that we shall never know how or when the universe began. Nevertheless, recent discoveries in astronomy have enabled us for the first time to contemplate rationally the question: Was there a natural beginning to the present order of the astronomical universe? A related question is: If the astronomical universe did have a beginning, are we entitled to suppose that the laws of Nature have remained unchanged? The two questions are clearly related.

Let me take the second question first. Have the laws of Nature remained the same? Can the universality of Nature's laws implied by Newton in his formulation of the laws of gravitation be extended to all time in a changing universe?

It is clear that over limited periods of time the laws of Nature can be assumed not to have changed. After all, the motions of planets have been followed accurately over the past three centuries – and less accurately over all historical times – and all we know about planetary motions has been accounted for with great precision with the same Newtonian laws and with the same value for the constant of gravitation. Moreover, the physical properties of the Milky Way system have been studied over most of its extent – and its extent is 30,000 light years. It can be asserted that the laws of atomic physics have not changed measurably during a period of this extent. And on the earth, geological strata have been dated for times which go back several hundreds of millions of years. In particular, the dating of these strata by the radioactive content of the minerals they contain assumes that the laws of physics have not changed over these long periods. But if during these times the astronomical universe in its broad aspects has not changed appreciably, the assumption that the laws have not changed appreciably during these same periods would appear to be a natural one. The questions that I have formulated, to have a meaning, must be predicated on the supposition that there is a time scale on which the universe is changing its aspect. And if such a time scale exists, the first question is: What is it?

That a time scale characteristic of the universe at large exists was first suggested by the discoveries of Hubble in the early twenties. There are two parts to Hubble's discoveries. The first part relates to what may be considered as the fundamental units or constituents of the universe. It emerged unequivocally from Hubble's studies that the fundamental units are the galaxies of which our own Milky Way system is not an untypical one. Galaxies occur in a wide variety of shapes and forms. The majority exhibit extraordinary organization and pattern.

To fix ideas, let me say that a galaxy contains some ten thousand million or more stars; its dimension can be measured in thousands of light years: our own galaxy has a radius of 30,000 light years. Further, the distance between galaxies is about 50 to 100 times their dimensions.

The second part to Hubble's discovery is that beyond the immediate neighbourhood of our own Milky Way system, the galaxies appear to be receding from us with a velocity increasing linearly with the distance. In other words, all the galaxies appear to be running away from us as though, as Eddington once said, 'we were the plague spot of the universe'. Hubble's law that galaxies recede from us with a velocity proportional to the distance was deduced from an examination of their spectra.

Now suppose that we take Hubble's law literally. Then it follows that a galaxy which is twice as far as another will be receding with a velocity twice that of the nearer one. Accordingly, if we could extrapolate backwards, both galaxies would have been on top of us at a past epoch. More generally, we may conclude that if Hubble's relation is a strict mathematical one, all the galaxies constituting the astronomical universe should have been together at a common point at a past calculable epoch. Whether or not we are willing to extrapolate Hubble's law backward in this literal fashion, it is clear that the past epoch calculated in the manner I have indicated does provide a scale of time in which the universe must have changed substantially. Current analysis of the observations suggests that the scale of time so deduced is about seventy thousand million years.

With the time scale established, the questions I stated earlier can be rephrased as follows: Have the laws of Nature been constant over periods as long as say thirty or forty thousand million years? And, what indeed was the universe like seventy thousand million years ago? These questions cannot be answered without some underlying theory. While there are several competing theories that are presently being considered, I shall base my remarks on the framework provided by Einstein's general theory of relativity. This theory appears to me the most reasonable.

This is clearly not the occasion to digress at this point and describe the content of the theory of relativity. Suffice it to say that it is a natural generalization of Newton's theory and a more comprehensive one. On Einstein's theory, applied to the astronomical universe in the large, it follows, that at each instant the universe can be described by a scale of distance which we may call the radius of the universe. At a given epoch it measures the furthest distance from which a light signal can reach us. This radius varies with the time. Its currently estimated value is ten thousand million light years. But the most important consequence that follows from the theory is that this radius of the universe was zero at a certain calculable past epoch some seventy thousand million years ago. In other words, the conclusion arrived at by a naive extrapolation backwards of Hubble's law, interpreted literally, is indeed a valid one. That the theory predicts such a singular origin for the universe is surprising; but it has been established rigorously, with great generality, by a young English mathematician, Roger Penrose.

And finally, it is an exact consequence of the theory that the ratio of the wavelengths of an identified line in the light of a distant galaxy to the wavelength of the same source as measured here and now, is the same as the ratio of the radius of the universe now and as it was when the light was emitted by the galaxy.

During the past few years a dozen or more objects have been discovered for which the ratio of the wavelength I mentioned is about three. Precisely what has been found is the following. In a laboratory source, hydrogen emits a line with a wavelength that is about a third of the wavelength of the visible extreme violet light. But this same line emitted by the stellar object in the remote past and arriving here on earth now is actually observed in visible light. The fact that all the identifiable spectral lines in these objects are shifted by the same factor of about three, means that the radius of the universe at the time light left these objects was three times smaller and the density was some twenty-seven times greater than they are now. And a careful analysis of the spectrum shows that during this span of time at any rate the laws of atomic physics have not changed to any measurable extent. To have been able to see back in time when the density of the universe was thirty times what it is now is, of course, a considerable advance. But even this ratio is very far from what it would have been if we take the relativistic picture and go further back in time when the radius of the universe was, say ten thousand million times smaller, not merely three times or a thousand times smaller. Does it appear that this extrapolation is meaningless and fanciful? But the general theory of relativity gives a theoretical meaning to such a question since a state of affairs attained by such extrapolation is predicted as an initial state for our present universe. In other words, the question is meaningful and one can reasonably ask: Is there anything we can observe now that can be considered as the residue or the remnant of that initial singular past? But to answer this question we must take the relativistic picture seriously and determine what it has to say about that remote past. Such a determination has been made by Robert Dicke and his associates at Princeton.

Dicke calculated that at the time the radius of the universe was 10^{10} times smaller, the temperature should have been some ten thousand million degrees – in other words a veritable fireball. And as the universe expanded, radiation of this very high temperature, which would have filled the universe at that time, would be reduced. For example, its temperature would have fallen to ten thousand degrees after the first ten million years. As the universe continued to expand beyond this point the radiation will cool adiabatically, i.e., in the same manner as gas in a chamber will cool if it is suddenly expanded. And Dicke concludes that the radiation from the original fireball must now fill the universe uniformly, but that its temperature must be very low – in fact, 3° Kelvin – a temperature that is attainable in the laboratory only by liquefying helium. It corresponds to radiation at a temperature of 270° of frost! How can we detect this low temperature radiation?

It can be shown that this radiation at 270° of frost should have its maximum observable intensity at wavelengths in the neighbourhood of 3 millimeters, i.e., the radiation must be present in the microwave region. The remarkable fact is that radiation in these wavelengths has been detected; it comes with incredible uniformity from all directions; and they have all the properties that one might, on theoretical grounds, want to attribute to such fossil radiation from the original fireball.

With these discoveries I have described, astronomy appears to have justified the curiosity that man has felt about the origin of the universe, from the beginning of time.

As I said at the outset, man's contemplation of the astronomical universe has provided us with the one continuous thread that connects us with antiquity. And might I add now that it has also inspired in him the best?

nine

Indira Gandhi: Some Recollections[1]

It is an inverted form of egoism to recount one's own meetings with great historical figures. But for ordinary citizens there is not very much choice since what could a common person say of great historical figures like Indira Gandhi which does not relate to a few personal encounters? But I hope that the following few recollections of my conversations with the former prime minister, dispersed over the past two decades, might give the reader some feeling of the kind of person she was without the glare of publicity obscuring her personality.

Soon after her father's death, when Mrs Gandhi was a minor cabinet minister in Prime Minister Shastri's government, there was a small reception for her at the University of Chicago by her longtime friend Professor Theodore W. Schultz. I was at that reception; and during a brief moment when she was standing by herself I approached her with the remark, 'It must be very different now.' Her simple answer was, 'Yes, it is.' And she turned her head away.

---

1 From *Indira Gandhi: Statesmen, Scholars, Scientists, and Friends Remember*, New Delhi, Vikas Publishing House, 1985.

Later, in 1968, I had the chance to meet her on the occasion of the Second Nehru Memorial Lecture which I had the privilege of giving. I met her in an anteroom some ten minutes before the lecture, at which she, together with President Zakir Husain, was to share the chair. Mrs Gandhi came into the room obviously tired, without having had the opportunity even to freshen up after an oppressive day at the Lok Sabha (where, as I learned from the papers the next morning, she had been shouted at and heckled). The first thing she said to me was, 'You can have no idea as to how impossible it is to do something positive in this country; everyone wants to criticize and to find fault; and yet there is so much work to be done.' Before I could respond to that, President Zakir Husain came into the room and protocol had to take precedence. Soon we were in the lecture hall and Mrs Gandhi introduced me, without notes and without preparation, with a speech that was faultless both in its form and in its content. And I hope I will be forgiven if I quote from the published version of her speech.

> Our own eminent lecturer today is an American citizen, but I am sure that that does not make him less of an Indian or diminish our admiration for him. He himself may perhaps be remembering some of the frustrations when he wanted to serve the land of his birth. And how can we forgive ourselves?
>
> The time has come, if it is not already too late, when we must make an all-out effort to break the bonds of defeatism which envelop science in India. Many of our scientists working within the country, and some working abroad, are rated amongst world leaders and can be the pride and adornment of any institution. We must do our utmost to give them the best deal by creating conditions where they can give their own best to the country and the world. There is no time to lose.
>
> Much despondency is due to our pattern of administration in which the scientist is subordinated to the bureaucrat.

Later that evening there was a dinner at her home. Everyone was seated when Mrs Gandhi arrived a little late. It was apparent that she had the time to change; but she still appeared to be in a state of tension. When

I got up to usher her into her chair, she said, 'Don't help me; I am not used to being helped.' This remark dampened everyone at the table. And to break the ice, I asked her if the account I had read in one of President Kennedy's biographical memoirs was true. The occasion was when Mrs Gandhi was on a visit to the United States before her first tenure as prime minister. The statement in Kennedy's memoir that I quoted to her was that, when she was in New York, President Kennedy had called her on the telephone; and finding that she was to appear on *Meet the Press* on NBC the following day, said, 'Appearing before Mr Spivak and his panel is like being thrown to the lions.' Mrs Gandhi vouched for the veracity of that report and added, 'The following day when I appeared at the NBC studios some ten minutes before we were to go on the air, Mr Spivak asked me, "Can you recite the Gettysburg address?" and I asked, "What for?" He answered, "To see how well you know the United States." And I responded that President Kennedy had called me the previous day and had warned me that appearing before him and his panel was like being thrown to the lions; to which Mr Spivak responded, "Oh, no, Madam Gandhi, we are all very kind and very polite." To this, my answer was, "Oh, yes, I have just returned from East Africa; and I saw there many lions. They were also very kind and very polite."' This recollection by Mrs Gandhi eased her tension and broke the ice; and during the rest of the dinner she was an exceptionally gracious and vivacious host.

The last occasion my wife and I had the privilege of meeting Mrs Gandhi was at her home 1, Safdarjang Road in February 1982. She was gracious enough to give me an appointment for the asking of it and for no particular reason. I began by asking her whether I was wrong in thinking that the pride and the hope which characterized India of the twenties and the thirties were no longer the characteristics of the India of 1982. She responded with a certain grimness, 'I am afraid that is so. National pride is no longer a national commodity; instead criticism and distrust seem to be the present national pastimes.'

My last question to Mrs Gandhi before leaving was, 'Are you optimistic about the future of India?' Her instant reply was, 'I cannot afford not to be optimistic.' At that, her face which had hitherto been grave, broadened into a most charming smile. She was a great lady if ever there was one.

Part II

Family Reminiscences

one

My Everlasting Flame[1]

Lalitha Chandrasekhar

Can one's determination to live to finish one's undertaking conquer over what fate has determined for you? I have a feeling that Chandra had that will and succeeded, although he had the constant fear that he was going to die before me. 'Chandra, we can't be sure who will die first. It may well be that I will die before you.' The question was raised but we did not know the answer then. The undertaking was his *Principia*. The steel of his determination won over the threat of Fate, as we shall see later. In this indomitable conflict, Fate had to accept defeat for a while!

We had planned to leave for Wales on Saturday, the 26th of August. Chandra had written to Bernard Schutz at Cardiff for travel brochures to plan our trip. He had also intended to discuss with him his papers in the series he was writing with Valeria Ferrari on the non-radial oscillation of stars. A week before he died, Chandra said to me: 'I don't see why I have to discuss the paper with Bernard Schutz since it seems so right.' Chandra was extremely enthusiastic about the way the problem was

1 This article originally appeared in *The Man behind the Legend*, Ed: Kameshwar Wali, Imperial College Press, 1997.

resolving itself. It was all very clear in his mind, but he had not described it in detail on paper before he died. I collected his manuscripts at home and in his office at the university and emailed them to Valeria. She worked on the problem as best as possible but could not discover what Chandra had on his mind. I urged her to look into the matter again. It is my sincere hope that in the course of time, others besides Valeria will study the problem. I had a feeling that Chandra was on the verge of something very deep and profound which would throw a new light on things. If he had lived, he would have succeeded in explaining his ideas to Valeria. This had happened a couple of times before with some of the earlier papers in the series.

***

There is no question that one of our strongest memories of India was its music. Chandra loved to hear me sing. In the days when Chandra used to drive every week from Williams Bay to Chicago to give lectures and also to attend to the journal work, I used to sing to him during our long drive back to Williams Bay. This good habit of mine slackened somewhat after we moved permanently to Chicago. But the interest returned fortunately, and I would say I sang to him very often during the many months before he died. A week before he died, I sang a song to him about Krishna lifting the Govardhana mountain to cut off the sunlight during the great war of the Mahabharata. 'Won't you sing it again?' he asked. 'No, Chandra, there is another song I want to sing to you now; but I will sing it again later.' But that 'later' did not happen. The day before he died, I had planned to sing still another song to him that I had heard years ago at a concert and which I had never learned to sing before! Somehow, it came back to me and it was beautiful. It was about Ganapati, son of Shiva. 'Shall I sing it to you, Chandra?' 'No, Lalitha, I am not feeling well. Some other time,' he replied. That 'some other time' did not come since Chandra died the next day. He left soon after breakfast to see Dr Kirsner at the hospital. He had a massive heart attack on reaching the hospital and died just four hours after he left home.

It was a shattering experience for me. How could it happen so suddenly and without warning? I consoled myself by saying that he didn't suffer. But we had hoped to be together some more years, and that was not to be.

Chandra's body was cremated and I sprinkled his ashes on every spot that he frequented in the university campus: the place around the Moore statues, the grounds of the Court Theatre, the Laboratory for Astrophysics and Space Research, the Crerar Library, the Administration Building, Mandel Hall, the Regenstein Library, and the Seminary Co-op Bookstore, in that order. I had requested Mr Sonnenschein, the president of the university and Mr Kleinbard, the vice-president of University News and Community Affairs, to accompany me when I sprinkled Chandra's ashes. They were very kind in agreeing to do so. Finally, Mr Kleinbard drove me to the promontory point jutting into Lake Michigan, where I immersed the last of Chandra's ashes to be churned in time into the Atlantic Ocean and from there to all the oceans of the world.

Chandra did not want a memorial service after his death. The idea that I might have a reunion of Chandra's friends and colleagues on an informal basis occurred to me when several of them expressed the wish to have an occasion when they could express what they felt for Chandra. About seventy-five of them from the physics, chemistry, mathematics, and astronomy departments of the University of Chicago, and some friends from outside Chicago gathered at Swift Commons on 18 October 1995, about two months after Chandra's death.

I thanked those who had accepted my invitation to come to the reunion and described in brief how our life in this country started with Chandra accepting a position at the Yerkes Observatory at Williams Bay, Wisconsin. This institution was a part of the University of Chicago, and Chandra's decision to join it in preference to the Harvard College Observatory was, I am sure, because of the magnetic personality of President Maynard Hutchins of the University of Chicago, and also because of the young and enthusiastic faculty that Dr Otto Struve, director of the observatory, had assembled at Yerkes.

He entered his new appointment at Yerkes with enthusiasm, and did a fair amount of teaching, often bearing upon his own research. He felt very strongly that teaching was the best way to clarify one's thoughts while doing research. Apart from teaching, Chandra had also accepted the task of running the Yerkes Library and was, in addition, put in charge of running the weekly colloquia. So far, the colloquia had been on astronomical subjects. Chandra felt that astronomy needed the infusion of physics to make it expand in an astrophysical sense. He persuaded the physicists in Chicago to come to Yerkes to give their colloquia. He also persuaded the astronomers to go to the Chicago campus to present their colloquia in order to influence the physicists. In the same way, chemistry and geophysics were also drawn into the picture. Chandra's vision grew wider still and he soon felt that a scientist's life would be richer if it included, among the various influences, art and music. This culminated in the Ryerson lecture he gave in 1975 on 'Shakespeare, Newton and Beethoven or Patterns of Creativity'.

Going back to the colloquia he ran at Yerkes, he used to number them and keep a record of the date and title of each colloquium in a notebook. When the number reached 100, he celebrated the occasion with a cake decorated with that number! He got a special cake made on the 1000th colloquium, with the grand and impressive number showing at the centre. Twenty years had elapsed and Chandra felt that it was a good time for him to pass the job on to someone else. A few years after we had moved permanently to Chicago, he went back to Yerkes to retrieve the colloquia notebook. It could not be found. Someone had discarded it! Why anyone would do such a thing was beyond our understanding. What a fine record it would have made for us! It was too bad!

Chandra was the managing editor for *The Astrophysical Journal* for nineteen years. But if you add the six years when he was an associate editor, and that effort was in no way minor, it can be said that Chandra was associated with the journal for a quarter of a century. Chandra thought the job was important. If no one else was willing to do it, he had to do it. One day I asked him: 'Chandra, for how long are you going to be stuck with this journal? Is it going to be forever? It is standing in the way of our having a fuller life together. Should you not think about my needs too?' There was a moment of poignant silence. Chandra was then swept out of that inner world of his and into a stark realization that he had neglected me. He was moved to tears and said, 'I am sorry, Lalitha. I should have known better. It will take some time for me to make the necessary arrangements so that I can leave the job.' He had to find another managing editor. Chandra had taken care of *Letters* and *Supplements* too, but no one he asked was willing to take on the entire load. So far, Chandra had managed all that in addition to his regular research and teaching.

The job had to be split between Helmut Abt as the new managing editor and two further editors for *Letters* and the *Supplements*. In addition, Chandra raised the position of Jeanette Burnett, who was his editorial assistant so far, to that of an assistant production manager. In addition, he had to make arrangements for the American Astronomical Society to take charge of the *Journal* and turn over to them the half-a-million dollars he had accumulated in a reserve fund.

Once all this was done, we could think of moving permanently to Chicago. Initially, we rented an apartment at 5550 Dorchester in order to get a feel of what life in Chicago would be like. We would stay there for only one or two nights a week. Then one day, while driving past the new apartment building we had seen coming up at 4800 Chicago Beach Drive, I said to Chandra: 'Let us go in there and see what kind of apartments they have.' 'You mean now?' 'Yes, now.' We went in and saw a three-bedroom apartment we liked and signed the lease right away! That was a huge triumph for me. We were finally ready to escape Yerkes. We had been there too long. A new life was about to begin and we were looking forward to it. Chancellor Hutchins had been asking Chandra for a number of years: 'Chandra, when are you going to move to Chicago? I think you should do it soon.' We had finally done it! We stayed at 4800 before we moved into our present apartment at 5825 Dorchester. This time it was Chandra who made the move, since this house was closer to the university. He had signed a lease for a three-bedroom apartment. 'Why three? I thought they had four-bedroom apartments,' I asked. 'Why do we need four bedrooms?' Chandra asked, puzzled. 'Well, we had a common study at 4800. With four bedrooms, I can have my own study,' I replied. Chandra made the change and we have been here for almost thirty years.

Chandra would remark, 'Why do I have to continue doing science? A moment should come when I can say "No more; no more writing papers, no more of this incessant grind drafting the text, entering the equations, the proofs, etc." and turn to my other interests in music and literature.' Nobody believed he would stop or could stop.

The Mathematical Theory of Black Holes was written and published – a monumental undertaking. That was the period of his collaboration with an extraordinary person – a student, a colleague, and a dear friend – Basilis Xanthopoulos. His assassination by a deranged student in Crete was a shock that Chandra could not overcome. *The Mathematical Theory* was followed by a series of papers on colliding waves, in which Basilis also collaborated. Then followed the series of papers on non-radial oscillations with Valeria Ferrari. Yes, no one believed Chandra would or could stop! And when the three-hundredth anniversary of the printing of Newton's *Principia* was celebrated and Chandra was asked to give a talk on the occasion here at the university, Chandra's early desire to read the *Principia* which he had set aside came to the forefront and he took it up enthusiastically. To begin with, he was planning to study only a few propositions bearing upon the universal law of gravitation; but as time went on, his interest expanded. He studied the lunar theory, the figure of the earth, the theory of tides, comets, velocity of sound and conic sections. There was excitement when he described the Brachistochrone problem, the initial value problem and the ascent and descent of bodies. He was thorough in verifying every equation, every corollary, and when Newton just stated the result without providing a proof, he would investigate and find out how Newton must have proved it. One of the most exciting moments in his study of the *Principia* came about when we visited the Cambridge University Library archives in Cambridge, England, to look at Newton's papers. Chandra had drawn a diagram the way he thought Newton must have drawn it when he proved a particular corollary. What did Chandra find? A diagram identical to the one he had drawn! I was most impressed and said to him: 'Chandra, you have succeeded in entering Newton's mind and discovered how his mind worked.'

Chandra was quite afraid that he might not live to finish writing his *Principia*, and when he had finished writing it, to see it through the publication by the Oxford University Press. But fortune was kind and it was published, and he finally had his own personal copy of the book that he could hold in his hand and turn the pages of. But the most exciting moment for me was when he called me from his office to say that he had received ten extra copies. 'The first of these copies is for you. May I come over right away and give it to you?' 'Oh, please do. I can't wait to receive it.' He came over right away and presented me with my copy. I turned the pages, and was overwhelmed on seeing that the book was dedicated to me! 'Chandra, how good of you, it is an honour, but I am not sure I deserve it.' 'Of course you do. You have been with me all through the writing, supporting me, and following my efforts with great interest. When we were at the Oxford University Press to see the galley proofs of the book, I had told everyone, particularly Mike Mansfield that this particular page should not be in evidence, and you did not notice the absence!' he said, having ensured that I would not get to see the dedication page in the proof stage. 'It is such a beautiful idea, and is all the more meaningful to me. Thank you for making this moment so very precious to me.' Chandra had that rare ability to give special meaning to such moments. Chandra watched me as I turned every page to see the carefully drawn diagrams, the explanatory text, and the superb printing by the Oxford University Press. 'Beautifully done,' I told him, and remembered Mike Mansfield telling me: 'This is the best book we have published.' Chandra used to say that he had discovered something new in almost every page of the *Principia*. It was our intention to go through the entire book together, but unfortunately, we were able to go through only about a third of it. August 21 had arrived to take him away.

Chandra used to say that he would probably be remembered more for his work on the *Principia* than for his other scientific contributions. That he would be remembered for his work on the *Principia* is, without question, true. But I have no doubt that he would be remembered equally for all his scientific work. The interest, use and influence of any of Chandra's work is due to the way in which he approached the subject under investigation: he looked into every detail, found out what had already been done on the subject, what was still to be investigated, and what were the errors that had entered into the field and caused confusion in scientific thinking. The problem became particularly serious if a well-known scientist had introduced the error and people failed to notice the error out of respect for him! When every detail in a subject had been carefully looked into, the subject began to reveal new secrets. These were the discoveries Chandra made since the subject lay transparent before him. He would stand back and get a perspective of the subject. I had an input in the way he looked at a subject. I called the arrangement of all the details a formal garden; the errors were the weeds which had to be pulled out.

There is another thing that Chandra will be remembered for in this university. This was put in a nutshell by President Hutchins to me when Chandra and I went to hear a lecture of his. He had already left the university to head the Center for the Study of Democratic Institutions at Santa Barbara in California and had come to Chicago to give his lecture. At the end of the lecture, we went to tell him how much we enjoyed hearing his lecture. Mr Hutchins then held both my hands and said to me: 'The best thing I did for the University of Chicago was to appoint your husband to the faculty.' Chandra heard him say it and said to me later: 'He is exaggerating.' A year later, we were in Santa Barbara. 'Chandra, we should visit Mr Hutchins,' I said. 'I don't know if we really should,' Chandra replied. 'We really should,' I insisted. Mr Hutchins received us graciously and, again, as we were leaving, he took my hands and repeated: 'The best thing I did for the University of Chicago was to appoint your husband to the faculty'. This time, there was no denying the sincerity of that statement. He seemed to mean every bit of it and it touched our hearts. We were glad we went to see him since he died soon after. Now, why did Mr Hutchins make this statement to me on two different occasions? There is no question he must have remembered how Dean Gale of the physics department had refused to allow Chandra to lecture at the campus. The refusal was blunt: he did not want this black scientist from India to lecture in his department. Hutchins had written a one-line reply to Mr Struve, the director of the Yerkes Observatory, who had been in a dilemma, and who brought the matter to Hutchins' attention. 'Mr Chandrasekhar shall give his lectures.' The lectures were given and many who had heard them have remarked about their mathematical elegance. The full purport of Hutchins' remark to me was that Chandra had paved the way for other non-white members to be appointed to the faculty.

But Chandra had been lecturing at Yerkes Observatory long before all this. News of these remarkable lectures spread and students came from all over the country to hear him, and to do research with him to earn their Ph.Ds. Fifty-one students in all received their Ph.Ds with him. A few of these were from overseas. There were also post-docs and scientists who came to work with him.

I used to attend Chandra's lectures at Yerkes too. Not many people know that I was a student with Chandra in the physics department at Presidency College in Madras, India. He was a year senior to me. Some of the classes were common for both of us. I used to sit in the front row. Immediately behind me was Chandra. I knew his presence and he knew mine. In this way, a friendship arose, which in later years, Chandra used to describe in the following words: 'There was a girl I knew then. I left for Cambridge, England. After seven years, I returned and married her; and we have lived together happily ever after.' That 'ever' lasted almost sixty years. We were planning to celebrate our sixtieth wedding anniversary in 1996 by going to the Lyric opera in Chicago to see Wagner's *Ring Cycle*, just as we had been to Bayreuth in Germany to celebrate our fiftieth wedding anniversary by watching the same opera. The tickets came, but Chandra wasn't with me to see the operas. I took others and we remembered.

There was an azalea plant which was given to Chandra by a friend of his. It bloomed for a while and then there were no more flowers. But I watered it anyway and it became a handsome plant with beautiful leaves but no flowers. After a few months it sprouted buds. Chandra and I used to watch these buds, hoping they would bloom some day. They didn't. But after he died they bloomed, one by one. The flowers were larger and brighter in colour than those that the plant had before. 'Chandra, you are blooming for me,' I said to myself. I called the plant 'My Everlasting Flame.'

Chandra's remark about standing in the valley below and waiting for the sun to rise over the Kanchenjunga has often been quoted. That was the last sentence in his essay on the 'Pursuit of Science'. Now I am standing in the valley, looking at the summit of the Kanchenjunga. I feel that he is there at the top, looking at the universe. He has reached the summit and has found peace.

two

My Anna[1]

S. (Purasu) Balakrishnan

Pen in hand, I pause to think how I can render in words even a faint impression of the respected and beloved man – brother, scholar, gentleman and genius – who made our circle special by just being in it and is now no more.

We were four brothers and six sisters living in a spacious bungalow called 'Chandra Vilas'. Two-storeyed and beautiful, with two high arches framing a front verandah in each storey, and a fair-sized compound around it. It was situated in the elite locality of Mylapore in Madras, at that time home to eminent judges, lawyers, scholars, authors and musicians.

All of us brothers were born in Lahore, now in Pakistan. Our father, Chandrasekhar Subrahmanyan Ayyar, was in government service in the finance department and was liable to transfers all over (then undivided) India. There was a gap of about two years each between the three elder brothers (me being the third), and of twelve between me and the fourth,

1 This article originally appeared in *The Man Behind the Legend*, edited by Kameshwar Wali, Imperial College Press, 1997. Anna: The Tamil word for 'elder brother', the appellation by which Chandrasekhar was known in our circle.

Ramnath. In my boyish fancy, I used to think that we were like Rama and his three brothers (in the epic Ramayana), and that there was an affinity between Anna and me, just as there was between Rama and Lakshmana. Truth to tell, I sensed early on that my two elder brothers, Chandrasekhar and Visvanathan were closer to each other. The bond between Anna and me developed later, after he left for England on 1 August 1930. This separation had the effect of bringing us together in spirit, making our comradeship abstract, shorn of every disfigurement of reality, lifting it to the ideal, lonely world of communication by letters.

Of the younger days of eager, striving idealism, the time we spent before he left for England, I retain few but vivid memories. The first picture that comes to my mind is of us walking – while returning from school in Triplicane – on the Marina Beach in Madras in the evenings, he with quick long strides, I keeping up with him somehow, drinking in the breeze like a horse (and I should add, a diminutive one) and receiving his sparse words with silent assent and admiration. His words were few indeed, and none in the grand style, but they created a thrilling atmosphere on the breezy seashore. He loved the beach of Madras greatly. I remember how, when he had the privilege of enjoying a car ride along the Marina with Prof. Heisenberg of Germany (a Nobel Prize winner), who was at that time visiting Madras, Chandrasekhar told our mother exultantly that the professor had been charmed by the beach. This little event occurred when Chandrasekhar was a student of physics – the precise date being 14 October 1929 – and like some of the little events in great men's lives, I imagine, this personal contact with the celebrated foreign physicist had a great influence on him at that time, for Heisenberg's name was often on his lips. 'Heisenberg,' he told me once, 'can be compared only with Einstein.' And again, 'What a genius! And when very young he had flashed across the scientific world with his meteor-like brilliance!' Chandrasekhar came in contact with another great foreign scientist during his college days: Professor Arnold Sommerfeld of Germany. By no means were these the first influences in Chandrasekhar's life, for he laughingly told me once how, as a schoolboy, he would go to the beach to be alone, and there prostrate himself devoutly on the sands with the prayer: 'Oh God, may I be like Newton!' 'What days they were!' he would add with a smile after a moment.

In August or September 1936, during his short visit to India, as we were walking on the beach road in Madras, he observed: 'The relationship between a man and a woman, I think can never be perfect as between a man and a man, such as, for example, exists between you and me. We don't demand anything from each other and there is perfect understanding between us. But it is different in the case of a man and a woman. One always demands something from the other. The relationship is never ideal.'

***

This native wistfulness of his nature became emphasized during his prolonged exile from his country. Our mother's death, less than a year after he left home, affected him greatly. But his mind was made of the stern stuff of discipline.

Year after year, in the midst of his hectic schedule, and the stream of his publications, the moods of his pensive mind asserted themselves, probably accentuated by his controversy with Eddington, which would have been ruinous but for his phoenix-like quality of rising from the ashes. He wrote to me from Cambridge on 26 June 1935:

> It is ages since I heard from you ... For the first time in months I feel homesick. I shall return surely before June next year – that is, in less than a year! How I look forward to it! I shall be different, and so will the others be. Six years! How long! You see, I can hardly imagine how things are at home. Memory fails, not because I cannot recollect, but because memory recalls what is no more. Whenever I think of home, the scene that almost always appears before me is mother lying on the easy chair in front of the house. I do not know why I always recollect her in a red saree ... All gone ...

Despite his homesickness, he felt at home in Cambridge, a fact that is demonstrated by his letters. He was invited as a visiting lecturer by two

American universities. He crossed the Atlantic on 30 November 1935 on board the *Brittanic*. Two days before his departure from England, he wrote: 'I am going to Harvard as a visiting lecturer in cosmic physics ... Do please write to me during your Christmas holidays, particularly as I shall appreciate letters from home when away from my second home at Cambridge – if you understand what I mean – I love Cambridge!'

At Harvard, he delivered a course of ten lectures; and from there he wrote to me on 23 March 1936:

> I was planning to reply to your earlier letter from the boat. As things stand, it is more than probable that I [will] return home for some weeks during the month of July, August and September ... You might know that I have more or less decided to accept an invitation from the University of Chicago to join the Yerkes Observatory as a research associate. It is a fairly good position, and it will be of great value to me personally to be attached to one of the really great observatories of the world. I visited Chicago and Yerkes about two weeks ago. I had a very enjoyable time at Yerkes. The Yerkes Observatory is situated on the bank of a beautiful lake: Williams Bay, and behind it are wild woods – a truly inspiring place. Dr Struve, the director, was very nice, and the prospects are altogether fair ... So it does seem that we are to work our lives' purposes in different countries ... Perhaps I am selfish. But science has the tradition only of itself, while art is true in only so far as it weaves human forces in the network of nature, especially of one's own country. Perhaps I am too sweeping, but I am having in my mind Turgenev and Tolstoy. To say this, however, is not to deny the international appeal of really great literature.

This letter gives the origin of his connection with the Chicago University, where he is now a legend and a tradition by himself. He received a similar invitation from Harvard University, of which, however, he did not avail himself. It is also a testimony to the literary strand in him. It is to be noted that he mentions Turgenev before Tolstoy.

He left Chicago for a while for Cambridge and packed for India – after six years.

He sailed from Genoa on 31 July 1936 and arrived in Bombay on 12 August. He married Lalitha, whom he had known as a student in the physics honours class in Presidency College, on 11 September 1936, and left with her for England on 17 October.

I recall, on two evenings, we walked on the Marina of Madras. He was a recognized scientist. He had shot into the Indian sky like a meteor, or shall I say like Professor Heisenberg in the German sky. But I saw walking beside me an earnest, eager student, thinking only in terms of the pursuit of knowledge, warmed immediately by the mention of high endeavour in any sphere, persuading me, without being patronizing, to think highly of myself. Truly, here is the seed of greatness, I thought.

* * *

Although I have mentioned the important event of his wedding, I shall not forgive myself if, on account of the interlude, I pass over a comparatively trifling incident: his visit to Mrs Janaki Ammal, the widow of the late Ramanujan. Chandra and I went together to her modest lodgings in one of the dark and dingy by-lanes of Triplicane. Later, she called at his house, and he introduced her to his sisters and even succeeded in making that shy lady feel at home. He told her how the great professors across the seas revered the memory of her late husband as that of a guru, a master. 'The other scientists here,' he told her, 'are worth only the dust on his feet.' He informed her that one of the professors in England was writing a book on Ramanujan, and to illustrate it, a good photograph of Ramanujan was necessary. The available photographs of him were disappointing. Could she help in the matter? She said that it was a pity that she had no photographs of her husband. However, she did have his passport with her. Chandrasekhar replied that he would like to have a look at it. He went with her to her house and got the passport. The tiny photograph of Ramanujan was a find!

When Anna left India, he entrusted the passport to me, asking me to make copies of the photograph to be sent to him, and to return the passport to Ramanujan's wife. When I carried out his instructions (keeping, however, one copy of the photograph with me), he wrote to me from Williams Bay on 18 October 1937: 'Your letter and Ramanujan's photograph. Thanks very much for sending them. I think it is extremely fortunate that we arranged to have this – really the first fairly good photograph of Ramanujan. I think it will become the official one as Hardy will probably publish it in his book on Ramanujan.'

It is a measure of the man's thoughtfulness that despite years having passed after the incident, on 19 July 1942, he wrote to our father acknowledging my role in procuring the photograph:

> I was interested to know that you have read Hardy's *A Mathematician's Apology*. I also was enthusiastic over it. Incidentally, have you seen his book on Ramanujan – a book in the Cambridge University series – a companion to Ramanujan's 'Collected Papers'? In Hardy's book on Ramanujan, there is a frontispiece photograph of Ramanujan – a photograph which is, in a sense, a discovery – though Balakrishnan had a lot to do with it.

It was from this photograph that forty years later, on the initiative of Richard Askey and Chandrasekhar, four busts of Ramanujan were made by the sculptor Paul T. Granlund of Gustavus College, Saint Peter, Minnesota, USA. One of them was commissioned, through donations secured by Richard Askey from the international community of mathematicians, to be presented to Mrs Ramanujan, which was done in the autumn of 1983. Richard Askey acquired one; Anna and Lalitha two. Anna kept one in his house, and presented the other to the Raman Institute in Bangalore. Later, he presented the bust in his possession to the Royal Society of England.

* * *

America proved a grateful and congenial home to Chandra. He joined the Yerkes Observatory as a research associate in 1937 and was promoted to a full professorship in 1943. His papers and those of his colleagues and collaborators became a regular feature in *The Astrophysical Journal*, of which he became editor. He was recognized, in the words of an American astronomer, as 'one of the leading authorities in the field of galactic dynamics', and became an integral part of the progress in the field of astronomy in America. Throughout his years in America, Chandra wrote to me about his life in America, about his work and his feelings about home and the people he had left behind.

To continue here, however, I may perhaps indicate my association with him through the years in the world of books. In his Cambridge years (1933–34) he presented to me a copy of J.W.N. Sullivan's *Beethoven* and a copy of Sir James Jean's *Mysterious Universe*. I used the former in my article 'From Schiller through Browning and Beethoven to the Upanishads: A Crescendo of Joy', which appeared in the *Literary Quarterly* of Mysore in January 1993. I used the latter in my book, *The Big Bang and Brahma's Day*, which came out in 1995.

On his brief visit to India from Cambridge in 1936, he made a present to me of a set of fifteen volumes of Chekhov – comprising thirteen stories and two plays – translated by Constance Garnett. Apropos of this splendid and sumptuous gift, I may mention that I wrote a biography of Chekhov in Tamil which was published in 1947.

All through his life and after his death (I shall explain the latter phrase presently) I received gifts of books from him. These comprised: Victor Robinson's *Story of Medicine*; Quentin Bell's *Virginia Woolf: A Biography*; two volumes of *Pediatric Clinics of North America* on my request since I needed them in connection with writing some medical articles; three books by Oliver Sacks: *The Man Who Mistook His Wife for a Hat*, *Awakenings* and *An Anthropologist on Mars*; Arvid Paulson's *Late Plays of Henrik Ibsen*; *Julie and Other Plays* by August Strindberg; Peter Brook's translation of Jean-Claude Carriere's play *The Mahabharatha*; T.S. Elliot's *Collected Poems*.

Chandrasekhar also gave me some of his own books, like *Eddington: the Most Distinguished Astrophysicist of His Time* and *Truth and Beauty: Aesthetics and Motivations in Science*.

I have set aside for separate mention in order to quote the inscriptions that they carried: J.A.B. Van Buitenen's translation of *The Mahabharatha*, Books 2 and 3, and Henri Troyat's *Chekhov*. The inscriptions respectively were as follows: 'For Balakrishnan, in grateful remembrance of the fortnight I spent at his house in Bangalore, 1975, S. Chandrasekhar' and 'For Balakrishnan and Shyamala, in remembrance of the most relaxed and refreshing two weeks in your home, Anna, 1987'.

He regularly sent me all his published articles, even the scientific ones, although I have no pretensions to understanding them.

On 19 July 1995, a month before he passed away (on 21 August 1995), I received a copy of his book *Newton's Principia for the Common Reader*. He had called me up earlier that he had instructed the publisher (Oxford University Press) to send me a copy. Acknowledging receipt of the book over the phone, I told him: 'It is a glorious book, magnificently produced. I am overwhelmed. You have spared a copy for me when I cannot understand a word of it.' 'No,' he replied, 'there are some quotations in it; you can understand them.' He was probably referring to the covering quotation for the book by Dr Samuel Johnson which he used to explain to the incredulous reader why he had given the name, such as it was, to the book. It was his swansong. He had told me several times over the phone that, with this book, he would put a stop to all his research and writing. There is something appropriate to this being his last work, something akin to rounding off his life in terms of his boyhood prayer: 'O God, may I be like Newton!', or in terms of his dictum: 'the last of life for which the first was made'.

About three months after he passed away, I received a book, a splendid one: *Rabindranath Tagore* by Krishna Dutta and Andrew Robinson. It was mailed to me by Seminary Co-operative Bookstore Inc., Chicago, with a letter from the manager dated 14 November 1995:

> Dear Dr Balakrishnan,
>
> Before Professor Chandrasekhar died, he had asked the bookstore to send you a recent biography of Tagore which has only now been published in the US. We send it to you now with our compliments, knowing that Chandra wanted you to have it.
> Sincerely,
> Jack Cella
> Manager

The list of books that I have given above is long, but I must add that, over the years, he has gifted large sums of money to me, and that without his help I could not have gone to the USA and Canada to qualify myself further. My brother was the kind of man who would bestow favours as if receiving them.

I am yet to mention what perhaps is the crowning item in this list. When he came to India some time after receiving the 1983 Nobel Prize in physics at Stockholm, he gave me a replica of the Nobel medal which the Swedish Academy gave its laureates in addition to the original gold medal. He told me: 'I do not know what to do with it. I am giving it to you.' I am at a loss as to how best to preserve it for posterity. Incidentally, I also do not know what to do with the four lovely porcelain plates with exquisite hand-painted flower, leaf and bird designs (from the Smithsonian Institute, if I remember correctly) that he gave me.

On my part, I may mention that I dedicated my first book (*Pon Valayal and Other Stories*, in Tamil, 1942) to him with the inscription (in Tamil) 'Dedicated to my brother Dr S. Chandrasekhar, who shines in America to the glory of the motherland'; and my book in English *Ramalinga, Poet and Prophet* (1984) with the inscription 'To Subrahmanyan Chandrasekhar, who made our world special by being in it'; and another book *The Big Bang and Brahma's Day* (1995) with the inscription 'To the memory of S. Chandrasekhar'. Through the years, I sent him copies of my published books and nearly all my stories, poems and articles as they appeared in periodicals. He was always receptive and eager to respond and comment graciously.

***

On being awarded the 1983 Nobel Prize in physics (which the scientific world knows came to him forty years late) he wrote to me on 4 December 1983, in response to a letter of mine:

> First I must express my sense of being overwhelmed by the 'happiness' which all of you seem to have shared in the announcement of the award on October 19.[1] And this fact that

the award has given so much happiness to those whom one really cares for and loves is the only aspect which has given me and Lalitha unalloyed pleasure. For the rest, the award, while gratifying, is not one that I sought, or indeed one that I considered relevant to a scientific career. I am afraid that its significance has been very greatly exaggerated, and it distorts the perspective. Thus: A lady asked me the other day: 'The work that has been recognized was done fifty years ago. What have you been doing since?' I responded, 'They also serve who stand and wait.'[2] To which she asked: 'Have you been waiting for the Nobel Prize all these years?' My answer was 'There was no Nobel Prize in Milton's time!' She had not heard of Milton (apparently). And the moral?

... We are leaving for Stockholm tomorrow and shall be returning on 15 December. That leaves me hardly three weeks before we go to Zurich to give the Pauli lectures (a commitment made some eight months ago) and to receive a 'Tomala' prize of the principal university of Zurich. Remember my story of the bedecked general?[3] As you know, the original plan was to come to India directly from Zurich. But even apart from 'constraints' mentioned by you, the idea of undertaking a further long journey is more than I wish to contemplate now. The fact is that I am very tired – physically, mentally and emotionally. It was only with the greatest effort that I could concentrate sufficiently to write out the lecture I am to give in Stockholm next week. I feel totally drained.

To return to other matters: I found your reminiscences of our years before 1930 most tastefully written: truthfully written, yet excellent.[4] It vividly brought back to me those years. I well remember the 'I doubt it' incident – yes, it was mother. I shall write again either from Stockholm or soon after our return.

---

1 Incidentally, Anna's date of birth is 19 October 1910.

2 Quoted from Milton's 'Sonnet on His Blindness'.

3 The story is that a general had his whole chest covered by medals and when somebody asked him, 'How is that you have so many medals?' he replied, 'the first was a mistake, and the rest simply followed.'

4 I have not used these reminiscences in the present article.

***

In connection with his later years, I may dwell on one point of our association which brings out an important aspect of his nature.

In the Colloquium on Nuclear Policy, Culture and History, held in Chicago in March 1987, in its third session devoted to 'An Ethics for Nuclear Policy: The Bhagavad Gita, or Gandhian Non-Violence or the Middle Way?' he said:[5]

> I now wish to comment on what has been said about the Gita. I should like to preface my remarks with a personal statement in order that my later remarks will not be misunderstood. I consider myself an atheist.
>
> ... It so happens that my brother, Dr Balakrishnan, residing in Bangalore, is a Sanskrit scholar. I had an extended correspondence and discussion with him on the Gita ... He said that if one views the Gita as the proclamation of standards of conduct by God, then none of the problems that I had encountered will arise. For example, the statement has been made around this table that the Gita instructs Arjuna to kill – but, according to my brother, that is not the way it should be read. As we know, the Gita starts with Arjuna expressing his moral conflicts in having to kill his elders and teachers and many whom he continues to love. But the fact which is often overlooked, to which my attention was drawn, is that when Arjuna expresses his doubts and misgivings, Krishna reveals that the end of the war has been ordained and that his elders, teachers and all he loves are destined to be killed. Indeed what is going to happen *will* happen and does not depend upon what Arjuna does or does not do. Krishna's particular advice to Arjuna derives from the fact that what will happen has already been ordained and that the only choice before him is to play the role as best as he can in a part that has been assigned to him.

5 *Nuclear Policy, Culture and History*, Milton Singer, University of Chicago, Centre for International Studies, University of Chicago, Chicago, Illinois 60637, USA, 1987, pp. 84–85.

> Therefore it is not an instruction to kill or not to kill; it is rather the part he has to play in a sequence of events whose end cannot be altered; and that the future has already been decided. In other words, the Gita does not give you the luxury of playing a decisive role in the shaping of events. The choice open to you is to play your own part as well as you can under the circumstance in which you happen to be involved.

Commenting on the discussion on the *Gita*, Professor Milton Singer, editor of the Report, observes:[6]

> In spite of the varied interpretations of the Gita's message there is one underlining interpretation which almost all speakers seemed finally to accept. This interpretation was first suggested by Chandrasekhar when he pointed out that Krishna's advice could not be interpreted as advice how to act in the future, because Krishna reveals a future to him in which the battle has already been fought and Arjuna's kinsmen are already dead.

The discussion between Anna and me on the *Gita* and the report on the Chicago Colloquium edited by Milton Singer (a copy of which Anna sent me) resulted in my book *The Bhagavad Gita and Nuclear Policy*, published by Bharatiya Vidya Bhavan of Bombay in 1993.

* * *

After the voyage in strange seas of thought alone, I come now to the last phase of my brother's life. Loneliness had marked him for her own. It was a way of life for him, as he once told Professor Kameshwar Wali. His last phase was sombre.

I remember him telling me more than once over the phone that he sometimes wondered whether all that he did and accomplished in his lifetime was really worth the price. And also:

---

6 Report on the Chicago Colloquium, Editor's preface, p. 9.

> I have a strange feeling with regard to my book *Principia*. It does not seem to be mine, whereas my previous books seemed to be mine. Having finished the book, I have only the exalted feeling that I had been in the company of a great mind. The previous books represent to me years of hard work and attainment of an overall perspective of their themes. The feeling with *Newton's Principia* is different. I don't feel it to be mine. I recall only having been in the company of a supreme intelligence.

Again, when he was in Madras in December 1994 (a visit he undertook to see our sister Savitri, who was ailing with a terminal illness), he told us that he had vague apprehensions of going into nervous exhaustion and a distinct foreboding of a breakdown. In response to this, I wrote to him in my letter dated 21 January 1995 when he had returned to Chicago:

> It was disquieting to me to know of your state of mind which you mentioned to me. Your sense of foreboding and your sense of events happening outside of you, including your work and giving you unrest is a vague yet real disquiet. This state of things falling away from one is deemed desirable by the Upanishads, according to the teaching of which, however, there should be no accompanying disquiet or restlessness but on the other hand serenity.

Then I wrote to him on 8 July 1994:

> I feel good getting phone calls from you. You seem to be in a very troubled spiritual state, and to this I am responding: To me you seem to belong to the class of men, in the words of Emerson in the essay 'Character', 'the individuals of which appear at long intervals, so eminently endowed' that they 'seem to be an accumulation of that power we consider'. The power that Emerson was considering was, in his words, 'character which is nature in its highest form'. He describes such persons, borrowing a phrase from Napoleon, as 'victory-organized'. What appears like a continuation of this

> enunciation occurs in his essay 'Fate': 'When a strong will appears, it usually results from a certain unity of organization, as if the whole energy of body and mind flowed in one direction. All great force is real and elemental ... Where power is shown in will, it must rest on the universal force ... I know not what the word 'sublime' means, if it be not the intimations in this infant of a terrific force.' Arjuna, in the Gita, got this intimation from Krishna ... Similarly you *had* to do your life-long, life-filling and life-propelling, and shall I add, life-denying scientific work ... You have been an eminent and pliant tool of this elemental force. Perhaps there is no room for regret ...
>
> Another thing I want to write to you is in regard to your 'strange feeling', as you put it, that all your books, all your hard work, when the books have been written and the work has been done, seem not to be yours, seem to be something extraneous, entities by themselves, separate and different from you. This is a mystic intimation, on the intellectual level, proclaimed by the Upanishads which in fact gives this sense of non-cognition even to one's body, senses and mind. (Note that the mind is included in the list.) The Gita also teaches that once you have performed your work, you should have no further concern with it and that it belongs to God. I see that after all Hindu blood runs in you.

And then came a phone call for me in Bombay on 22 August 1995 at 7.30 a.m. (Indian Standard Time) that Anna had passed away at noon (US time) at the University Hospital, Chicago, on August 21. With pain in his chest, he had driven from his house to the hospital himself, parked the car, and gone to the doctor's office. The doctor immediately recognized that his condition was serious with a heart attack and admitted him to the Intensive Care Unit. Lalitha was telephoned and she had a chance to exchange a few words with him.

I may only voice for myself the mourning of Heraclitus's friend for Heraclitus (in the words of William Johnson Cory):

> They told me, Heraclitus, they told me you were dead,
> They brought me bitter news to hear and bitter tears to shed.

I wept, as I remembered, how often you and I
Had tired the sun with talking and sent him down the sky.

And now that thou art lying, my dear old Carian guest,
A handful of grey ashes, long long ago at rest,
Still are thy pleasant voices, thy nightingales awake;
For Death, he taketh all away, but them he cannot take.

three

A Walk through Chandra Vilas

Vidya Shankar

S. Chandrasekhar was our eldest brother. He was 'Anna' to his seven younger siblings and 'Ayya' to his two elder sisters. I was ten years old when Anna left for Cambridge, but have many vivid memories of the times when all of us were together in our home 'Chandra Vilas' in Madras. The house stood on a one-acre plot at the blind end of the eighth lane off Edward Elliots Road (now Radhakrishnan Salai), next to the petrol pump. Chandra Vilas was built by Babuji, our father, in the early 1920s. It had the distinction of being marked in the topographic sheet of the Survey of India. Babuji proudly showed this to us children. Chandra Vilas has now been demolished and replaced by an apartment block. But the façade of the new building bears the same old marble plaque displaying the name 'Chandra Vilas' in bold black letters.

Anna studied at The Hindu Higher Secondary School in Triplicane, Madras. About the institution, he once recalled: 'It was a beautiful school with a friendly atmosphere, and the years spent there were memorable. There is one fellow I cannot forget: the son of our milkman. He joined me in the second form, and now he is Balakrishnan's classmate! Quite a record!' (Balakrishnan was four years junior to Anna.) According to him, the teachers ranged from 'highly respectable to amazingly idiotic'. He wondered whether they ever prepared for their classes. It seemed as though they were tongue-tied at home, and so just prattled away when they came to school!

Anna then went on to do physics honours at the prestigious Presidency College, University of Madras. The college had, and has, a magnificent building facing the sea. It had an invigorating intellectual atmosphere. About his classmates there he said, 'I don't know why girl students should be given seats in the first row. A huge lady in gaudy-coloured saris, and with too many flowers in her hair, effectively blocks the view of the students at the back.' Perhaps Anna experienced the stark contrast as compared to the petite, fair Lalitha, with her tidy, beautifully curled hair.

Anna loved strolling along the Marina beach, 'the second-longest beach in the world', he would say proudly. In his later visits to Madras, he would keep aside time to renew his acquaintance with the beach and with Presidency College by walking along the beach fronting his alma mater. And he could never control a smile of amusement when he saw the Fyson clock adorning the college dome, which never showed the correct time. Indeed, his bond with the Marina beach was so strong that many years later, Lalitha was to scatter his ashes on its sands.

On one of his visits to Madras, Anna was requested to inaugurate the Astrophysics Association in his alma mater. The venue was the Physics Lecture Hall. A host of us followed him; we were given seats in the first two rows. None of us understood a word of his lecture. As his neat handwriting filled the blackboard, he raised the panel to bring down the second unused one. As he did so, there was a loud screeching sound. Anna exclaimed, 'Oh! The same squeaking sound I heard years ago while I was sitting there!' pointing to the end of the fourth row. The audience burst into laughter and we joined them. We had finally understood something that he said!

* * *

Life at Chandra Vilas was never dull since there were so many of us living there, each one doing something or the other all the time. There was a garden in front. My sister Savitri was very fond of gardening. One day she was digging the soil around a coconut tree with a small spade when we heard her scream. She came running in, crying, '*Ayyaiyo*! A big frog jumped on me!' Anna immediately said, 'There are no frogs around coconut trees, only toads. They look like frogs; but if a toad falls on you, your hands will become gnarled like a toad's skin!' Savitri sobbed even more. I vigorously washed her hand with Dettol disinfectant as Anna looked on with a mischievous smile!

Anna spent most of his time reading books. One day, seeing him engrossed in a book as usual, Babuji said, 'Don't keep reading in the house like Asamanjam. Go to the beach and get some fresh air.'

Anna retorted in response: 'How many rupees worth of fresh air should I get?' However, like an obedient son, he took the cycle, hid a book under his arms, and buzzed off straight to his friend Ramachandran Rao's house, where he could continue his studies undisturbed. He returned after an hour and said, 'Let nobody disturb me for an hour before dinner,' and went upstairs to continue his studies.

***

Anna had the habit of cycling around the small backyard near the kitchen, making everyone sit on the side steps so that he could chat with the family as he cycled. Once, he exuberantly decided to have a spontaneous singing session. He started thus: 'We are all talented. Here is Savitri with her sonorous voice, Vidya, a musical genius, Sarada, the guide, Balakrishnan, with his soft voice, Visvam with his thunderous voice, and I, the conductor, and of course Amma, the musician-composer. Let us joyfully sing '*Pasiyal melinda nari onru*' (The fox and the grapes) which every one of us has learnt from Amma.' And the Choir members, aged between six and eighteen, proceeded to sing with great enthusiasm – 'singing' their best at the top of their voices.

A neighbour living three houses away from us got alarmed on hearing the cacophony, and thought some disaster had befallen the family. He came running over to Chandra Vilas, panting: 'Any burglary?'

The band fell silent. Then Anna went forward with a welcoming smile and said, 'Music, sir, music!' All of us burst out laughing. Our poor neighbour looked stupefied, and went home quite disappointed.

***

Anna had a very neat and beautiful handwriting. When he wrote, he could not bear a single scratch or a corrected word, nor the '/\' sign in a sentence to insert extra words. The moment the need came for this, he would tear off the page and start on a new one. These discarded sheets would later be stitched together and used as rough notebooks. Rajakka would be furious with the leniency shown to Anna, but there was little she could do about it. So she would recite this nursery rhyme in an attempt to get even:

> What are little girls made of?
> Sugar and spice and everything nice ...
> What are little boys made of?
> Frogs and snails and puppy-dog tails.

Years later, when Anna received Babuji's letter giving him the news of a third son being born to Rajakka, Anna wrote to Rajakka:

> Happy news ...
> And what are little boys made of?
> Frogs and snails and puppy-dog tails!

Anna's letters would be in chaste English, in his beautiful handwriting. Apropos his writing, I must recall an incident here. When I visited him in America, he showed me one of his hand-written manuscripts which he took out from a drawer. It was so beautiful that I remarked, 'Anna, you should publish your works in your original handwriting and not in ugly printed stuff.' Anna just smiled in appreciation and closed the drawer.

This humility was a hallmark of his and there are any number of such incidents that one can recall. On his first visit to India in 1936, a group of college boys came to Chandra Vilas. Anna, clad in white dhoti and a white half-sleeved shirt, was standing in the front verandah. One of the boys excitedly asked, 'Can we meet Prof Chandrasekhar?'

Anna, nodding his head, said, 'Yes.'

Another boy followed up with 'the renowned astrophysicist Prof Chandrasekhar'.

Anna repeated: 'Yes.'

A third boy spoke up. 'We would like to fix up an appointment with Professor.'

Anna replied: 'You can fix an appointment for tomorrow.'

The students had obviously not been able to recognize him, though they had come specifically to meet him. There was nothing in his demeanour to suggest pride or unapproachability and the students took him to be just someone residing in the house.

* * *

Anna had a deep attachment to our family home Chandra Vilas. It held nostalgic memories of a carefree childhood, and of our mother Amma whom he loved with a profound emotion. On one of his visits to Madras, his few words revealed that he could relive incidents of his childhood and feel the presence of his mother in the places she most frequented when alive.

One morning, both of us took a walk through the ground floor of Chandra Vilas. It turned out to be a pilgrimage.

We walked in from the front gate. To the right of the entrance is a tap (#10 in the Chandra Vilas floor plan sketch). Anna gleefully remembered how, as a youngster, he used to terrorize all of us with the water from the tap. He would place his palm under the running tap so that the water sprayed out in the form of a wide jet. He would manipulate it so expertly that anyone who passed by would get drenched.

Stepping onto the verandah which overlooked the front yard, Anna was overjoyed to see the neem tree to the left. It had grown to a great height over the years, with spreading branches. This tree was planted by Amma, who was a great believer in the therapeutic value of neem leaves. Anna recalled Amma saying how the air filtered through its branches and leaves was purified and made fresh. He then glanced to the right where a shrub 'manoranjitam' used to grow. He recalled Amma's dejection when

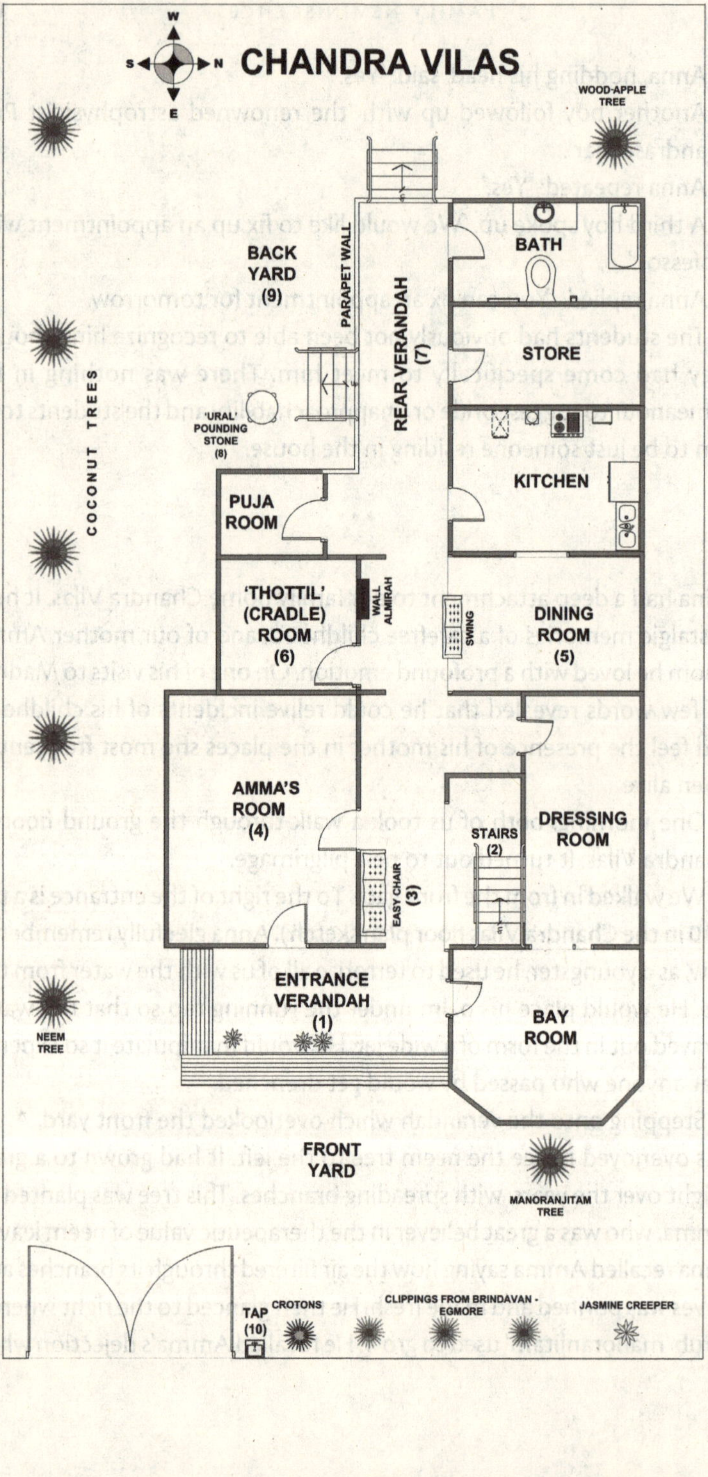
CHANDRA VILAS
W
S
N
E
WOOD-APPLE TREE
BACK YARD (9)
PARAPET WALL
REAR VERANDAH (7)
BATH
STORE
KITCHEN
'URAL' POUNDING STONE (8)
COCONUT TREES
PUJA ROOM
'THOTTIL' (CRADLE) ROOM (6)
WALL ALMIRAH
SWING
DINING ROOM (5)
AMMA'S ROOM (4)
STAIRS (2)
DRESSING ROOM
EASY CHAIR (3)
ENTRANCE VERANDAH (1)
BAY ROOM
NEEM TREE
FRONT YARD
MANORANJITAM TREE
TAP (10)
CROTONS
CLIPPINGS FROM BRINDAVAN - EGMORE
JASMINE CREEPER

it was cut down on Babuji's orders. The shrub bore highly perfumed flowers, but unfortunately also attracted wasps and snakes. One day, a snake came into the house – hence Babuji's orders. So upset was she by the destruction of her favourite plant that Amma did not speak to anyone for two days.

Sharing these memories, Anna walked up to the entrance through the front verandah (#1) and remarked, 'It was here that Amma used to wait for her Sanskrit teacher every morning. Later, she taught some Sanskrit slokas and songs to us.' *Gajamukha-deva* was a favourite which Anna still remembered.

We then came to the entrance hall. Anna looked at the stairs (#2) on the right leading to the first floor and he commented that he could not remember ever climbing those stairs one-by-one. He would always stride up two or three steps at a time. Then he glanced at the long reclining easy chair (#3) and said, 'This is where Amma used to rest whenever she was tired.' He gazed for a while at Amma's room (#4) but made no comment. I could see the sadness in his eyes which were full of memories.

Entering the dining room (#5), pointing to a corner, Anna remembered, 'Amma used to sit here and play the veena, and you used to sing with her.'

A large swing dominated the dining room right from our childhood days. The swing brought to Anna's mind the many hours spent swinging to and fro, singing songs. He looked at the wall almirah and could not resist a loud chuckle of amusement. It was a two-door wall cupboard, but had only one door; the other door had fallen off when we were children, and it continued to be in the same state. This amused Anna a great deal. 'Some things at least do not change,' he said.

Anna recalled how he used to curl up in the 'cradle room' (#6), resting his head and legs on the raised sides of the cradle, and study there, undisturbed, for long hours.

The rear verandah (#7), which was partly open and had a low parapet wall, was the venue for the relay races that Anna used to conduct with us. From the verandah one could see the ural (pounding stone, #8). He remarked that he has never ceased to be amazed at the perfect synchronization of the two women pounding grains with alternating strokes of their ulukkais (long heavy wooden staffs), without ever clashing with one another.

We walked out to the backyard (#9) which was very much Anna's domain. He would perpetually be whizzing around there on his bicycle, threatening both life and limb of anyone who dared to invade his territory while he was cycling. On the left of the backyard was a wood-apple tree. This brought to Anna's mind the concoction that our great grand-aunt, Athai, a youthful old lady, used to make with the ripe fruit and jaggery (eaten by us not without protest) as it was considered to be anti-toxic and good for stomach disorders.

His eyes were then drawn to the coconut trees. He recalled that Amma used to quote Avvaiyar's sayings about the coconut tree. He did not recall the actual words, but did remember the gist of it – gratitude for a favour or gift received should be like that of the coconut tree; in return for the water given to it at its roots, it gives back sweet water, a hundred times over, from its crown.

We walked back, wrapped up in memories of a shared childhood, some memories sad and others joyous. The house was still. I am sure Anna must have mentally said goodbye to Chandra Vilas, the house that embodied his childhood and was, for him, permeated with the spirit of his dearly loved Amma.

four

Impressions

Vasanti Ram

It was a cold wintry morning. Christmas 1960. It was vacation time and I had gone to Williams Bay to spend the holidays with Ayya Mama and Lalitha. From Calumet City in Illinois I took a train to Walworth, the station where I had to get off. As the train chugged along, I thought of Ayya Mama who had been painted larger than life at times. But my mother – in her forthright, honest way, and in the true spirit of the elder sister who worked away at mundane household chores while her little brother pored over his books – had often brought him back to size and exposed him as a spoilt, favoured brat.

Arriving at Walworth, I looked out and saw Ayya Mama walking in his dark overcoat flecked with snow. I got off the train. I was young enough to feel no embarrassment. 'Hello, Vasanti! How was your journey?' he said in his slightly hoarse voice, which I found very attractive. We went out in the cold to his car and drove to his home – a beautiful, small house which had snow all around. Lalitha came out with a welcoming smile.

Christmas fifty years ago. What do I remember? A bit here, a bit there. Are things really continuous? It was like travelling through new lands. I see a single tree on a rock jutting over the blue Pacific Ocean; a luminous point at sunset in the Grand Canyon; the blue of Lake Louise in the

Rockies. Which did I see first? What order? They are recalled, relived, but I remember no sequence. So it is with memories and meetings.

Ayya Mama took me to see the lake behind his house. It was frozen. 'Would you like to walk on it? Come on.' He took me along and as I stepped carefully on the sheet of ice, he said that there were more broken legs in winter than at any other time! 'And do you know,' he said, 'that the ice is just one inch thick?' Good Lord, why did I pretend to be brave?

Ayya Mama had easy and cordial relations with the university staff. They called him 'Superman Candysucker' – a far easier way of saying Subrahmanyan Chandrasekhar. He obviously enjoyed this nomenclature. Once when his younger brother Ramnath visited him, they exclaimed, 'Oh Chandra! And we thought *you* were handsome!' He chuckled as he narrated this. Ayya Mama was a wonderful raconteur. Whatever he related had the element of a story – one wanted to know the end. He was a treasure-trove of anecdotes about Fermi, Dirac, Euler and Einstein. They came alive as people though their science probably passed me by.

In those four happy days we heard a lot of music – Telemann and Couperin, Bach and Beethoven – and talked of Eliot, Wordsworth, teaching English in India, and so on. Sometime during the conversation, I mentioned Parker 51, the most coveted pen in those days, and how Chinanna had promised to give me one if I visited him in Jamshedpur. Ayya Mama left the room and came back in a few minutes with a Parker 51 – dark blue with a silver cap, the classic combination. 'For you,' he said. I still have the pen. On the day I was to leave, he gave me a cheque. 'A gift from us. Lalitha and I would like you to travel in Europe.' And I did. That was certainly one of the best gifts I ever received.

***

I got married to Ram and moved to Delhi in 1963. Ayya Mama came to India quite a few times. We always made a point of meeting him. The most memorable were a few evenings with my grand-uncle, Ramudu Mama. Uncle and nephew were just a couple of years apart, and had been close friends in their younger days. Whenever they met, they shared old memories, punctuated by Ramudu Mama's hearty guffaw. His was the most childlike laughter that one ever heard. Here I must mention a little incident. Ramudu Mama, who was the director general of the Meteorological Observatory in New Delhi had just published a book titled *Climate during the Indus Valley Civilization* and was immensely proud of it. He was showing it off to Ayya Mama. Conversation continued and we, Ram and I, indulged in our usual teasing of Ramudu Mama. 'Every morning we read reports in the newspaper about the daily weather stating that it may be cloudy with the possibility of rain or that it may be sunny and so on. Do we require a big meteorological department with a big director (Ramudu Mama) to say this?' Ramudu Mama and the others guffawed as always. Ayya Mama cut in quickly. 'Ha,' he said, 'Ramudu may not be precise about the weather in *Delhi* today, but you should ask him about the weather in the *Indus Valley* 5000 years ago – he would be absolutely precise!'

***

In 1979, I went to the USA and spent a few days with Ayya Mama and Lalitha in Chicago. Thinking back, I have never seen Ayya Mama in anything but impeccably tailored trousers and shirt sleeves. However early I got up, there he would be all dressed and working away. 'I don't have much time. I have so much to do,' he would say. It seemed like a perpetual race against time.

Lalitha went about her chores in her meticulous, organized manner. Everything she did was with utmost care for detail. Then there were those four o'clock walks to the Henry Moore sculpture on the campus. Before we set out, there would be an interminable question-answer session on the likely weather in the next half hour. Lalitha would wonder if she should take a shawl, maybe a jacket; was it windy? A scarf might be just right, or should she take a light sweater; then the wind-chill factor would be ascertained from the weatherman. Ayya Mama would patiently mumble a monosyllabic 'yes' or 'no' each time.

One evening, as we went through the campus, Ayya Mama pointed out to a person and said, 'That is Isaac Singer.' A little later, he nodded at a passing gentleman and said, 'That was Robert Millikan,' and in the elevator, as we got into it, was Saul Bellow. I gaped – three Nobel laureates in the space of ten minutes!

It was a short visit, but again it was cordial and easy. Once, in a pensive mood, he said, 'Where do I belong? I don't belong here, I don't belong in India. I don't know what to say to the young people I meet,' – a sudden admission of loneliness, from which he shook himself off and talked about books and music.

This time he gave me a record of Eliot's *The Four Quartets*. Before I left, he played for me the song '*The Farewell*' from Mahler's *The Song of the Earth*.

Yet this sensitive man with his love for literature, music and the arts could hurt people. He could be downright rude. He could simply refuse to meet gentle, diffident relatives who would never have expected a rebuff and his strong likes and dislikes could make one tentative and self-conscious. At times, he would sit with his family inducing silence, not conversation; distance not camaraderie.

His silence at times was as expressive as his speech.

five

My First few Meetings with Ayya Mama

Uma Parameswaran

Stained Glass Windows

I saw him walk up the halls of learning.
Scholars rose to their feet in reverent awe
As he went past them to the inner sanctum.
There Fermi and Von Neumann greeted him
With open arms; there Dirac leaned forward
For a handshake, and Hardy smiled at him.

I saw him walk between sculptured pillars
In the modern temples of his native land
Where acolytes shouted hallelujah
And all the priests welcomed him
With rosewater and sandal paste,
Clad him in sanctified vestments
And anointed him with high titles.

After the ceremonies, outside the temple,
The acolytes met him one by one,

And poured out their hopes and fears
As one would to a deity
    remote but always there.
And he heard them patiently
    as would a deity
    remote though always there.

I walked with him down the halls of memory
Past Fermi, Von Neumann, Dirac,
To the inner chambers where the rooms grew barer
And the air was insistent with echoes.
The windows were boarded-up, the shelves empty.

Then we came to a room, bare except for a pendulum
Of clustered memories that flung shadows
On the bleak walls.
I traced a single beam of light
to a closed door
Which we opened.
And entered.

This is the first part of a longer poem. The reference to the modern temples, as Nehru called research centres, came to mind from an anecdote about Ayya Mama recounted by my husband, Parameswaran. When he asked Ayya Mama what he felt about being put on a pedestal like a god, Ayya Mama answered that he had no control over that perception.

It was a privilege to have been able to spend some time with Ayya Mama, listening to some of his memories. It was like looking at stained-glass windows from the inside, when there is brilliant sunshine outside. The second part of the poem, which is not included here, is about how memories in that bare room are like stained-glass windows from the outside when there is no light within the building.

* * *

My first meeting with Ayya Mama was when he visited India in the 1950s, but I don't remember much about that visit. I also met him during his 1961–62 visit. There was an extended-family group photograph taken on that visit and I remember the bustle trying to get everyone together. Of this visit, I also remember a scene – many of us in a room, with a bench in the middle stacked with a lot of new saris brought from the famous store 'Nalli's'. I have no idea why there were so many saris. My sister Vasanti picked up a sari – I think it was off-white, with a turquoise border – and said that it was the best of the lot. Then she looked at the price label and said, 'No wonder it is the best of the lot.' Ayya Mama told her that he would like to gift it to her, but she said 'Oh no, no!' and refused to let him do so.

***

I left India in 1963 to join Indiana University in Bloomington. That school year, I visited Ayya Mama and Lalitha Mami twice, once during fall and again during my spring break. On the first visit, I took a bus from Bloomington and dozed off as we neared Chicago. When I opened my eyes, I said to myself: 'Oh my god, I must have boarded the wrong bus and reached New York!' because outside the bus window was a vast, billowing sea with high waves. It turned out that it was just Lake Michigan, but it sure seemed like an endless expanse of water.

Ayya Mama met me at the bus depot and we walked to his office at the university because he had a few minutes of work there. He insisted on carrying my overnight bag. I sat in his office, looking at the famous framed picture of a man halfway up a ladder. Then he started talking to me, and asked me a question. I was halfway through the answer when the phone rang. He picked up the receiver, did not ask who it was, but just told the person that he was busy at the moment and asked that person to call back later. I was amazed. So different from most of us, who tend to excuse ourselves from our visitors and respond to the phone. He is the only person I have met who actually gave priority to the person he was talking with, above the ring of a telephone!

We drove to Williams Bay later, and I recall us spending the evening listening to an opera – *Madame Butterfly*, if I remember right. I also remember that when I went for a shower next morning, having been thoroughly spoilt during my three-month stay in the US with the luxury of long hot showers, I used up all the hot water and then screamed that the water was now *cold*, and Lalitha Mami came running and boiled some water on the stove so I could finish washing my hair. My bed had an electric blanket, and I was pretty scared of the idea of sleeping under a web of wires. I tried not to use it, but this was Wisconsin winter I am talking about, and there was no way out!

By the next visit, I had decided to get married, and I told Ayya Mama all about Parameswaran. Aware of Ayya Mama's ever-neatly-pressed trousers and ever-neatly-knotted tie, I added that Parameswaran did not care much about what he wore. Ayya Mama said, 'Everything else you've said about him seems just right. You can work on the dress problem in due time.' (I never could, as anyone who knows Parameswaran can vouch for!)

I got married in Princeton, where my brother Sadasiv lived at the time. He was at the RCA lab where they were working on the first camera that went to the moon. The wedding was held at the house of one of his friends (they had gone away on a long vacation) and was officiated by a heavily-built Justice of the Peace. Parameswaran and I exchanged garlands that had a hundred roses each. Ayya Mama and Lalitha Mami were there along with Professor Martin Schwarzschild and his wife. Apart from them, there was a cousin from New York who wove the wedding garlands and cooked the wedding lunch as well! Finally, there was my close friend Linda from Bloomington. Ayya Mama and Sadasiv signed as witnesses. Linda was completely bowled over on realizing that she was in the presence of two of America's ten top scientists! I had the rare privilege of thirty per cent of the guests at my wedding being among America's best scientists.

Parameswaran and I went to East Lansing, where Parameswaran was to be a visiting professor. Within two days of our reaching, Ayya Mama and Lalitha Mami drove all the way from Chicago and brought a whole lot of linen, kitchenware, cutlery etc. It was very kind of them to do so.

They just shrugged away the trouble of driving that long distance as though it was routine. I had made lunch for them but they said they had stopped on the way, which was just as well because my culinary skills were – and continue to be – at the low end of the scale. They headed back in a couple of hours. It was wonderfully generous of them to come all the way, both to the wedding and to East Lansing. I still have a blanket that they brought at the time, of English wool.

***

Many of us have letters from Ayya Mama that we treasure. I would like to share the first letter I received from him, dated 21 December 1956. I had written a short piece on Chandra Vilas and sent it to Babuji who got it typed and sent back a copy to me. He sent a copy to Ayya Mama as well, for I got a letter soon after. I do not think it necessary to say what I had written, for his letter refers to it in a self-explanatory manner.

> My dear Uma,
>
> Babuji sent me a copy of your 'Tract on Chandra Vilas'. It is a beautifully written essay and it brought back for me memories long submerged by the weight of years.
>
> I lived in Chandra Vilas during its first years: 1925–1930; and in my recollections of Chandra Vilas, I have always superposed my impressions of those years on the present. And reading your sensitively transcribed impressions of the present, I felt as embarrassed as one caught in the act of looking through the wrong end of a telescope ... Yes! To you, Chandra Vilas stands 'there as far as memory can stretch', but from my end of the telescope, Chandra Vilas has always appeared freshly built: the very building of it having been a novel adventure. Do you know, Uma, that when Chandra Vilas was built, we resided in the house next door, and that I kept the roll of the workers – charming, carefree men and women whose joyous faces I can still recall – masons and helpers who poured the concrete and laid the bricks? I can even recall my first visit to the freshly broken ground when the foundations were being dug. And

certainly, you cannot recall, Uma, the lovely centre of us all during those lovely long-gone days – your grandmother, my mother ... To you, 'the huge easy chair placed bang in the middle of the passage' is an incongruity. But do you know that when we returned to Chandra Vilas six years ago after a lapse of fifteen years, I should have felt disconsolate if the Chair had not been there? There, on that Chair, Uma, your grandmother used to rest during her long and painful illness; and I cannot recall Chandra Vilas without her lying in that Chair, with that anxious devotion for us all ... And the beaded archway you mention, that was a decoration, Uma, your grandmother beaded herself; and I can recall the joy that suffused her face as she first put that up.

... Those days are beyond the stretches of your memory; but your portrayal of Chandra Vilas brought back nostalgic memories in me. The memory of the freshly built Chandra Vilas and the memory of my mother, and I do want to thank you for your beautifully written essay on Chandra Vilas.

With best wishes,
Yours affectionately,
Ayya Mama

I met him several times in later years, but the memories of those early visits are what I treasure most. Ayya Mama concentrated so keenly on whatever one said to him – listening as though one were at his level of thinking and feeling – that a young person could not but feel gratified by his courtesy and graciousness.

six

Interaction with Prof. S. Chandrasekhar

V.H. Ram

I first met Ayya Mama in 1951 when he and Lalitha returned to India after an absence of almost fifteen years. Some family members had been invited along with Ayya Mama by Lalitha's sister for lunch. All of us were sitting on the floor in front of plantain leaves, in the traditional manner for a South Indian feast. I found myself seated next to Ayya Mama. While talking about education, Ayya Mama asked me whether I understood theorems better after I worked out some calculations based on them. I said, 'Yes, I understand a theorem only after I work out a few applications based on it.' Ayya Mama was surprised. He said that he always understood the theorem, and that the working out of applications did not enhance his understanding of it. I did not wish to dwell upon the differing levels of intellectual powers!

The second time I interacted with Ayya Mama at some length was in 1973 when he had come to New Delhi to give a lecture. After the lecture, my wife Vasanti and I met Ayya Mama, and Vasanti asked him to come to our home for lunch, to which he agreed. I had to pick up Ayya Mama from Ashoka Hotel where he was staying and drive him home. I picked him up and deliberately drove slowly, taking a longer route than the regular one. I plied him with questions on certain science subjects and he answered them patiently and with interest. One major question on which I wanted an eminent scientist like Ayya Mama to express an opinion was the apparent contradiction between the Second Law of Thermodynamics and the origin of life and biological evolution. There seems to be a paradox unless one assumes the existence of God! Ayya Mama then explained in some detail how there was no paradox – not even a contradiction – and the explanation which he gave was very obvious and simple!

The next time I interacted with Ayya Mama was in 1989 when he had come to Madras to see his sister Savitri. Ayya Mama and I were sitting in the verandah. I told him that I had read his biography by Wali. 'And what did you think of it?' asked Ayya Mama. I told him that I liked it overall but I had some reservations. I felt that there were some scientific subjects – radiative transfer, for instance – that Wali had merely touched upon and mentioned in passing without going into the subject even a little. I felt that a book on a scientist should also contain something about the science involved. Ayya Mama said that that was one possible view, but he personally disagreed with it. He said that if a reader was interested in any of his subjects of study, like radiative transfer, he should take the trouble of reading his, Ayya Mama's, books on that subject. I could not agree with Ayya Mama and as an example I said that any biography on Napoleon should deal with military tactics, the weapons used, and also in general with the art of war of that period. However, the conversation remained inconclusive and we were not fully convinced by each other's argument.

Apart from his obvious interest in science, Ayya Mama was a man of varied interests and vast knowledge – a fact I became aware of when we started discussing his book *Truth and Beauty*. When speaking of 'Patterns of Creativity' in the Nora and Edward Ryerson lecture, Ayya Mama had presented the hypothesis that whereas a scientist was most creative only at one point (after which his creativity dropped), in a music composer's case, his creativity increased progressively till the end of his productive life. He illustrated his point using Newton and Beethoven as examples. I said I was not sure whether this was true of musicians in general. His hypothesis was correct in Beethoven's case but could it be generalized? Ayya Mama cut in immediately: 'What about Verdi? Isn't his last opera *Falstaff* his greatest?' Ayya Mama had me floored. I never dreamt that he knew so much about operas!

I then touched upon his work in the 1930s which stated that stars of mass greater than about 1.4 times that of the sun would collapse even beyond the white dwarf stage. I said that in the 1960s the discovery of the pulsar by Antony Hewish and Jocelyn Bell had borne out the validity of his work, particularly since the pulsar was subsequently identified as the neutron star. I asked Ayya Mama whether science had indeed found a black hole. A little bit brash of me, I confess. Ayya Mama replied a bit curtly, with just the suggestion of a smile, 'Of course yes! That is why I got the Nobel Prize!'

seven

Ayya Mama: In Retrospect

V. Chander

When I saw him face-to-face for the first time, Ayya Mama had come to India after a lapse of fifteen years, in 1951. I was sixteen years old at that time. People in the family talked highly of Ayya Mama. To me, he was just another uncle whom you respect like all the other elders. What used to surprise me, however, was that the decibel levels of the voices of all my uncles and aunts, which used to reach a crescendo at family gatherings, would drop dramatically in his presence. In the early mornings and evenings, people would sit around to have a chat with him. At times, a deathly silence would descend upon the whole place. If I got caught in a situation like that, particularly in the evening, I would quietly sneak out to play with my friends.

I had another uncle who revelled in making cynical remarks. If he was present at any such get-together, he would sit in the verandah smoking, and reading a newspaper or a book. If he caught someone going in to join the forum, he would ask him in Tamil: 'Enna sannadikku ulle poraya!' ('What! Are you going into the sanctum sanctorum too?')

One morning, I got caught alone with Ayya Mama just outside the Chandra Vilas annexe that we lived in. Face-to-face with him, I wished him a good morning. He responded similarly and asked me if I was Chander, Bala's second son. I replied in the positive. He asked me what

I was studying. I told him that I was in the first year of college. He then asked me what my subjects were. I told him that besides English and Sanskrit, my subjects were mathematics, Indian history and commerce. He remarked that it was a strange combination of subjects, and asked me what I proposed to do in the future. I told him that I wanted to pursue commerce and, if possible, go in for chartered accountancy after B.Com. He said, 'Very good.'

Feeling that this was a good point to end the conversation, I was about to leave when he said, 'Where are you running away? Please get me your English prose book.' I went and got it. He went through it and asked me a few questions, which I answered. He then came to a chapter on Einstein's Theory of Relativity. Right on top, I had scribbled 'David O Selznick's *Duel in the Sun* starring Gregory Peck and Jennifer Jones.' He saw it and asked me: 'What is this you have written, and that too in your prose book?'

I hastily replied that, as per syllabus, this chapter was excluded and so I had indulged in the writing. He did not accept my explanation and reprimanded me for disrespecting the book. I just kept quiet.

After this glimpse into his dedication to education, I caught a glimpse of his exactitude too. He then told me that I spoke English well and asked me if I did any reading. I told him that I had read all the books by Charles Dickens, Sir Walter Scott, Alexander Dumas, Thomas Hardy, and others from Babuji's library. He was pleased to hear that and told me to keep up the good habit. He asked me if I could give the meaning for words. I said I could. So then he asked me the meaning of 'obstinate'. I replied: 'adamant'. He told me to get the Oxford dictionary, which he took from me and turned to the word 'obstinate'. He informed me that the exact meaning is 'phlegmatic'. The first meaning given in the dictionary is the correct one, though the second meaning given is 'adamant' and it is also a usage of the word.

That little interlude ended there. This was perhaps my only substantial one-on-one interaction with him, and it has remained etched in my memory.

***

I was just a few months old when Ayya Mama and Lalitha Mami left for the US in 1936. My mother – known as Chinakka to most in the family – was just a year elder to Ayya Mama, and he called her 'Bala', a shortened form of her name Balaparvati. She was the gentle-natured one among her siblings. In one of his letters to her, Ayya Mama comments: '... indeed, you are incapable of hurting anyone'. She used to correspond with him fairly regularly. I have read some of the letters written by him in his meticulously neat handwriting and flawless English, as also some written by my mother, which she used to hand over to my father for correction before sending to her brother. I think the best way to end this essay would be to let the readers get a feel of the person that Ayya Mama was and to give them a taste of the kind of beautiful letters he used to write. I am enclosing excerpts from two of his letters, one of which is a scan of his original letter, which reveal some of the innermost thoughts and feelings of the family man and avid letter writer who regretted his inability to stay in touch with his family as much as he would have wanted to. There are many more letters from which one can appreciate his wide spectrum of thoughts, but I have restricted it to just these two, which I feel provide a window into his way of thinking.

Excerpt from letter dated 14 August 1965:

> My dear Bala,
>
> I am ashamed to find that I am still to reply to your letter of December 26; and worse still, that I did not hasten to write to you and PV congratulating you both on the occasion of his 'Shashti Abtha Poorthi' about which Seetha wrote to me in April. I cannot honestly say that I could not have found the time to write to you; but I can say that since January there has been no day I could sit, close my eyes, think of home and Madras, and feel entirely natural in writing. What I *see* in front of me and what I have to do are both so unrelated and foreign to what I have to imagine so as to feel natural, that very much more than the time to write a letter is needed for the necessary composure. But having said this, I still feel guilty that I have not written before.

Excerpt from letter dated 16 November 1981:

Our lives have been lived separately for 50 years; and we have grown from youth to old age with no knowledge—I mean, literally no knowledge—of our mutual lives. By knowledge, I do not mean a knowledge of the principal dates, names, and places. Lives lived apart with only intermittent birthday greetings, wedding announcements, and the whereabouts of the principal characters, do not provide the texture and tenor of ones thoughts, feelings, and emotions; and sharing in thoughts, feelings, and emotions are essential ingredients for mutual understanding. Only a persistent effort at communicating ones thoughts, feelings, and emotions can give meaning and substance to mutual relationships. Without the effort—and alas! none of us have taken the effort—thoughts and feelings are sterile and dry. It is in, my judgement, pretense to imagine otherwise.

You say that one can escape from oneself—you replace 'loneliness' in place of oneself—by the expediency of a visit and a reunion. Loneliness—if that is the correct word—is a way of life. as one has lived one's life of three score years and ten; and one cannot escape from one's life by any expedience.

Well! I am not at all sure that what I have said makes any sense or meaning to you. But in all events, there is no cause for any self accusation on your part—or on the parts of any others. As one says life is a one-way street—has a beginning and an end; and no one can change it

eight

Chandra: Re-inventing an Uncle

Shiv Visvanathan

My father was my childhood hero. He was strong, wonderfully intelligent and an extraordinarily caring man. But the one man my father was proud of was his elder brother, my uncle Chandra. My father loved him, was proud of his achievements, and they shared a wonderful friendship. Their file of letters was a great read, full of confidences. They were like two squirrels sharing the best nuts. My father had filed all the letters that he received from his brother. But one of my aunts borrowed them and somehow lost the file, an act I could never forgive. The letters were not only precious, but a testimony and a testament to a friendship which was theirs alone.

My uncle was real because my father made him real. Otherwise he would have been a photograph in an album, an elegant picture rather than a flesh-and-blood human being. My father encouraged us to write to him. For me, letter writing was worse than the 'I will not talk in class' lines that I wrote about 500 times a week. I was shy, dreamy and erratic at school, and he was this paradigm of perfection, famous even in faraway Chicago which was the world of Al Capone and my uncle. I secretly loved the city that could contain both of them, the classic gangster and the even more classic scientist. My only complaint about him was that his letters had the same postage stamp, a dutiful uniformity that I could never forgive. Life was worse when he wrote to Appa in immaculately addressed aerogrammes. I felt a bit like a male Alice who wondered what use a letter was if it didn't have a festival of stamps. But my uncle stuck to Washington and Wilson, making them the two presidents I was tired of.

One of the few talents I had as a kid was that I could write what went as poems. Encouraged by my father, I wrote one about *My Uncle in Chicago.* I still remember the first stanza. I do not recollect if it had a second. Even if it did, it was forgettable. The piece went something like this:

My uncle is a man of vigour and vim,
And many a man has heard of him,
Through his wisdom and vision,
He has accomplished many a mission,
But sad to say that this is all I know,
About my uncle in Chicago.

As I grew up, I discovered that there were two variants of my uncle. One was the sane, elegant and aesthetic man who was my father's brother. The other was the one that some of my aunts (my father's sisters) had constructed. One of them would round us up and order us to ask Periappa 'intelligent questions'. Intelligence was anyway in short supply before this formidable man who sat elegantly in a white veshti, waiting quietly while his sister played a school principal conscripting questions.

My memories of these encounters are that they were utterly unbearable and atrociously funny. One waited dreamily for something to happen. The silence would be palpable. On one such occasion, my aunt's son obligingly shot his hand up and asked, 'Why do the planets go around in circles around the sun?' That did it. My uncle flared up like a latter-day Savonarola and retaliated: 'Don't you know that it is not a circle but an ellipse?' It was as if a tsunami had struck my congress of cousins. Copernicus was distant enough, but an ellipse became a thing of beauty and joy forever. We woke up, like little Rip Van Winkles, to the beauty of the Copernican revolution, to the genius of Kepler, and a strange man called Tycho Brahe. I loved the sound of this last name. My poor cousin had to recite the corrected version for the next two days, much to my glee. An ellipse, for all its geometrical elegance, was one of the moments of comedy in my life. Every summons to intelligence from my Dahlia of an aunt reminded me of my 'Copernican cousin'.

After that day, my uncle became a split-level figure, the official scientist my aunts doted on and the loveably elegant man my father was so close to. Years later, Appa explained that my uncle left for Cambridge when some of his sisters were still very young. They knew little about him, understood him less. Yet they doted on him, his dedication, his discipline and his sense of vocation. But the die was cast. I loved the split-level world of two uncles in one. It made life more meaningful and delightful. Given my dim-witted sense of math, I named him U1 and U2. I loved his visits. They were like newspaper events – full of excitement, a carnival into themselves. I used to go around claiming that my uncle was an astrophysicist, unclear about what it meant.

Chandra fascinated me. He used to recite anecdotes the way my Jesuit teachers presented theorems. I remember the first time he talked about Newton. Newton compared himself to a child collecting shells on the seashore, while the whole ocean of knowledge lay unexplored before him. Chandra loved the anecdote. It made him feel closer to a giant like Newton while conveying a sense of the innocence of science exploring the mysteries of the universe. I loved it, but more because I loved anything to do with beaches. My cup of life was full. But more curious than Newton was a strange Indian that my father and he repeatedly talked about. His name was Ramanujan. My father and uncle would discuss him incessantly. My uncle would tell us stories about how it was rumoured that Goddess Namakkal rolled her tongue, unravelling the theorem for Ramanujan. Given my difficulties with math, I could have done with such heavenly aids. But what followed was the more poignant story of Hardy visiting Ramanujan as he lay dying and Ramanujan asking him the number of the car he had arrived in. One realized that for my father and uncle, numbers were a wonderful world, alive with a rationality and meaning that I could not comprehend. I loved story books but cricket scores was the limit of my math skills. It drove Appa to despair but I was, I confess, immune to mathematics. However I loved stories about mathematicians like Euler,

Fermat, Pythagoras, Boole and Euclid; I loved the way their names tasted, but it stopped there. Anecdotes were welcome but theorems eluded me. Much later, when I became a sociologist of science, my uncle sent me a piece on Ramanujan, a sad note about the innumerable letters he wrote from Cambridge to his wife. Ramanujan's mother – like a typical Bollywood mother-in-law – appropriated all of them. I had already read about this in Ashis Nandy's *Alternative Sciences*, but the fragment my uncle gave me was more moving, and more Victorian. A sense of tragedy suffused the three stiff pages he sent me.

As I grew up, memories of my uncle grew bigger. Stories about him multiplied. Chandra and Raman were like secret, maybe not-so-secret, recommendation certificates I carried. Their contrasting styles were stunning. Raman was loud, exuberant, like an obsessed leprechaun and half Rumplestiltskin. Chandra was quietly elegant, aesthetic, restrained. They were like two parallel forms of life, two kinds of science, one home-grown and crassly obsessive, the other understated, quietly elegant and even more expressive.

My uncle Periappa found the utterly authoritarian attitude of his father, my grandfather, quite unacceptable. Babuji was like a character out of Samuel Butler's *The Way of All Flesh*. My father and Chandra would have long and quiet discussions on Chandra's distance from his father. It was a distance my father tried to soften, but Chandra felt it had the inevitability of a physical law. It was a deep but relentless hurt that he carried, the poignancy of which came out in his letters. It was the cross of a father whom he could not reach or fully understand. But one understood this since my grandfather was one of those tyrants who declared a state of emergency five days a week.

As one grew up and went to college, one felt closer to Periappa. He was curious about Indian politics and cared deeply for India. He was a proud nationalist even while being deeply cosmopolitan. He felt an aesthetic affinity to Nehru, and was personally fond of Mrs Indira Gandhi. He liked her intelligence, her ability to listen; but most of all, he was a sucker for elegance. We loved talking about politics and he was intensely curious about it. I could never figure out whether it was curiosity about India or a love for politics. There was a time when he used to visit India every year. He would make it a point to visit the physics department at Delhi University especially when his friend D.S. Kothari presided over it. We had a standard ritual: I would walk over to the physics department from Delhi School of Economics and wait till the lecture was over. We would then drive down to Ashoka Hotel or to my granduncle's house where coffee, laughter and science mingled in happy nostalgia. I must add that the physics department was not one of my favourite places. It was ruled by a tyrant with a bushy moustache called Faquir Chand Auluck. I remember a time when Chandra was having tea with Auluck and some senior colleagues. I walked in a bit late and asked to meet my uncle. Suspecting foul play Auluck turned rabid, insisting that Chandra was not my uncle. Tired and a bit irritated, I snapped back. As we bared our teeth, my uncle saw me and came over to claim me. The transformation in Mr Auluck was amazing. From a roadside bully, he metamorphosed into a liberal, lovable professor, a native Mr Chips. Sensing his embarrassment, I grinned wickedly. Chandra was oblivious to it all, content that he had met a bunch of intelligent students and happy to have met three teachers he was fond of: Panchapakesan, Rajaram and Mitra. He felt their presence made the visit worthwhile. I don't think he even *saw* Auluck, which added to my obvious delight.

Chandra enjoyed conversation and liked people who could make a particular type of conversation: a conversation of ideas, where anecdotes were scattered generously like nuts in a rich cake. I was lucky to have been brought up in such a world. Yet, I sensed that one would feel alien if one did not live in such a space. Touch poetry, politics, philosophy or music and he would soak it in like an elegant village gossip. Talk the everyday-ness of marriage, homework, children, shopping and he blinked in turn like a Martian who had landed in a strange planet. He realized this, but felt helpless. I remember an instance when we were discussing Virginia Woolf. Sitting near him, one of my aunts was talking boisterously about her grandchildren. Chandra turned around and said, 'Why don't we talk about something interesting?' It was a plea for connection, half intolerant, half prayer. His sister, a celebration of life in her own right, snapped back. 'We are talking about what interests *us*, cooking, and our grandchildren. You may talk about what interests *you*.' This imperial affirmation left him helpless.

There was sadness, a recognition of parallel worlds even among his own siblings. He recognized it but felt a sense of defeat about it. Once, as we were riding in the same car, he admitted that he could not relate to the enthusiasm of some of his nieces and nephews. He felt particularly helpless with one niece who was exuberant about the mathematical abilities of her son, and gushed voluminously about it. My uncle would sit autistically through the flow and then get impatient or wait to be rescued.

I loved the moments in Delhi when my father, my uncle and grand-uncle Ramaswamy would settle down to talk. Conversation flowed like vintage wine, a toast to friendship and life. The three men loved and sensed each other's worth, each an outstanding scientist, each a wonderful being. Memories moved over the years like an accordion being pressed back and forth. Laughter, banter, argument marked an affirmation of friendship. Three men celebrated life, science and a life of science, arm-wrestling over ideas. I secretly called it the South Extension Solvay Conference. It revealed my uncle at his best – relaxed, elegant, open, thoughtful, happy, and at home.

Preliminaries would end with coffee and ideas would flow. Once, the three of them had a huge monsoon map spread out like a carpet and were debating a little morsel of data. They were like three birds grumbling over something new. My grand-aunt looked at me and said, 'Look at them grumbling. I tell you they are completely happy, like three children. Nothing else bothers them.' She was right. All three had had the exuberance of children for life and science. It was magical. Three men, three styles of science, blending in a symphony of friendship. I sensed a depth of understanding – a play between the said and the unsaid – that was strangely moving.

It was a part pilgrimage into the past, with comments tied neatly like thoughtful presents. I remember him once telling my mother while they were talking about dance and music: 'With MS (Subbulakshmi) and Bala around, India does not have to worry.' Balasaraswati was a wonder, an original he admired. The great dancer had that little extra which one calls genius.

He was proud of his commitment to teaching, took delight in the fact that he drove miles to teach a class of two students. Then came the punch line. He said with puckish delight: 'My entire class won the Nobel Prize.' He was talking about Yang and Lee, delighted in their achievement. Years later he added sadly: 'They don't talk to each other any more.' No details were provided. The obituary of the friendship was the silence itself.

I used to discuss my travails as a young academic. The department was in a state of civil war and I was deep in it. He asked me if I read Chekhov, referring to a story about a village that fought over something for so long that people had forgotten the origin and cause of the quarrel. 'Department politics is a bit like that. Move on,' he nudged gently. There was an economy to these moments which I treasure. Wisdom was encapsulated in a classic story which saw and said things better.

Once, we were talking about reading the enormous volume of scientific research that one confronted. He talked about Enrico Fermi who was aghast that Chandra spent so much time reading for the *Astrophysical Journal*. Fermi explained that he did not find reading worthwhile, adding that he knew all the relevant people in the field. A few critical conversations meant more than all the articles in the field.

Chandra was precise in his judgements about other scientists. We were discussing Satyen Bose and his relationship with Einstein. Chandra said that the 'Bose–Einstein paper was classic'. But Einstein was not enthusiastic about his later work and Bose lost his zest for research. I asked Chandra about it. He said, 'Geniuses, like lightning, have to strike twice. Bose wilted after the first. To be seen as great, you need *two* insights. One remains a flash in the pan. Bose faded when Einstein withdrew support.'

Two names surfaced repeatedly: Arthur Eddington and K.S. Krishnan. Eddington virtually destroyed Chandra's career by slighting his work. My uncle left for the US soon after. Reminiscing over it, he was specific in his details. There was sadness but no bitterness. Someone asked, 'Was Eddington racist?' Chandra blinked. The thought had never occurred to him. He said, 'It would never have occurred to Eddington.' It was seen as a difference in view points and science had vindicated him. Years of pain must have condensed into that Haiku of a reaction.

We often discussed the Raman–Krishnan controversy about the contentions that Krishnan should have shared the prize. My uncle felt that the Krishnan diaries should have been published. The secrecy around them was unnecessary. He felt that once the truth of the collaboration was out, 'neither would be the lesser man'. It was a one-line judgement but one sensed it compressed years of thought. Chandra sent me a longer piece of his recollections of the debate. I wish *Current Science* had published an equivalent. He was matter-of-fact. Like science, the history of science too was a field of scholarship. As long as the normative held and held elegantly, life was live-able.

One thing always worried me and that was his judgement about politics. We often quarrelled about it, but he was unapologetic about his opinions. He would listen thoughtfully and smile wistfully. The one thing I could never forgive him for was his support for Indira Gandhi's emergency. I ranted, raved, told him about the torture, the violation of rights and the family planning programmes. He agreed that it was unfortunate, but claimed, 'Discipline was the need of the hour'. I was horrified but he stuck to his point. I accused him of being a performing flea for the regime, but he felt that Mrs Gandhi was intelligent and forward looking, the best bet for India. That was a moment when I found myself getting distanced from the man my father loved. It always bothered me.

Years after he passed away, I visited Chicago to give lectures at two seminars. Academic chores over, I walked over to visit my aunt Lalitha. She was a spry, alert woman I was fond of. As she talked, Chandra came alive in a different way. Suddenly, I realized that it was she who was acutely sensitive about politics. She talked of the early years at Chicago, about racism, both overt and tacit, about President Hutchins' commitment to Chandra. She added quietly, 'Chandra had no sense of racism. I used to cut out newspaper cuttings and place them before him. He used to say there is too much to do, do not bother with this.' That made sense. He survived racism, fought it with a different kind of tenacity, as if he was marching to a different drummer.

When my father died, I moved away from his family. Except for a few, they did not make sense to me. It was as if it was my father's presence that had made them real. I met Chandra occasionally. I remember his concern as I babbled on the phone the day Appa died. He stayed with my mother on the next visit. He was caring, did what the occasion demanded and tried to sustain the relationship but it was as if I had moved on. We met occasionally.

Once he told me about Edward Shils, the sociologist on Chicago's Committee for Social Thought. Shils was one the evaluators for my Ph.D. He was delighted with it and met my uncle and discussed it enthusiastically. Shils added, 'He is a bit like you.' Chandra smiled and said, 'Naturally, he is my nephew.' I liked the quiet, laconic way he recounted the event.

The Nobel Prize came a few years later. My brother-in-law Narayanan told me that the day the announcement was made public, Chandra was in class. When he walked out, he saw the press, but assumed that they had come to meet someone else. Only then was he told of the announcement.

The Rip Van Winkles of science had finally woken up. I knew my father would have been delighted. That much was enough.

nine

Periappa[1]

Malathi Ramanathan

Reminiscing about Indira Gandhi, Periappa wrote, 'It is an inverted form of egoism to recount one's own meetings with great historical figures. But for ordinary citizens there is not very much choice since what could a common person say of great historical figures like Indira Gandhi which does not relate to a few personal encounters?'[2] He had a beautiful way of conveying his thoughts and these words come to my mind as I attempt to recall my memories of an uncle who was a great scientist. Since my childhood, his presence was deeply felt with affection and reverence. All of us, the grand-children of Chandra Vilas – our family home in Chennai – shared this feeling for him. What made it special for me and my sister Revathy was the bond that existed between my Appa,[3] S. Balakrishnan and his 'Anna',[4] which translated into our thoughts on him. I shall write about a few of those special moments of our lives as we interacted with him through the long years, when he visited us in India or when we visited him at his home in Chicago. Given our hesitant, often

1 Periappa: Tamil word for uncle, the elder brother of one's father

2 Chandrasekhar, 'Indira Gandhi: Some Recollections'

3 Appa: Tamil word for father

4 Anna: Tamil word for elder brother

tongue-tied, attempts at dialogue when we met him in person, what I remember is Periappa putting us at ease by narrating incidents related to his life and anecdotes about his interaction with other scientists, said, at times, with a tongue-in-cheek humour! His memory for minute details, dates and observations never failed to astound me.

The correspondence between Periappa and Appa since 1930 is a veritable treasure in terms of the thoughts, experiences and ideas on life and work that are contained in the letters. A recent reading of these fascinating letters that Periappa wrote to Appa has enabled me to know them and their mutual relationship better, and also to understand the times that they lived in. Thus the venture to write about Periappa has become for me a trek back in space and time.

Almost fifty-nine years ago, at the age of seven, when I first met Periappa in Madras (Chennai), I remember telling Amma[5] (my mother, Shyamala) that he looked like Appa. I probably missed my father who was away in Canada, studying for his F.R.C.P. and working at the Children's Hospital in Toronto for three long years. Later, when Appa was working in the Safdarjung Hospital, New Delhi, and I was a teenager doing my honours in history, Periappa and Lalitha Periamma[6] stayed with us. During this visit, Periappa came with me to Lady Shri Ram College, where I was studying and later sent me my photograph taken in front of the college building.

We – Periappa, Periamma, Appa, Amma, Revathy (who was about seven years old), I and a few other close relatives – went in two cars to visit the Taj Mahal in Agra. What I remember of the trip is that Revathy was in the car other than the one in which Periappa was; about halfway back to Delhi, it was found that Revathy was not in the second car either. Finally, it turned out that she had been asked to hide under the seat of the second car as a joke – to give the impression that she was missing! Periappa insisted on making her sit with him all the way back home!

Of this visit, I remember that Dr Vikram Sarabhai had come home to meet Periappa. We went with Periappa when he visited Prof. K.S.

---

5 Amma: Tamil word for mother

6 Periamma: Tamil word for aunt, father's elder brother's wife

Krishnan in his house.[7] As I look back, meeting these eminent men as a teenager was inspiring to me. I was now grown-up enough to appreciate Periappa's extraordinary ability to explain the theory of black holes in simple terms. More important to me was his attitude and eagerness to ensure that everyone could understand it, whatever be the age or discipline of study. We attended a lecture of his in Delhi. It was an inspiring experience though the talk was way beyond my understanding! Attending his talks whenever we could was an established practise that we considered our privilege.

My husband Ramanathan and I met Periappa and Periamma for the first time after our wedding when they stayed with his youngest sister, Sundari, in Bombay. During their visit to India a few years later, I recall a picture of Periappa and my sons, Sharad and Arvind (aged nine and six), sitting in the drawing room, with Periappa explaining the theory of black holes to them. Periappa, as always, had made it easily understandable and I could see the keen interest with which they listened to him. On his return to Chicago, he sent a cartoon – of him beside the picture of a black hole that was published in a newspaper in the US – to Sharad, along with a comment that Sharad had asked him the best question put to him on the subject during his visit.

Once, Periappa's uncle Kunjappa,[8] who had retired in Mumbai, expressed his wish to come to our home to meet Periappa. On hearing this, Periappa said he would like to see him at *his* home, instead of his coming all the way to ours. There was much laughter and banter between the two of them, which was a pleasure to watch! Many years earlier, in Delhi, I remember Periappa teasing Kunjappa that he would drop by at Kunjappa's office at the Meteorological Observatory and call him 'Ramudu' as he was called at home. This had Kunjappa protesting, since he feared that Periappa would make good his threat!

One of my treasured memories is of a morning at breakfast that stretched to four hours of intense, interesting discussions, repartees and

---

7 Dr Vikram Sarabhai and Prof. K.S. Krishnan were renowned scientists.

8 C. Ramaswamy, younger brother of C. Subrahmanya Ayyar (Babuji) and C.V. Raman

laughter in the Sandoz guest house. Seated around the table were Periappa, Periamma, Appa, Amma, Periappa's sisters Vidyakka and Savitriakka,[9] and Ramanathan and me. The topics ranged from the Bhagvad Gita (on the question of accepting Lord Krishna as a personification of God and discussions on the teachings in the Gita) to many a scientific subject, to music and books, and their combined childhood memories. Each of the brothers and sisters was as well read as the other and each had something special and unique to convey – often quoting from a Sanskrit verse or a poem or a well-known author and what was more important, his or her own opinion on the topic concerned.

This was Periappa's first visit after receiving the Nobel Prize and the others had come to greet him in Mumbai where he and Periamma had landed first. Periappa told us many a story about the Nobel he had received and the attendant attention that he had had to deal with – 'the effect' as he put it! He showed us the Nobel Prize and it was during this trip that he gave the replica of it to my father. I have cherished these hours spent amidst some of the best among men and women who had high ideals and who have inspired me and made me aware of belonging to a unique and very special family. The Diwali that year was spent amidst this family – as memorable as one could wish for!

Our trip to Pune to hear Periappa's lecture on 'The Series of Paintings of Claude Monet and the Landscape of General Relativity' in IUCAA was memorable. Ramnath Chittappa[10] stayed in the same hotel as Ramanathan, Arvind and I. Arvind got to know Chittappa well for the first time and remarked how interesting it was to talk with him. Appa and Amma stayed in another hotel, along with Periappa and Periamma. As he told us later, Periappa felt that he could not connect with the audience while speaking since the light was focussed more on him than on the audience during the lecture. I recalled this talk given on the lawns of IUCAA in the quadrangle encircled by its building when I saw

9 Akka, Tamil word for elder sister; they were addressed as Akka in the family

10 S. Ramnath, the youngest brother of Periappa and Appa; Chittappa – Tamil word for uncle.

the paintings of the haystacks by Monet in Periappa's house in Chicago in July 1994.

* * *

Innumerable memories crowd the mind as I remember the two trips that Ramanathan and I made to Chicago to stay with Periappa – the visit to the Chicago University and his office, a painting of him in the hall, his picture amidst the other Nobel laureates of Chicago University and the visit to the museum and a bookshop. We sat in his house listening to Mahler's music and to his talk about the years spent in Cambridge, Williams Bay and Chicago. He also told us about the incident of Eddington severely critiquing his theory and his comment to himself later that night – 'this is how the world ends, not with a bang but with a whimper'.

He narrated how the staff at the *APJ* (*AstroPhysical Journal*) had agreed to work overtime during a weekend to publish the news on quasars on the condition that he explain quasars to them later – which he did on the following working day. They had wanted to know why it was so important that it be included in that issue of *APJ* in the very last hours of its publication. The news on quasars made the frontlines of *Time* magazine and from then on the staff agreed unconditionally to whatever decision he made as the editor with regard to publications!

As we sat on a bench outside the museum, amidst trees and the green lawn, scientists that one had heard or read about like Bohr, Dirac, Fermi, Heisenberg, Penrose and Pauli came alive as Periappa recounted incidents from his interactions with them. He had flown across the Atlantic thrice to meet Prof. Roger Penrose in England, just for a day on each occasion, to talk over the problem that he was working on at that point of time, to clear his mind, as he put it! When Periappa visited a critically ill Fermi, the latter wondered, with wry humour, if he would be born an elephant in his next birth.

It was during our second visit to Chicago in 1994 that Periappa showed us a copy of the second edition of Newton's *Principia* which he had bought, the expense not being a deterrent to owning such a treasure. He was then working on what was to be his last book, *Newton's Principia for the Common Reader*. He showed us the pages of some problems that he was then working on. The obvious excitement, almost bordering on reverence, with which he showed us the book remains in my mind's eye. One could see that his heart was set on completing the work and getting it published on time.

I remember, that in the midst of some discussion, I was a little surprised when he said that the word 'enjoy' was misleading. I had remarked that maybe he was enjoying his work on Newton's *Principia*. He said that was a different matter altogether; there was a sense of marvel at the way Newton arrived at solutions to problems, but this in no way qualified it to be an enjoyment to be working on the *Principia*! As I now read his letters to Appa, through the decades of his life in America, I understand a little of what he meant then. During dinner that evening, Periappa said that he was an expert in making pancakes, which he prepared in that meticulous way of his. It was then that he said to me: 'Ask Sharad to visit us. If not physics, I shall teach him how to make pancakes!'

Now from the sublime to the ridiculous! In December 1986, when he came to Bombay to give a talk at the Tata Institute of Fundamental Research, Periappa and Periamma were staying at the Taj Hotel. My convocation for the doctoral degree was on the same day as his lecture. Ramanathan and I went to meet him at the hotel the next evening. Periappa told me that he had looked for us the previous day and I explained why we were unable to be there. That morning, the *Free Press Journal* (19 December 1986) carried on its first page a picture of the first woman vice-chancellor of the Bombay University, along with the vice-president of India, the ex-officio chancellor and four student degree holders entering the convocation hall. By chance, I happened to be one of the four students in the picture. The report on Periappa's lecture, with his photo, was featured on the third page. With an amused look, Periappa told me that I had taken precedence to be on the first page! I would have shrunk into invisibility in my chair, had it been possible!

Once, in the early sixties, he had told me and Appa[11] that I reminded him of the Ajanta frescoes. Many years later, he asked me if I remembered what he had once told me about the Ajanta frescoes. A little taken aback (of course I remembered!), I shook my head. His smiling reply was: 'No woman ever forgets a compliment!' The remembrance of his comment has been a morale booster whenever I needed one!

It was fortunate for me that on most of his trips to India, his return flight to Chicago was via Mumbai, giving me and my husband the opportunity to be with him and Periamma. Hence, he and Periamma have come to every house that we have lived in.

Periappa would spend some days with Appa on all his trips to India. His arrival signalled a family get-together of a week or two when his brothers and sisters and sisters-in-law, and a sprinkling of nephews and nieces came to be with him. Added to this were the visitors, both scientists and others, who dropped in to see him.

Holding fort at home in Bangalore, with tremendous grace and élan, was my mother. She was beautiful, gracious and gentle. Amma would plan and cook breakfasts, lunches and dinners for a houseful of guests, and be impeccably dressed from morning till night, also ever ready to go out with everyone! She had come a long way since 1941, when Periappa had written to Appa: 'How very glad I am to hear of your marriage. I am sure that the woman of your choice will be a true companion to you. I would like so much to make the friendship of your wife.'[12]

This did come true, as in 1977 he wrote: 'So here I am writing to you – in fact the first person at home to whom I am writing after I went to the hospital for cardio-catheterization on 21 September which was soon followed by surgery – and you know the rest ... Let me say, finally, that during my illness, the picture of you, Shyamala and I sitting on the bench in Lal Bagh gardens came to my mind several times. And I long

11 He referred to it in his letter to Appa dated 7 October 1968, after seeing my wedding photograph.

12 Letter dated 12 July 1941; all the letters referred to in this article are from Periappa to Appa.

for the time when we could do so again.'[13] This wish was to be fulfilled several times in the coming years. Morning walks in the Lal Bagh gardens, whenever Periappa and Periamma came to Bangalore, were a pleasure to look forward to. Along the pathway in the garden, Periappa would be talking, with the others listening intently, or Appa expressing his thoughts. At home there would be peals of laughter, interspersed with talk. The neighbours used to tell us that they felt quite envious of these family reunions!

During the course of these years, I received several books from Periappa as presents: *The Essential Confucius* by Thomas Cleary, *It does not Die* by Maittreyi Devi, *Awakenings* by Oliver Sachs, *Five Plays* by Strindberg, *The Wild Duck* and *Hedda Gabler* by Henrik Ibsen, *The Annotated Shakespeare* by A.L. Rowse and two books authored by him, *The Mathematical Theory of Black Holes* and *Truth and Beauty*. Then there are two beautifully painted ceramic plates from the 1979 Chicago collection. In the early sixties, he had sent me his photograph and the photo of his office in Chicago University. A very treasured item, again given by him, is the cassette of an interview of his by the BBC, recorded several years before he got the Nobel Prize. I had reason to accept money from him on two occasions, and on display was the art of giving where it looked as if the person accepting the money was doing the donor an honour!

On his last visit to India, I spoke with Periappa from Aligarh where I had gone to attend the Indian History Congress. He was in Radhika's[14] house in Delhi, on his way back to Chicago. He was back from Madras where he had been to Savitriakka's house after her recent passing away. He sounded tired. It was a difficult time for him and I could feel his deep sense of loss. His voice remained with me for many a day.

The family reunions in India meant a great deal to Periappa. In 1962, he wrote to Appa: 'There were so many occasions which were deeply satisfying and moving ... I need not say how much my having been together with you and our brothers and sisters has meant to me ... Like

13 Letter dated 2 October 1977

14 Radhika, Ramnath Chittappa's daughter

all things, they have also receded into memory; but I believe that we are all, to some extent, ennobled for having come close together.' Had it not been for the letters between Periappa and Appa, I would not have gauged the extent and depth of their close relationship, though I *did* know that they were fond of each other and exchanged letters often.

Periappa once said that to praise a person too much without any real base is to do as much injustice as to underrate without base.[15] For me, Periappa was the embodiment of a gentleman in the finest spirit of the term. His innate courtesy, humaneness and sensitivity, the way he interacted with the family and the affection that he bestowed on us are beyond compare. He once wrote: 'A scientist has something significant to say ... He always creates his own atmosphere ... With all this, life centred only on one's own profession is not entirely satisfactory.'[16] In his pursuit of science to the exclusion of everything else, he had made sacrifices aplenty in his life. He reached great heights as a scientist and as a wonderful person.

It was a coincidence that my son Arvind landed in the USA to pursue his doctorate on the same day that Periappa passed away. In Appa's copy of Periappa's last book *Newton's Principia for the Common Reader*, Appa has noted in pencil on the first page: 'Received from Anna on Wednesday 19/7/95. Scheduled to leave for Bombay on 29/7/95', and again a terse 'Anna passed away yesterday (21 August, 2 p.m., US time). Received a phone call from Lalitha to this effect at 7.30 a.m.' The first note was written in Bangalore and the second in Mumbai. Though Appa said little and became silent as was his wont when he was deeply sad, I could sense that with Periappa's passing away, he had lost someone with whom, in Appa's own words, there had developed a 'comradeship' that was 'abstract, shorn of every disfigurement of reality, lifting it to the ideal, lonely world of communication by letters'.[17]

---

15 Letter dated 17 July 1961

16 Letter dated 22 September 1948

17 Purasu Balakrishnan, 'Subrahmanyan Chandrasekhar: My Anna', in Kameshwar C. Wali ed., *S. Chandrasekhar, The Man behind the Legend*

When Periamma came to India for the first time after Periappa's death, she stayed with us for two days on her way back to Chicago from Chennai. A few years later, in 2000, when Ramanathan and I went to visit her in Chicago, she gave Periappa's pocket watch to be given to Ramnath Chittappa. When we visited her again in 2008 along with Revathy's family, she was well past her mid-nineties. She made the visit memorable for us when, lying on the sofa in the drawing room, she sang three Tamil songs by ancient Tamil poets and a Thyagaraja kriti. Before singing '*Saadinchane*' by Thyagaraja, she told Ramanathan how she had reminded him, during their visit to Thane, of some of the words of this song! While I sang along with her in one song, she asked me to sing one more for her. Though her voice was frail, her rendering of the songs and the perfect recollection of the words spoke volumes for how well she must have learnt them years ago!

PERIAPPA AND APPA

The correspondence between Periappa and Appa through the years (from 1930 till Periappa passed away in 1995) reveals not merely their close relationship but also their hopes, struggles and aspirations. Of interest is their reflection on current events and persons. An objective realism is the hallmark of these letters. Not having read the letters that Appa wrote to him, for my piece I rely on Periappa's letters to Appa. The photocopies of these letters have been meticulously kept by Appa in files, the original ones having been given by him to be kept in the Chicago University archives.

It is not surprising that there was a regular exchange of letters between the brothers, since almost till the seventies they were the main – and probably the only – source of communication between people, with telephonic conversations being rare and used only during emergencies. Periappa told me once that he wrote to Babuji[18] every week, as would Babuji to him. Periappa and Appa wrote to each other often, especially during

18 C. Subrahmanya Ayyar, Periappa's father, was addressed as Babuji in the family.

the first four decades after Periappa left India for Cambridge in 1930. From the late seventies, the letters are shorter when compared to the three- to fourteen-page letters of earlier times. This was probably due to increased conversations over the phone. Till the end of their lives, one constant factor was the exchange of books and articles authored by either of them, or of the talks and lectures given on important occasions by Periappa.

The tone of the letters was set with Appa's note to Periappa just before he left for England. Periappa saw it after he reached Bombay and replied on 31 July 1930: 'It came to me as a surprise that I had unconsciously anticipated the question in the station (at Madras), and said as to what I could possibly advise you.'[19] He went on to write a list of books, along with the concerned chapters to read, for Appa's perusal.

These letters between Periappa and Appa contain their discussions on several subjects, changing with changing circumstances. Covering a period of over sixty years, the letters are witness to their growing up: from teenagers, ever so gradually, into men in their prime, and then on to mature men in their fifties, sixties, seventies ... working and growing in their respective fields, lending emotional and moral support to each other. I shall try to recapture their refreshing candour. Reading the quotes from his letters, one can almost visualize Periappa and hear him speak! I have tried not to add too many of my own comments or digress, but to let the letters and Periappa's writing tell the story in his own words. I have also tried to portray a little more of the early years of his life since I found them quite fascinating.

On Writing Letters

A few months after his arrival in Cambridge, Periappa wrote: 'Your letter did relieve me of so much monotony which has become part of my life here. All day long equations and German. Nobody to talk to. Books before me or scrolled manuscripts. I must add, however ... one gets the quiet enjoyment of books, a moral satisfaction of having learnt something more.'[20]

---

19 Chandrasekhar's letter to S. Balakrishnan dated 31 July 1930

20 Letter dated 6 November 1930

Commenting that he treasured Appa's letters because of the 'moving' nature of the letters and because 'they seem to me such exquisite examples of perfect letter writing', he wrote: 'A letter is one which is a perfectly open-hearted, sympathetic revelation of one's thoughts in its contact with other minds through the medium of language. This letter of 2 January 1931 oscillates between Kalidasa, Milton and Shakespeare and your intellectual reaction to the rhythm of their thoughts ... I can pride myself on having a record of your fervour for the great thoughts of three great men!'[21]

A year later he wrote, 'There is such a lot of harmless trivialities one could write about ... One could make letter writing a more pleasant occupation than even conversation. But then the writer should be confident that he to whom one writes will be in sympathy – I use the word sympathy in the fullest possible sense – with the writer. Well! It is really a long time since I wrote in such a style (I used to before). In the joys and sorrows of life – "joys" and "sorrows" in the recognized sense of the terms – one has always companions: one's parents, brothers, sisters and friends. But there are "joys" – more exactly "sorrows" – of the nature of personal feeling, for which consolation has to come entirely from the self. One feels sad, one does not know why – a vague haunting sense of want, a vacancy, an oppressive feeling and a moral disgust. These are sorrows which cannot be shared. Character, courage, cheerfulness and hope, these are our eternal friends, and consolation is from a habit of mind more than anything else ...'[22]

In 1958 he commented: 'I have one difficulty: the matters about which I can write are limited; and it is a difficulty which is commonly shared when time and environment separate two persons. And since this must needs be so, I shall, somewhat in the manner of your letter, simply record the state of my mind as of the present moment.'[23] How true is this statement on time and environment even today, in spite of the existence of the most modern means of communication!

---

21 Letter dated 2 February 1931

22 Letter dated 27 April 1932

23 Letter dated 10 August 1958

On Living in Another Country, Far Removed from Home

Quoting Appa's letter, he wrote in 1942: 'My feelings are best expressed in your own words: "It is a sad spectacle that human relationships offer us ... In the early years we keep close together, but later, time and space and the loneliness of spirit divide us ... We look at one another across the widening gap and feel sorry for one another ... and the gap still widens under our feet." That is from your last year's letter and how well you describe the feelings! And now looking across the still widening gap a vague nostalgia fills me and how I long to be near you – but the gap widens even as I write.'[24]

He wanted to know how the World War had affected the hopes, feelings and attitudes of family and friends. On a similar vein, he continued: 'You see one pays a terrible price for living in strange lands ... You cease to be yourself and you vainly try to be anything else, at home nowhere, a stranger everywhere. A strange intoxication comes over you ... You live as in a dream, you work as in a dream, you become inhuman ... You live in proportion to your ability to share and your inability to share, you lose contact with life ... I do not know if I make myself clear ... The fact that I am an Indian gives me a strange feeling and I feel stranger that I am in America. A frank but monstrous confession. But for one thing I hunger: what is it that affects you and all those whom I love in this crisis of our times? ... Perhaps you are puzzled by this letter and maybe this letter will confirm you in the ever widening gap in the loneliness of our spirits. But believe me, your hopes and aspirations are mine as well ...'[25]

As for himself, 'The war has upset a great deal of my world and the continual worry, nervousness and helplessness of it all has been deadening in every way: even my work has proceeded, (if at all) only on account of the inertia of past momentum ... Last two years have been sterile and that sterility has been accompanied by lassitude. I try to shake it off. But each

---

24 Letter dated 28 May 1942

25 Ibid.

day brings its own tale of disaster and woe ... Would that the war were soon over – but even in this wish, I would rather have war than Nazi victory (which would reduce all peoples, certainly Indians, to slavery)'[26] After his first visit to Poland to attend a conference on General Relativity, he wrote: 'How can one express one's expression of Auschwitz where man, degrading himself beyond measure, planned and executed the extermination of man, coldly, methodically and with all the resources of science ...'[27]

By 1948, the dilemma of living in another country apparently assumed a new dimension when he wrote, 'Living so far so long, you cease to have a home. You are a foreigner if a slice of your life has no meaning, strikes no chord in the average norm of your surroundings, and I know we shall always be foreigners wherever we are, even if we were to return to India – twenty years is a large enough slice to distinguish one from the norm'.[28]

In 1954, after becoming citizens of the USA, Periappa commented: 'As for ourselves, as I said, the past year has been the most harassing one: first we became citizens of this country. It was not an easy decision for us and I am afraid that it has not been received too well: a fact which only emphasizes that having lived twenty-four years abroad is to have traversed a bridge so long that it does no longer seem to matter that the bridge indeed exists ...'[29] Indeed, they had travelled far – in terms of time and environment – away from Babuji, who was hurt by their decision to take up American citizenship. For him, this meant that they would not return to India. Also, for him, the perceptions of nationhood were vastly different.

The Indian Context

No matter how long he had been away, India touched a chord in Periappa, as did Appa's writings. On receiving a letter from his brother Visvam[30] in

26 Letter dated 12 July 1941

27 Letter dated 7 April 1963

28 Letter dated 22 September 1948

29 Letter dated 17 July 1954

30 S. Visvanathan was Periappa's younger brother and elder to Appa.

1943, telling him that Appa's first volume of collected short stories had been published with a dedication page carrying his (Periappa's) name, Periappa wrote:

> I wish I knew how to thank you or tell you how very much this means to me. You know how I feel about this: As I have expressed to you on several occasions, I have always regarded the full development of your artistic abilities as a matter of utmost importance. For, at a time like the present, when our country is going through the birth pangs of a new era, it is only sensitive artists like yourself who can feel the pulse of the new life germinating and thus inaugurate a fresh renaissance in a new country which will be the India of tomorrow ...
>
> How I long for a free India when you and I can strive after the ideals, proud of our independence, proud in our leaders and creating in our midst the heritage of tomorrow ... I cannot help feeling that out of all this suffering and frustration, out of all the multitude of injuries inflicted on us, we shall all gain a new stature in a newly won confidence, courage and self-respect. And if we can have this faith, a faith which has nourished our greatest men, why can't we find inspiration in our very misfortunes and strive after what surely will be the pride of future generations? And with these thoughts deeply felt, I commend you the responsibility of nourishing and developing your art ...
>
> Just imagine! To create a new literature born of the people and for the people! Imagine a new theatre in which Shakespearean plays in your Tamil version will be enacted, thus bringing for the first time, to the salt of our country, the salt of an earlier age![31] ... And so with this wish, deeply felt, I shall conclude, thanking you again for the dedication,
>
> Yours ever,
> S. Chandrasekhar

31 In his letter of 26 September 1945, Periappa wrote: 'In 1936 you read out to me your translation of Shakespeare's plays. They produced a particularly strong impression on me.'

This was the independent India of his dreams, which would be nurtured by his generation!

On receiving Appa's letter about the happenings on the day of India's independence, 15 August 1947, he wrote: 'It was nice having your impressions of Independence Day. They gave me more of what the day meant than anything I had read in the papers in this country.'[32]

When Gandhi was assassinated on 30 January 1948, he wrote: 'Your letter of February 25 moved me once again as I had earlier been moved by our cruel loss: It is indeed, as you say, as though the Himalayas should roll and tumble. I was in New York on that fateful day and I wandered all day without aim and purpose. I did not want to see anyone: I felt too choked for words ... But I felt since, a pride, only vaguely felt before, that I am a citizen of His country ...'[33]

During India's war with China in November 1962, replying to Appa's letter of seven months ago, he says: 'The daily, common pressures of life do not allow one to let free play for one's emotions: too many crudities intervene and block. You must know this feeling ... Still, this morning has been quiet and free; and I resolved to write. But what an unhappy occasion to write: what with the insecurity and the calamity of the war enveloping all activities and feelings. Lalitha and I have been sick over the events of the last month, and so must you be all, only even more so.'[34]

In April 1963, he wrote: 'Well! The last two months have been quiet on the Chinese front. I hope it does not flare up with the melting of the snow.'[35]

On Nehru's death, he replied to Appa: 'He (Nehru) has critics indeed; but I share your own different judgement.'[36]

Concerns Regarding Choice of Profession

These discussions were held mostly between the years 1931 and 1939 when Appa was torn between his literary aspirations and the choice of

---

32 Letter dated 12 January 1948

33 Letter dated 23 February 1948

34 Letter dated 25 November 1962

35 Letter dated 7 April 1963

36 Letter dated 30 October 1963

a medical education as a means of making a living, each often running contrary to the other. Periappa was his sounding board and counsellor. Apart from the personal nature of the issues concerned, it brought up a lot of interesting observations on education, freedom of choice, profession, security and aspirations to build a new literary tradition in the renascent India. It is good to remember that at this time they were both in their twenties! It is also interesting to note that Periappa wrote dates the Indian way till 6 March 1933 and that from 28 June 1933 onwards as 1933 June 28 – in the year, month, date order! Periappa is the cheerleader in these and many other letters, almost till the fifties, providing moral and emotional support to Appa. There seems to be a slight reversal in roles in the latter years of Periappa's life, with Appa's letters providing philosophical grounding and support, as evidenced in Appa's writings on 'Anna'. A certain friendship and affection permeates all the letters.

In making the choice of subjects to study (given that Appa wanted to do creative writing), Periappa wrote: 'Now you have asked me as to what I regard as your proper course for the "coming years". I have thought carefully about it and I have not arrived at anything definite. But I feel that I can place before you certain canons of judgement which ought to enable you – if you have not already done it – to make the choice easier in any case.'[37] This is one of the longest letters that Periappa wrote to Appa, comprising of fourteen pages! He felt that he could not overemphasize the fact that 'by a hasty choice, you do not mutilate some of your finest aspirations'.[38] And that 'if you think however that you can submit to the call of a doctor and be satisfied with the leisure hours to spend on your studies from the "Book of Nature", and have the contentment from the high kind of social service which a doctor renders, then I should be the last to dissuade you'.[39]

As for himself, he wrote: 'Take me, for instance. I was fond of mathematics. I am now working in astrophysics. But the essential fact remains that I always had an ambition to be a "speculative natural

---

37 Letter dated 12 May 1931

38 Ibid.

39 Ibid.

philosopher". It is just that ambition that guides one. Paths may differ but the soul of the thing is not changed.'[40] Yet, he had his moments of doubt too, as when a month later he wrote: 'Astrophysics gives me no satisfaction. The whole thing is so speculative. I wish to deal with concrete problems and join hands in my work with those of the pure 'theoreticians' like Born, Dirac, and others. You will charge me with too vain ambitions. I merely submit to your criticism. But that is my weakness and won't you excuse me?'[41]

Replying to Appa's query on the difficulty of taking science as a subject of study and finding newer things in science, Periappa wrote: 'You think it possible that in this big world there really exist any untrodden path? There can never exist anything really "brand new". History (as well as science) is a perpetual becoming. There really is no discovery. Discovery is not the finding of an unknown thing, but only the bringing to prominence what others have dimly recognized. Even Newton's Laws of Gravitation were anticipated by Hooke, Kepler, and others. Faraday's Laws of Induction were independently discovered by a Polish physicist. Every man in his respective life follows no untrodden path but only follows the beaten track along which hundreds have gone before. I do not see how the track can become more "overtrodden" for one.'

He also wrote: 'Every worker in science recognizes at the outset his inferiority to a thousand other workers – known and unknown – but one does not on that account keep silent.'[42]

Questioning the ideals of education as they existed in India, he said: 'All of us should realize that no aspect of knowledge can be inconsistent with another. It is of course an unfortunate circumstance that education as conceived amongst us and the atmosphere in which we all have been educated has not had any idealism in it at all. The attitude has always been the suicidal point of view that education is a means to get a comfortable setting in life – I hate that very phrase and I am sure you also do so.[43]

40 Ibid.

41 Letter dated 24 June 1931

42 Letter dated 3 September 1931

43 Letter dated August 1933

Later, he wrote encouragingly: 'Life is long and all will be for the best. Only imagine how great a foundation you can lay for yourself and how much satisfaction it will give you and us all to see your fulfilled desires, for can full knowledge of so human yet so all embracing a science as medicine fail to give satisfaction? It is wonderful how science makes progress and what great discovery in one particular branch has not had repercussions on science at large?'[44] Then, in 1936, he wrote: 'That it was Chekhov – or was it one of the other great Russian writers? – who once said that every artist must undergo the training of a medical doctor to fully understand human suffering in the large, perhaps this prescription is somewhat analogous to Plato's suggestion of Euclid as the first introduction to philosophical thinking. You can readily comprehend why I should just now recall Chekhov – I think it was Chekhov who in early life was a doctor.'[45] Appa had by now finished four years of medicine.

Answering another of Appa's letters and calling upon Appa to break away the chains if that was the only way he could pursue his writing and be happy, Periappa wrote: '"Living" and "Security", these are conventional watch-words which carry no meaning to me, and I am sure they carry no meaning to you. I recall once a conversation with Hardy (the famous mathematician who discovered Ramanujan): "If anybody asks you why you are an astronomer and what use is astronomy, then to such a philistine the correct answer is astronomy may not be useful, indeed my work may not be of importance in any sense, but I am convinced that my work in astronomy is at least the most important part of my personality."'[46]

In effect, the emphasis was on pursuing one's aspiration and spirit of creativity to the exclusion of everything else.

These years were witness to Periappa facing the storm of Eddington's criticism. His angst is almost poetically described in this letter of January 1935:

44 Letter dated 11 February 1934

45 Letter dated 23 March 1936

46 Letter dated 17 June 1939

> Involved in the puzzles of the interior of stars, battered by differential equations, boxed by numerical calculations, impeded by ignorance, rushed at by the dawning of the new year, I have at last emerged out not indeed with the anticipated joy with which I began by diving into the crucibles of nature, but burnt and smoking, dissatisfied and tired.
>
> But having emerged I would delight in knowing how shapely corpses attended by their pageantry of scissors and knives dance in your dreams and skid beyond unawares with the oncoming of the blizzard of 'papers'.
>
> May New Year prove a ship with 'sails of silk and masts of gold' for you to voyage forth across the ocean of human knowledge – for is not medicine the science of Gods and healing the art of the most worthy? Why, why need you feel downcast; is not your ship laden 'with sugar in the cabin and apples in the hold? Onward, onward with courage, determination and good cheer! Excelsior!'[47]

In the same letter, he goes on to explain how some controversies with Eddington during the past year had upset his enthusiasm a great deal.

A few months later, in June 1935, he wrote that after his mother's passing away 'memory fails not because I cannot recollect but because memory recalls what is no more', at home in Chandra Vilas. 'I recollect too our reading together – how I used to bore you reading all my texts? –Ruskin especially – blown bag pipes for friends to pipe with! ... As you wrote to me on my election to the Trinity Fellowship, for work we sacrifice the richer things in life. But is it worth it after all? The world judges not by what we cherish, but by what we accomplish and even that only to forget ... Still, I know I would not be happy if I returned home just now ...'[48]

In 1937, on his life at Williams Bay, he wrote that it was 'a quiet and routine one of astronomers ... Sometimes the exhilaration of having found something new, sometimes the saddening effect of realizing one's own shortcomings relative to the giants, sometimes the old indifference

47 Letter dated 9 January 1935

48 Letter dated 26 June 1935

of deadened feelings ... still one gets out of any of these moods, to one's days of work of calculations, discussions, writing papers, correspondence, etc. That in short is the life of an astronomer and that in short is my own life ... Then one grows old and dies ...'[49]

It is evident that during this period, as in later years of their lives, they corresponded regularly, sharing their thoughts on matters close to their hearts.

On Board Ships

Periappa's allegory of the ships in his New Year greetings is reflective of the times they then lived in – when aeroplanes as a means of transport were absent. He wrote letters while on board ships, for example, the letter dated 8 December 1936 on board *Gunard White Star 'Laconia'*, from Cambridge on the way to Yerkes, USA, and the letter dated 23 March 1936 on board *Gunard White Star 'Bergenegaria'* from Yerkes, USA, to Cambridge. In his letter dated 17 June 1939, on board French line S.S. *Champlain* en route to Paris, he wrote: '4th day of our journey and at the moment, we are fog bound and so the boat is creeping at snail's pace and blowing the loud horn every few minutes' and adds that he has left his 'loyal spouse alone' because 'our finances would not have permitted our travelling together' and 'the French Foundation have persuaded themselves into the illusion of believing that my presence at the Conference is worth $600 (an illusion which is not necessary for me to dispel!!). P.S. I shall sail back by July 26. P.P.S. The fog outside seems to get worse. I hope this does not delay embarking too much.'[50]

On Being a Scientist

Periappa's letters of the early years have interesting observations regarding many scientists or about his own life as a scientist. These were the years when many eminent scientists were doing original scientific

49 Letter dated 22 June 1937

50 Letter dated 17 June 1939

work. The inspiring times are often reflected in these letters as also the frustrations and routine involved in the pursuit of science.

After reading Jean's 'Astronomy and Cosmogony' and going through his mathematics and not merely his awe at the perspectives of space and time, Periappa wrote in 1930: 'On a scale where the orbit of the sun is of the size of a point, the fastest nebulae is thousands of miles, the earth dwindles into an electron and will have to be magnified a million times to be resolved by the most powerful microscope. The inhabitant of the earth may well pause to consider his place in the scheme of the universe. And I pause for a while and as consolation repeat to myself Hardy's famous saying, "To feel the infinity of God's love in man's infinitismelness!"'[51]

This letter, written in 1931, has the hallmark of Periappa: 'I write this letter just to give you a very interesting (?) thing I have read: "Once when the famous Boltzmann had concluded a lecture on atoms and molecules, the equally famous Mach arose and said in effect: "You do not know that molecules exist." Boltzmann replied, "I know that there are molecules," Mach retorted, "You do not" and so the debate ended.'

Now I am not going to tell you where I took this from. Perhaps you read this already. Perhaps not. In any case where do you think the modern physicists stand – with Mach or Boltzmann? It is hardly necessary for me to add that your judgement is not to be clouded by the fact that while Boltzmann is the greatest physicist (other than Maxwell) of the 19th century (we have Dirac – the Boltzmann, and Heisenberg – the Maxwell of the 20th century) Mach is (a great philosopher, but) no physicist. In particular, with whom do you think I side?'[52]

He wrote: 'I wish always to remind myself that Weierstrass, one of the greatest mathematicians of Germany began work at 40 and still had 40 years not only to prove his extraordinary abilities as a mathematician with a very wide range, but also to be the father of a flourishing school of mathematics with such eminent representatives like David Hilbert,

51 Letter dated 1 September 1930

52 Letter dated 26 November 1930

Hermann Weyl, Edmund Landon, J. Von Neumann, Carl Runge, Clebsch, and many others. One can quote many such instances. Cayley began work in mathematics after retirement (he was a barrister) and any occasional visitor to any decent library cannot but be struck by 14–15 octavo volumes of Cayley's Collected Works. And then there is your own – rather our – Valmiki.'

A few months later he wrote, 'Dirac's lectures are masterly ... Now he has come to that region of quantum mechanics, where the demarcation between science and metaphysics is hazy (even as most people's notions are) and his lectures are profoundly philosophical and deep. The likes of it one can perhaps hear only in a few other places – Gottingen (Hilbert), Copenhagen (Bohr), Zurich (Weyl), Leipzig (Heisenberg) and Berlin (Einstein, Lane and Planck).'[53]

Enclosing the reprint of an article in *Nature* by Bohr, Periappa wrote from the Copenhagen Institut for Fysik: 'In reading the essay, you ought to bear in mind that each sentence has taken Bohr at an average more than half an hour to write ... One ought to bear this in mind because each sentence is pregnant with meaning and there is very much more expressed in each sentence than would even a careful reading indicate ... Just remember a moment that Bohr has been the guiding spirit in all the great difficulties all these twenty years – always at the top! A great teacher, thinker and philosopher, one who more than anybody else living has contributed continuously to the progress of ideas, one who is responsible for our ideas about atoms and more than all one who has inspired every investigator of science in modern times.[54]

His description of witnessing the solar eclipse of 9 June 1945[55] is worth recording. Hiltner and he drove with their equipment – on which they had worked all May and June – packed in a trailer, along the Mississippi, then up the valley of the Red River to Winnipeg, to Pine River, deep in Manitoba, where there was a curious little village with an entirely Russian population. Their selected site 'was a little ridge some three-quarters of a

53 Letter dated 21 January 1931

54 Letter dated 2 May 1933

55 Letter dated 25 July 1945

mile from the central track of totality, and which commanded a clear view of the eastern sky (the totality was to occur at 7.15 in the morning).' They prepared the place by clearing the bushes, putting up the tent, making foundations for concrete piers to mount the telescopes, all of which took a week. 'But during the nights I stayed on the site. Lying there in the tent, alone, and with the knowledge that no human beings were present for miles and miles around, I felt a strange quietness: It was a feeling which intoxicated me and I longed for the evenings every day ...' Though it began as a cloudy morning, as the clouds slowly cleared, '25 minutes before totality there was a clear band and the already partially eclipsed sun shown forth. A few minutes later, the eastern sky was beautiful and clear and everyone trembled with expectation. And the totality itself was the supreme climax. During the last minute darkness literally descended, for the moment a rim of the sun is broken into droplets of golden fire, then a flash, the prominences become visible and then the miracle happens: the sun suddenly blossoms and the faint delicate texture of the corona reveals itself. With this shining plumage, faintly green, with the darkened disc, it looks like a wild bird at bay... and the world stands still ... And then all of a sudden a blinding flash ... It is all over! But the impression of those 37 seconds will be permanent ... There was still another phase. It had been computed that the totality should occur at 7.15.45 seconds and in order that our observing programme may be carried, we had a counter, who started counting exactly one minute before the computed instant, from 60 backwards. And at zero, it was zero – and you have to live through that instant to feel the impact of man's genius charting the heavens ... We packed the trailer later in the day and early next morning started on our journey back and we arrived in Williams Bay on July 13.'[56]

In 1943 and 1944[57] he wrote that his life revolved around three principal 'duties'– teaching, research and routine business. Of these, research was a vague pleasurable pursuit involving ruminating and hunting for ideas. A scholar's life was uneventful: that is, in everything

56 Ibid.

57 Letters dated 19 May 1943 and 7 November 1944

except in the matters of his study, and these were likely to be of interest only to those in his profession. After a spate of hectic months, he wrote: 'I long for a time when I shall have more peace for calm and peaceful meditations even if the objects pondered upon include only "shoes and ships and sealing wax!"'[58]

As the years passed, the letters frequently refer to the ever-present stress of work. 'This constant effort to keep abreast of matters which continuously press and clamour for attention leaves no time for peace and quietness. And how I long for them!' Again, 'the pressure on my time is very considerable: the number of people and things which require my attention are many. The harassment of these many small matters prevent concentration on real scientific effort ... As you see that in many ways the life of a scientist is no different from the life of a practising doctor!'[59] This was, no doubt, in reply to Appa's similar refrain in his letter!

After his trip to India in 1969, he wrote 'since my return to Chicago, it has been one thing after another: after the tail, the knife, and so on!' humorously referring to a Tamil poem for children.[60] He went on to list nine items that needed his immediate attention – to complete a long-protracted calculation, mostly done prior to his trip to India but needing two more weeks of work; his book on ellipsoids; two papers of the preceding year to be completed, on one of which he was to talk in Princeton by the end of January; to give the Richtmeyer lecture in February. Meanwhile, the proof of his book had come and he had agreed to write a paper for a volume being prepared in honour of G. Wentzel, a colleague in the Department of Physics, and finally the *Astrophysics Journal* and his students! After a couple of more pages, he wrote: 'I hope I have not tired you. But I felt like rambling along.'[61]

His meticulous approach to scientific research and writing is evident in this letter: 'During the fall of 1967 and the winter of 1968 I had put together my work on the "ellipsoids" in a book. It was supposedly a

---

58 Letter dated 19 May 1943

59 Letter dated 10 August 1958

60 Letter dated 6 April 1969; *'Vaalu pochu kathi vandadu dum dum dum!'*

61 Ibid.

completion of a lot of unfinished work but it concluded with a statement that a particular problem (originally formulated by Darwin) had not been resolved. That seemed to me unsatisfactory aesthetically. So after some hard thinking I succeeded in solving the problem. The problem had to be solved: the proofs of the book were due at any time: if the solution had to be included in the book it had to be worked out, calculations and all, by January 15 and I confess to some luck in being able to do it.'[62]

In his Seferis lecture of 29 March 1989 on 'The Perception of Beauty and the Pursuit of Science', he quoted Penrose about the 'subtle role played by aesthetics, in connection with research, namely as a means for obtaining results'.[63]

Once, failing to obtain *Parables from Nature* by Maria Edgeworth from the Bodlein Library in Oxford, he wrote to Appa: 'I recall that when we were in school, we used to read a book called *Parables from Nature* in which there is a story titled (or with a moral, I cannot recall which) "Not lost, but gone before" – the story of a grasshopper (or dragonfly) hatched on the bed of a pond, which escaped after growing wings and vainly tries to return to the bed of the pond to relate to those left behind which are constantly perplexed as to what happens to the flies that leave and never return ... I would be grateful if you can trace the book and send me the text of the story. The story is a fine parable also for some recent discoveries in astronomy and I would like to use it in a public lecture (the Halley lecture) I am to give in Oxford in early May.'[64] In March, he asked Vidyakka if she could find the book in Ethiraj College, to which all the cupboards-ful of Babuji's books had been donated. There is no later mention as to whether he was able to get the text of the story!

When he went for a conference in Poland in 1973, he mentioned that the Polish Physical Society awarded him 'their Smoluchouski Medal – the first time it was awarded to a foreigner – to recognize some contributions I made during the early forties to a furtherance of Smoluchouski's ideas

---

62 Ibid.

63 The First Seferis Lecture (delivered on 29 March 1989), 'The Perception of Beauty and the Pursuit of Science'

64 Letters dated 29 January 1972 and 18 March 1972

– and Smoluchouski is one of Poland's scientific heroes'.[65] Commenting that he was not looking forward to the lecturing in the new quarter, he wrote '"life seems to have lost its savour" as Milne used to say. I suppose that is the result of growing old.'[66] It is a measure of the man that in spite of references to stress, he continued to work and be productive for many years to come.

In his convocation address in Roorkee, he tells about this quest for one's satisfaction in scholarly endeavours: 'In concluding, let me try to answer directly the question why one, fully aware of one's inherent and often insurmountable limitations, nevertheless devotes oneself to scholarship and to a life of constant endeavour, many failures, and fewer successes? The answer is, as T.S. Eliot has given in his *Confidential Clerk*: It is strange, isn't it, / That a man should have a consuming passion / To do something for which he lacks the capacity?'[67]

On Literature

Periappa and Appa shared a deep interest in literature. The letters are replete with references to the great authors and their books which they were reading. The earliest reference is to *The Collected Works of Charles and Mary Lamb*, which Periappa was sending to Appa, as he noted, 'one needs occasionally some kind of relaxation and I bought this book for a couple of shillings and read the whole book through one evening (the tales from Shakespeare omitted) ... All the essays are wonderfully "nice" but my "best" is "The Sailor Uncle" ... What is your "best"? – perhaps the "Young Motorman"?'[68]

Enclosing a copy of a lecture by Housman, Periappa wrote: 'A short time before I left for Europe, one evening when you, Krishnamurthi and I went for a walk along the beach – the evening when we discussed a variety

65 Letter dated 24 September 1973

66 Ibid.

67 The Convocation Address (Roorkee, India: 28 November 1989), a copy of which was sent to S. Balakrishnan.

68 Letter dated 18 March 1931

of things including the Uncertainty Principle of Heisenberg, I recollect very clearly your having said that evening: "Poetry is not the thing said, but the way of saying it" – when reading a review of Housman's lecture I was surprised to come across this sentence again. So I bought the book and on page 37 you will find your sentence – It is amazing … the idea of my telling you is how very delighted I was to live through again that very pleasant evening we had.'[69]

In 1943, he referred to having read Turgenev's *Fathers and Sons* again, Dostoevsky's *Blessed*, some Virginia Woolf and Tolstoy's *War and Peace*. After his heart attack in 1977, he wrote: 'After the first few days of discomfort, I actually enjoyed the convalescence by reading a new biography of Shakespeare, some of his sonnets and re-reading *Hamlet* and *Othello*.'[70] Also, since he had chosen to talk on 'The Patterns of Creativity in Science, Literature and Music', for the Nora Ryerson lecture, he was 'educating himself' since he was 'presently uneducated in these matters' and 'the experience will be a good one!'[71] Elsewhere he wrote that these general addresses were in some ways his 'literary efforts!'

Appa sent all his literary books, articles, short stories, poems and plays, both in Tamil and English, to Periappa and these are all individually referred to in Periappa's letters through the long years, often with a note of critical appreciation. For example, 'Today the copy of your article on Kalidasa arrived – I enjoyed this tremendously: the strength of feeling you bring to bear and the clarity with which the essentials are brought to focus are indeed most refreshing. Without intending to say something really nice, I do feel that your writing has a character and an integrity which is most unusual: Chekhov or Dostoevsky are the only others I can recall.'[72] In 1944, he wrote: 'In 1936 you read out to me your translation of Shakespeare's plays. They produced a particularly strong impression on me. And blank verse in Tamil was new. I think you should publish the

69 Letter dated 28 June 1933

70 Letter dated 17 September 1974

71 Ibid.

72 Letter dated 7 November 1944

translations of at least a few plays: they will create a new medium for the stage ...' Conveying happiness at Appa's play in Tamil being published by Bharatiya Vidya Bhavan, he wrote in 1963: 'Lalitha and I can never forget the evening at our home when you read out your play to us.'[73]

On receiving the parcel of a book from the USA (Rabindranath Tagore, *The Myriad-Minded Man*) in 1996, Appa automatically said, 'Anna has sent it', and then 'Oh! He is no more.' Indeed, 'Anna' had arranged to send it when the book was still in the process of being published! Two years later, when another parcel of the newly published book of poems by Appa, titled *Nineteen Forty Two and Other Poems on Indian Themes,* arrived in September 1998, Appa was not there to receive it. It had come a month too late. I quote this poem by Appa as a tribute to Periappa and Appa – the dreams, the struggles and the indomitable will of their generation:

The Anointed Generation[74]

Lo, we are the anointed
the chosen
We are the God-anointed
Men and women

We were the last generation
of slaves
And the first generation
Of free men

We broke
the yoke
And smiled at the foe
In friendship's glow[75]

---

73 Letter dated 30 October 1963

74 Purusu Balakrishnan, *Nineteen Forty Two and Other Poems on Indian Themes*, Bharatiya Vidya Bhavan, 1998, pp. 5–6

We followed Gandhi
And we were Gandhi
We sang with Bharati
And we were Bharati

We held our heads high
with Tagore
and we were lit by the spark
that he brought from the sages

We worked with Nehru
and we were Nehru
We walked with Vinobha
and we were Vinobha

And we were Vallabhbhai Patel
And Jayaprakash Narayan
We saw God in Ramana –
We were the God-anointed!

---

75 The first toast that Nehru raised for independent India was 'God save the King', thereby displaying a rare broadness of mind.

ten

REMEMBERING SUBRAHMANYAN CHANDRASEKHAR

S. Ramanathan

PROFESSOR CHANDRASEKHAR WAS BORN ON 19 OCTOBER 1910 AND IF HE were alive, this would have been his 100th year.

I had the privilege of meeting him a number of times both in the USA and India, thanks to my being married to his niece. Of those many meetings, the one I had in Chicago in 1994 was very special. This was mainly because, during that trip, I stayed with him in his apartment for a couple of days and he therefore talked with me at length on various subjects. With no pretence to understanding his field of work, my discussions were obviously general.

He lived on campus in the Chicago University. Within a few hours of my arrival, he first took me to his office room and then around the campus. We sat for a while near Henry Moore's sculpture *Nuclear Energy*. It had been unveiled in the place where Enrico Fermi and his team of physicists had achieved the first controlled self-sustaining nuclear chain reaction. Then Chandrasekhar took me to the Oriental Institute Museum and, with special permission, brought from the archives a sheet of paper with Leonardo Da Vinci's original handwriting. He spent considerable time talking about the various exhibits in the museum. From the store outside the museum, he got a bust of Nefertiti as a memento for me.

While we walked on the lawns of the university, I asked him about the most memorable incident related to the announcement of the Nobel Prize. He said that he had walked as usual to his office in the university and had opened the door when someone knocked. To his surprise he saw Robert Millikan, looking frail and weak. Millikan said, 'Chandra, when I got the prize, I felt you should have got it earlier than me. Congratulations.' What touched Chandrasekhar was that Professor Millikan, who had got the Nobel Prize in chemistry a few years before, was ill and was confined to his apartment, which was in the same building as Chandrasekhar's; yet he had taken the trouble of walking up to the office to convey his feelings.

During another conversation, Chandrasekhar said that he had received an invitation from the dean of a well-known university in the USA requesting him to consider joining their university, reiterating that they would provide for everything. He had replied to the dean that at his age, as per Hindu custom, one should give up everything and withdraw into the forest to practise vanaprasthashram. The dean had replied, 'We will be able to provide everything, but a forest may be a bit difficult!'

As we walked back to his building and entered the elevator, Saul Bellow, the Nobel laureate in literature, also got in. Later, Chandrasekhar remarked that many in that building were Nobel laureates and that they preferred the rented apartments to owning houses, since it meant that no time was needed to be spent on maintenance problems! This kept them free to concentrate on their work. He added that there was, of course, the risk that they could be asked to vacate any time.

At lunch, Chandrasekhar spoke about the need to motivate boys and girls in school to pursue pure science. He said that in the USA it was not uncommon for scientists like Fermi to give lectures to school students and it was considered an honour to be invited to give such lectures. He talked about the passion and dedication that one needs to achieve something worthwhile in scientific research. It requires sacrifices and working continuously for long hours without interruption or distraction. He said this was the reason why, despite having close relatives in the USA, he had not attended any important family function. In a lighter vein, he said that there was a Hungarian professor in the university and once meeting him in the corridors during the days of the Hungarian revolution, he had asked him whether his relatives were safe in Hungary, to which the Hungarian professor replied, 'Oh, no, something terrible has happened ...' and added after a pause: 'They are all here!'

Chandrasekhar had met Einstein twice and the first time after he was introduced, Einstein told him that he would be meeting him for dinner the next day. Chandrasekhar, a young astrophysicist in those days and yet to make a mark, was thrilled that Einstein remembered that he was in the list of invitees for the dinner next day. In reply to my statement that I had heard that Einstein was a very simple person, Chandrasekhar said, 'I am reminded of Bernard Shaw's remark on Gandhi. He said that Gandhi is a humble, simple man but he knows he is Gandhi all right, and this applies to Einstein as well.'

Later in the evening, he played two of his favourite music records, *The Music of the Minstrels*, and Bruno Walter rehearsing and recording Mozart's symphony no. 36. Bruno Walter had once come to his apartment for dinner and during the conversation Chandrasekhar spoke to him with his usual high emotion about Newton. Bruno asked him whether Newton is to science what Bach is to music. Chandrasekhar had replied, 'That is the only comparison I shall tolerate.'

The next day, I had to leave after lunch. He took out a 'visitors' book' and said that any person staying with him had to write comments and sign before leaving. I hesitated because the book contained names of a number of scientific luminaries and I did not fit in. Finally, I was forced to comply on his insistence. While I was turning the pages of the autograph book, I saw Paul Dirac's name and signature. Mrs Lalitha Chandrasekhar said that before Dirac came visiting, Chandrasekhar had warned her that he was a serious person and did not talk much. But Dirac, as soon as he arrived, changed into shorts, picked up a pickaxe and cleaned the snow in front of the apartment building – and did not stop talking with her!

I felt a lump in my throat as I left them, little realizing that it was my last meeting with Chandrasekhar. He died the next year on 21 August 1995. I did go back after a few years to meet Mrs Chandrasekhar, who continues to live in the same apartment, and who completed a hundred years this year. She talked about the launching of the X-ray observatory named after Chandrasekhar by NASA on Space Shuttle *Columbia,* and that she had been invited by NASA to watch the launch. Before that, they had asked her to give something that belonged to Chandrasekhar which they could send in the space shuttle and give back to her. She had given them Chandrasekhar's pocket-watch. Then she took out the same pocket-watch and requested me to hand it over to Chandrasekhar's youngest brother Ramnath who was then in Delhi.

As I left her and got into a taxi to go to the airport, I remembered Chandrasekhar's concluding statement in his speech on 'Newton and Michelangelo' that he gave at Lindau, Germany: 'When a supreme creative mind is kindled, it leaves a blazing trail that remains a beacon for centuries.'

I thought how true it was in his case.

eleven

A Miscellany of Memories

D. Ashok

My mother Sarada, like her siblings, had a lot of respect and admiration for her eldest brother – Ayya Mama to us. She had also graduated with honours in physics and could appreciate his work to an extent. She would browse through his lectures and books, which he periodically sent by mail, and would occasionally ask him questions about them. She would write long letters to him and Ayya Mama would reply to each one of them. Amma would show his letters to us and point out his beautiful handwriting in particular. One would not see a single word scratched out in his letters. It showed his clarity of thought. Amma had heard from Ayya Mama that some of his handwritten manuscripts were directly taken up for printing.

When Amma tried to encourage us to make him our role model, we would protest saying that he was a born genius. She would invariably correct us by saying that genius is a result of 99 per cent perspiration. I remember Lalitha Mami telling me that sometimes she would quietly peep into Ayya Mama's study when he was working and would find him in exactly the same posture that he had been in a few hours earlier. Such was his concentration and hard work; and I believe that anyone putting in such effort cannot but become one of the best in his field.

Though we were privileged to have two Nobel laureates in our family, I must say that I do not believe such genius runs in our family, or for that matter in any other family. Ayya Mama and Professor C.V. Raman, the nephew and the uncle, were of different genetic models. I have had the opportunity of talking to both at length and observing them closely. Except their passion for work and the fact that both chose their own partners at a time when love marriages were more the exception than the rule, they did not have much in common. Professor had a dominating personality. Ayya Mama, on the other hand, was soft-spoken. Professor was early to bed and early to rise while Ayya Mama's best hours for work were in the early mornings and late evenings. Ayya Mama almost always spoke in complete sentences. Over the years, I noticed the effort he would put in even in our day-to-day conversation, whether he was speaking or listening. He was an aggressive listener and in that respect too was very different from Professor.

After being conferred a Ph.D by Delhi University, Ayya Mama wrote to Amma (I am quoting from memory here): 'It was nice getting this doctorate in India in the company of good friends like M.G.K. Menon, and a bit strange to share the dais with ... [name of a few politicians] ... but it was a truly hair-raising experience to realize that one's work in science was equated to the level of MS's (M.S. Subbulakshmi) music.'

All of us have photographic memories of Ayya Mama's mischievous smile whenever he cracked a joke. The Big 10 – the four brothers and six sisters – surpassed each other in their sense of humour. On one occasion, our grand-uncle Kunjappa (C. Ramaswamy) was discussing his work at the Council of Scientific and Industrial Research, an organization he was working with after his retirement. They had posted him to the same building where just a few weeks earlier he had been occupying a huge room, being the director general. Ayya Mama asked him if his present smaller room was comfortable for his work. Kunjappa, with his characteristic innocence, replied that it was absolutely okay, except that it was next to the ladies' room. Ayya Mama's comment 'Ramudu, that should be no reason for complaint' drew guffaws from everyone.

I think it was in 1983 that we had Ayya Mama visiting us at our home in Madras. My mother had come from Puduchatram to be with him for a fortnight. My daughter Aarthi was about six years old and was intrigued by the fact that the attention that was normally her prerogative, was being diverted on that day to someone else. Typical of Aarthi, she took him head on. To impress him, she showed him some of her school notebooks where she had scored top marks.

Typical also of Ayya Mama, he took his time tackling Aarthi. He sat next to my mother on the sofa, munching murukku, sipping tea and conversing with her and my aunt Savitriakka, and of course giving some attention to Aarthi too. This was the first time that I saw Ayya Mama enjoying food or drink and even talking about it. He complimented my wife on the tea and asked her how she normally prepared it. It was more than just being polite to a hostess. I was, till then, carrying the baggage that a Chandra Vilas youngster was not supposed to be distracted by such trivialities as food, or he would not excel in his studies.

Aarthi, restless in the meantime, finally offered that Ayya Mama could ask her any question from her book, which she could literally recite from back to front – a Chandra Vilas trait. We were busy talking to Lalitha Mami when we suddenly realized that there was an argument in progress between Ayya Mama and Aarthi. We did not know what the subject was. At that point Aarthi was insisting in an intimidating voice that she was right because her teacher had told her so and that her teacher could never be wrong.

Ayya Mama then recalled an incident from a couple of years ago when back in the US he had had a similar argument with an American child a little older than Aarthi. The argument was regarding the temperature of the sun. The child insisted that the temperature of the sun was a uniform 11,000°F, and did not vary from 11,000°F on the surface to about 27 million °F at the core as Ayya Mama had mentioned. So Ayya Mama took her to the nearby library and showed her the relevant section in a book. The little girl appeared convinced for a moment. She then turned the book up and down, and examined it for a while. Then she said, 'No. I still do not agree. This book is written by *you* after all!' Ayya Mama went on to tell us that at Aarthi's age all children have the same sense of intellectual enquiry, but Indian children get so inhibited as they grow up that they rarely challenge the teacher or the printed word. I mustered enough courage to ask him whether our age-old system of gurukul did not deliver. After all Chandra Vilas and Babuji encouraged a daily joint student-teacher prayer before starting a lesson. Instead of replying to my question, he asked me if I knew the story of Ekalavyan, and his quiet smile packed it with a lot for me to reflect on.

twelve

Anecdotes from a Silent Admirer

D. Bharath

Ayya-Mama: A word that has always been uttered in hushed tones, with a great deal of awe and reverence. This is the impression that was indelibly etched in my childhood.

I did most of my schooling in my village in Thanjavur district and we used to visit Pattinam (the city that has renamed itself Chennai from its erstwhile name Madras – but it has remained 'Pattinam' to us in the village) once in a couple of years to visit Babuji, or to participate in the family reunions when my uncle Prof. Chandrasekhar – alias Ayya Mama – came to India. As a schoolboy, I could never interact with him freely, mostly due to the extraordinary awe that I used to sense in everyone around him; neither could he converse with me because of my inability to speak in English, and his inability to understand the Tamil that I spoke so fluently and eloquently.

I think it was in the year 1961 that we had a family reunion in Pattinam and we all went for a picnic. All of us children hosted a variety entertainment programme for Ayya Mama. I remember a young girl named Maya doing an act from Kalidasa's epic *Shakunthalam* in Sanskrit. I did a mono-act depicting a scene from the Tamil movie *Veera Pandyia Katta Bomman*. The dialogues in the movie were written in delectable Tamil by M. Karunanidhi (who is currently the chief minister of Tamil

Nadu) and enacted by the inimitable colossus of Tamil cinema, Sivaji Ganesan. All the other acts that evening were in English.

Despite my frequent meetings with him for many years – which included an eight-hour trip with him and Lalitha Mami in a car – the emotional distance between us remained. He too must have sensed my discomfort in his presence. He once tried to provoke me by saying that I came more to accompany my mother on such trips than due to any particular interest in meeting him. Like I always do in such situations, I remained silent, and just smiled and moved away.

Perhaps he never knew that I used to read all his articles, and was a great fan of his writings. Even today I keep recommending his book *Truth and Beauty* to others. I wish to possess all his writings, lectures and books. My regret is that his books are often priced high and are not in a layman's reach.

He also perhaps did not know that I gave myself the name Chandrasekhar as my official Hindu name during my upanayanam. He continues to be my hero of sorts. But the distance remained all the way.

***

An incident that I am always reminded of is the time he came to my house to participate in my daughter Anupama's birthday celebrations. It must have been her second birthday and my mother was staying with me in my house in Bangalore. My house was just a stone's throw away from Balanna's. Ayya Mama, as always, was staying with Balanna on his visit to Bangalore. This trip of Ayya Mama's was significant in the sense that it was his first after receiving the Nobel Prize the previous year. I had called my friends and colleagues for the birthday celebration, and they were all there in the room, along with Ayya Mama. But none of them recognized the great man in their midst.

The next day, on my way to work in the company bus, I expressed my surprise and disappointment that none of my colleagues had congratulated my uncle on his becoming a Nobel laureate. This set the cat amongst the pigeons. They 'accused' me of not letting them know that he was there, despite the fact that they were all sitting so close to him! I was amused by the fact that none of them recognized a celebrity, although it was in an unexpected forum. They immediately wanted to make amends by hosting a high tea in his honour. Despite my repeated assertion that Prof. Chandrasekhar was a very private person and that I could not approach him with such a ridiculous request, they wanted to me to try it for their sake. So I finally called up my aunt Shyamalakka and told her my predicament and asked her to convey the request on behalf of my friends. She came back to me with the reply that 'Anna' did not want to participate in any public function. I communicated the same to my friends, suitably admonishing them for expecting a Nobel laureate to accept being felicitated by such ignoramuses.

I thought that the chapter on this matter was closed and busied myself with my work. To my surprise, I got a call from Ayya Mama shortly thereafter, saying that he would accept the offer if it would make me happy. I was stunned at such generosity. I thanked him profusely and told him that such a get-together was not necessary at all, and that his time in India would be better spent otherwise.

Perhaps with that one act of kindness towards me, he came much closer to me as a loving uncle and a bigger hero. But he never got to know about that either.

thirteen

Conversations with Ayya Mama[1]

V.S. Mahesh

It is tempting for someone who hails from a family that has produced two Nobel laureates and several other great personalities, including a mother who published books in her nineties, to blindly support those who espouse the cause of 'Nature' in the on-going 'Nature vs. Nurture' debate. To claim one's right to be considered special by virtue of one's genes is an easy way out when the cards are stacked in one's favour. From Ricardo and Malthus to the evolutionary biologists of the 20th century, several arguments have been put forward to justify the special status claimed by self-proclaimed 'upper classes'.

I have never been a supporter of this school of thought, and abhor the negative extremes to which this logic leads, like racism and caste-ism. I support the school of thought that it is the *nurturing* of the younger generation by the older, and the atmosphere created for the transfer of intangible knowledge and values that is critical for development of people to their full potential.

---

1 *Ayya Mama* was how Dr S. Chandrasekhar was addressed as by his sisters' children

NURTURING, THE CHANDRA VILAS WAY

In this short piece, I wish to address the role of nurturing as was practised in the Chandra Vilas family during my formative years, with particular focus on my personal interactions with Ayya Mama. I owe a great debt of gratitude to my mother Vidya Shankar and her siblings, one of whom was Ayya Mama, for the time they were willing to spend with us, from engaging in conversations to role modelling and telling us the truth in the brutally honest Chandra Vilas way.

Nurturing in the Chandra Vilas family had its unique ways. It was not of the soft, handholding variety. Rather, it was a demanding, often very directive process. Working on and developing one's intellectual potential took precedence over all other aspects of one's younger days. My brothers and I had to be at our desk by 6.00 a.m. or so every morning, be it a school day or a holiday. The only exceptions were the first day of holidays after examinations – exactly three times a year. We had a desk each, with little chairs to sit on. Conversations were not allowed during those early hours of the day. While Amma worked on her music, writing and books, or was busy practising her veena, the three of us would be working on our respective school texts, supplemented by classics.

While this short piece is mainly about Ayya Mama, the picture conjured would be misleading to the reader if I talk of him without the right contextual background. Yes, he achieved much greater worldly success than others in the family, but worldly success is not everything. Seeking perfection in what one does without thinking about rewards is the essence of life, and that is what one learnt in the Chandra Vilas family. Ayya Mama, more than anyone else I know, symbolized this.

WE DON'T DO FALSE MODESTY HERE

Recently, an interviewer came to meet my mother and one of the questions he put to her was this: 'What was something really special about Prof. Chandrasekhar that you can recall from the early days that clearly set him apart?' My mother thought for some time and answered,

'I do not think he was particularly special or better than others. All of us were very special.' While the interviewer probably thought it was a very egotistical statement, I understood what my mother meant. She was just being honest, in the undiplomatic manner that is so typical of the Chandra Vilas family. I joked, however, saying that our family motto should be 'We do not do False Modesty here'. The fact that our family has never had a member entering diplomatic circles, let alone succeed in that arena should not surprise anyone!

My mother had four brothers, the eldest being Ayya Mama and the others, Chinanna (Visvanathan, the heavy-weight metallurgist who made unsuspecting nephews start on long bicycle rides and walks even before the birds woke up), Balanna (Balakrishnan, the gentle doctor and author of several books and short stories) and Ramnath (the youngest of the ten siblings but possibly the most worldly-wise of them all). Though we were a well-spread-out family, with none of my four uncles living in Madras when I was growing up, there were several occasions when I had the opportunity to interact with them on a one-to-one basis. The amount of learning these conversations provided outweighed the sometimes-unpleasant process of learning they entailed.

It would be beyond the scope of this piece to dwell on the role played by my aunts in this nurturing process, but it must be stated here that they played an equally important role. Their empathy, goodness, and understanding of the softer aspects of nurturing formed a critical part of our upbringing. But for Savitriakka (my mother's younger sister), I would not have passed my pre-university examinations! These aspects of nurturing will have to be dealt with separately.

To compensate for the distant presence of my uncles, my grandfather (Babuji) stayed a few houses away and he made it absolutely clear what he liked and what he didn't in a harshly honest way. There was no one to match his dictatorial style of communication. 'False Modesty' was not part of his psyche at all. In an introduction to one of his own books, he was 'honest' enough to inform the reader that other authors on the subject were charlatans whose publications were best avoided!

CONVERSATIONS BEGAN WITH 'WHAT IS YOUR CURRENT INTELLECTUAL PURSUIT?'

I must confess that these conversations and interactions – with my grandfather or with any of the uncles – were not particularly easy or enjoyable most of the time. Within a minute or two of meeting one of them, in some cases after a lapse of a few years, they would ask a question which more-or-less amounted to this: 'What have you being doing since we last met? I trust it has been a serious pursuit of an intellectual nature? If you have been wasting your time, then do not take up my time with inane conversations. I have no time to waste on such an aimless person.' As a youngster with other legitimate interests like playing cricket, reading Wodehouse, watching films, etc., meeting these uncles was indeed an onerous task, especially in the presence of a mother whose unconditional positive regard for her brothers elevated the meeting to a dizzy height of unequalled importance.

Despite all the tension these meetings caused in my early years, I believe they were some of the most important moments of nurturing for us, who formed the third generation of the Chandra Vilas family. To capture the flavour of these 'conversations', here are a few examples:

Babuji (circa 1957): My grandfather Babuji was reclining in the easy chair in the corridor adjacent to the library in Chandra Vilas. Two of my cousin sisters, well meaning, I am sure, had got him to agree to witness a performance by me, all of ten years old and as yet uninitiated to the norms of the family. I was asked by my cousins to present my histrionic talents to Babuji by enacting a scene from a Tamil movie. About three minutes into what was supposed to be a ten-minute performance, my audience of one walked out on me. Babuji got up, walked into his library and came out with the collected poems of Browning and told me quite curtly: 'Stop wasting your time. Read something useful.'

Ayya Mama (1961): Ayya Mama was visiting Madras, some time after Babuji had passed away. When he saw me, he asked me what I was studying and which subjects I liked most. The ham that I was, I promptly said, 'Physics.' He then surprised me by asking, 'Why do you like physics?'

I thought it a very strange question, coming from a world-renowned physicist like him. I attempted an answer, saying something like, 'It is so precise and unambiguous.' His response was: 'Ah! When you come to learn that most of advanced physics is based on what is known as the Uncertainty Principle, I wonder what you will have to say.' Not being familiar with Heisenberg or his work back then, I was dumbstruck by this answer. Ayya Mama spent some more time with me, talking about Newtonian physics and its limitations, the speed of light, probability theory, and so on, without once making me feel small or inadequate.

Chinanna (circa 1961): Chinanna arrived, as he uncannily did, the day before my mathematics examination. He began to quiz me on various aspects of arithmetic, geometry and trigonometry. He made scathing remarks about the textbooks prescribed, and about my lack of preparation. He made me do several sums, riders, etc., and managed to reduce me to a pulp on the night before my examination. I was back at my desk around 6.00 a.m. with Chinanna ready to *help* me with my preparation. As he measured around 46 inches around his chest and had a fantastic presence – with a doting sister (my mother) encouraging him to do whatever he wished to with his hapless nephew – I took it all unquestioningly. Stories of what Chinanna did to people who did not listen to him were part of family folklore; so I did not dare take chances. When the results were announced, it turned out I got a 100 per cent in mathematics.

At that time, I never understood how or why such a busy man heading a huge steel plant in Jamshedpur should arrive promptly before my examinations and spend time with me. It was much later in my life that I realized that he was playing a nurturing role in his own idiosyncratic style.

Balanna (summer of 1963): After finishing school, I was spending part of the summer vacation with Balanna in New Delhi. With three months to spend before the pre-university course was to begin, I was in a blissful state of idleness, or so I thought, until I ran into Balanna in his full glory. He asked me: 'What is the reading list you have for these holidays?' I did not have one, and it had never struck me that one was supposed to have one at the beginning of a well-merited break from studies. Here was a very busy doctor with patients to take care of and several other things to bother about, but he kept asking me about what I was planning to do to make the three months count. Before the summer holidays were over, I had read Walter Scott's *Ivanhoe* and translations of Homer's Iliad and the Odyssey. I was also introduced to Graves, Russell and several others. Balanna got me to read and discuss Ruskin's *Sesame and Lilies*, and to appreciate the great treasures contained in libraries, literally free for anyone with the time and dedication. Since then, till he passed away in 1998, Balanna always began his conversations with me by asking: 'So, what have you been reading of late?'

One conversation I had with him soon after his 80th birthday went something like this:

Balanna: I have a problem I am wrestling with. I am working on a new short story. I have also been persuaded to revisit some early work I had done in medicine since recent findings appear to support my earlier hypothesis. I have also been tempted to compile a series of my publications on a particular theme. The problem is that I have to choose which of the three to take up first.

Me: This is a great problem to have when you are 80 (and to myself, quietly, I wish I face similar problems if and when I reach that age).

Balanna: What has that got to do with age?

Ramnath (mid-1960s): In a refreshingly different twist, he talked of the student revolution in the US, the Kennedy presidency and the spirit of the '60s. John Kennedy had been assassinated, Bobby Kennedy was alive, and so was Martin Luther King. Ramnath wanted to know what the student population in India was doing and how interested I was in these matters. He had just returned after having lived for several years in Canada. Rumours of him having cold water baths in the Canadian winters and his non-standard approach to what life was all about had reached me. The only bearded uncle, he had a modern approach and a seemingly unlimited supply of time to engage me in conversation for hours on end. He was the perfect mentor to enable me to deal with my growing interests beyond the world of physics.

***

It is against this context of a unique family in which the older generation had the time and the inclination to engage in purposeful interaction and conversations with the younger generation that I present the interactions I have had with Ayya Mama. Two of these conversations were taped and are reproduced verbatim. Other conversations are from my memory and are not to be taken as verbatim quotes.

On How to Read

(Late 1960s, when I was a postgraduate student of physics in the Madras Christian College):

Ayya Mama: So, what are you reading these days?

Me: I am reading books and papers on quantum physics.

Ayya Mama: What books and which authors are you reading?

Me: (Gave him a list of books.)

Ayya Mama: How do you read them?

Me: (rather surprised by this question): Well, I just read from page to page, make notes on the margins, underline what I think to be important parts, and place question marks in the margins where I do not understand the subject matter clearly and which I have to revisit.

Ayya Mama: How well does this system of reading work for you?

Me: So far, it has worked but I must confess that I am struggling with quantum physics, especially with the core text by Schief.

Ayya Mama: I do not blame you. For one thing, that is a particularly bad book. For another, I am not sure if the system of reading you employ will work when you are grappling with a complex subject like quantum physics.

Me: What would you suggest I do differently?

Ayya Mama: First of all, change the book you are using. Read Landau and Lifshitz's book.

Me: But that is a real tome of a book and when I tried looking at it in the library, I found I got lost within a few pages.

Ayya Mama: That is to do with the way in which you read. Books of this nature, that deal with complex subjects, should be read first from cover to cover. Do not stop to make notes in the margins or take a pencil to the book during your first reading. Read the entire book, from cover to cover, almost as if you are reading a book of fiction. Get an overall picture of the subject first, and then follow your system of detailed reading. Keep a pad next to you and work out the mathematics yourself. The interconnected nature of the subject matter that you absorb from the first reading will help as you drill deep in the second reading.

And it worked like magic. I remember taking Landau and Lifshitz's book to the cricket grounds in the campus (when all the playing fields were completely empty in the early hours of the morning) and within three hours of continuous reading, I began to get a feel of the grandeur and the holistic nature of the subject matter. I have been using this approach for over forty years now. It is one of the best gifts I have ever received in my life. I try to get my students to do likewise. Most of them laugh it off as a quixotic approach to reading, but those who give it a serious try come back and thank me, just as I have been thanking Ayya Mama silently all these years.

The Indian Express Interview

Ayya Mama visited us in the early 1970s, when I was working as a journalist in Madras. I requested him for a formal interview that I could tape and use for publication. He readily agreed. He spoke about various aspects of life: of working in the University of Chicago, of the possibility of spending time in India, of working with his young students, and the collaborative thrust for learning in an interactive way and several things that mattered to him.

Chicago, 1978

In the summer of 1978, I visited Ayya Mama and stayed with him for a few days in Chicago.

On the first morning of my visit, I woke up around 6.00 a.m. and went to the kitchen to make myself a cup of coffee. As I passed Ayya Mama's study, I saw him working with his back to the door. He was already fully attired in the usual grey suit. His back was erect and head bent down and his attention was focussed on an assortment of papers and books under a reading lamp throwing light on his immaculately clean desk. The next day, as I walked past his study at 5.00 a.m., he was at his desk exactly like the previous day. In the course of that day, as we were walking through the campus to his office, our conversation turned to motivation. Here is my memory of the conversation:

Me: You were working in your study early in the morning today and yesterday. Is this your normal schedule of work?

Ayya Mama: Well, yes. I work on two or three problems or areas of investigation simultaneously. I work on one at home in my study and on another at my office. I find that it helps when I work that way.

Me: I have recently begun to work on the area of Motivation. One aspect that intrigues me is how people are able to sustain their motivation over extended periods of time. Could you please talk about how you deal with it?

Ayya Mama: I find that Motivation is like a brush fire, rather than a raging forest fire. One has to constantly keep lighting the fire. I find it useful to set a clear target, and announce it in a manner that even I cannot change the target. The pressure to achieve that target is important. As one grows in one's profession, there are fewer and fewer external targets. One has to create self-set targets that are demanding. One trick I employ is to announce a new course that I will teach or a lecture that I will give on a topic that I am still unfamiliar with. Once I make that target public and students know they can register for the course or attend a public lecture, I know I have no option but to achieve that target. As soon as I complete that task, I have to deliberately light another brush fire, by creating a new target. Yet another way to sustain motivation is to work collaboratively with colleagues or students. People with similar interests, who converse on a joint enquiry or research, help each other enormously. Working with young students, with all their youthful energy and focus certainly helps. The Socratic approach to learning through dialogues is a very useful one indeed.

I recall another incident that took place during that walk through the campus: as we entered a building, he walked by himself to see a display case and then asked me to come over. He explained that this case displayed recent achievements of faculty and students, and the reason for his wishing to see it first was to be sure that it did not contain anything about him! He said, 'A few years ago, I was taking a visitor along and when we reached this case, there was a lot of material about some work I had done. I felt very embarrassed. I did not want to make a similar mistake. Had there been something about me in that display case, I would not have shown you that case but walked around it.'

Milton, in his elegiac poem 'Lycidas' describes human need for fame as 'the last infirmity of a noble mind' and Victor Hugo describes popularity as 'Glory's small change'. Reading the thoughts of great minds is one way of learning, but a far better and stronger influence is actually witnessing the enactment of such thoughts. That little episode with Ayya Mama taught me a lot. Doing one's bit for the sake of doing it well, with no thoughts whatsoever for the recognition or fame that comes with it is, in many ways, the ultimate test for motivation. A few decades later, when my own research led me to understand that the quality of one's work actually improved when one is not concerned with the recognition or fame that the work could lead to, I remembered this little scene I witnessed in the campus of the University of Chicago.

Ayya Mama's 'Holiday Trip' through India

In the mid-1980s, a few years after he was awarded the Nobel Prize, I met Ayya Mama in Chicago briefly when he was thinking about making a trip to India. People were falling over each other to 'felicitate' him on his success and he was quite annoyed with it all. He was anyway planning to visit India to see the family and was reluctantly accepting a few of the invitations. He was going to visit Delhi, Bombay, Bangalore and Madras, and was working on his schedule. When I suggested that he and Lalitha

Periamma take a little time off to visit a few other places by themselves, he said that he had always wanted to do so, but was not sure how easy it would be. I took the responsibility of arranging his trip to Agra, Jaipur and Udaipur, along with making local arrangements for travel and stay, and safe, vegetarian food. Almost like a child, he was very happy to visit these places, which he had never seen before.

I met him a few times during that trip, and recall a few conversations and incidents.

While having breakfast at a hotel in Delhi, Ayya Mama told me about a very curious incident. He said that he was visiting Dr Jayant Narlikar, founder-director of IUCAA, at his flat in Bombay and as he came out of the lift, he found the place filled with several people he did not know at all. One gentleman, who was apparently the occupant of a flat directly opposite Narlikar's, insisted that Ayya Mama step into his home for a few minutes. As Narlikar also seemed to wish it, he agreed. As he entered, someone began to ring a brass hand-held bell of the sort that one sees in temples, another lit some camphor and the host and his family prostrated at Ayya Mama's feet, embarrassing him immensely.

Another incident happened at the Taj Mahal Hotel in Bombay. My wife Hem and I were sitting with Ayya Mama along with a few others in the moonlight suite at the Taj Mahal Hotel (one that was to get tragically burnt during the 26 November 2008 tragedy). A cocktail-dinner had been arranged by local scientists in one of the banquet rooms of the Taj a few floors below, with Ayya Mama as the chief guest. As a strict teetotaller who disliked such events and avoided socializing whenever he could, Ayya Mama had chosen to skip the cocktail hour altogether. He was talking of a Wagner festival he had gone to in Austria and got into an interesting conversation with Hem on Bertolt Brecht.

Hem happened to mention Brecht's play *Galileo*. Ayya Mama was very critical of Brecht's treatment of the subject since, according to him, the play had factual errors. Hem tried to argue in favour of Brecht and defend his artistic or dramatic license. But Ayya Mama held his ground and was not going to let Brecht or his defender get away with factual distortions of a historic figure, and a scientist at that. The conversation then veered to two other plays of Brecht, *Exception and the Rule* and *He who says No, he who says Yes* – Hem was assisting with the direction and production of those plays at that time. Ayya Mama, unfortunately, was not a fan of the first one, but the second one happened to be one of his favourites. With palpable relief he added, 'I am so glad we can agree on something.' This honesty was typical of him. While he was genuinely pleased that he could express his enthusiasm at least over one of the plays and concur with his partner in the conversation, he was not going to make polite but meaningless remarks for the sake of propriety.

It was a very pleasant evening, till we went down to the banquet room. Ayya Mama's mood changed dramatically as we entered the banquet room and this is what happened: The buzz around the room was rather loud and raucous. A fairly inebriated physicist came up to him and told him how much he admired him, slurring as he did so. Ayya Mama cut him down, turned and asked me to direct him to the table where he was to be seated. Soon, everyone was seated. Three senior scientists spoke at length about Ayya Mama and his work. One gentleman, a top-ranking physicist at that, said he understood only the first two pages of a recent paper Ayya Mama had written, and many in the audience laughed. I was looking at Ayya Mama and whispered to Hem that Ayya Mama was being pushed to the brink of his patience. After almost half an hour of eulogizing, the one presiding over the function requested Ayya Mama, to address the audience. Ayya Mama got up and said, 'I note that many of you are happy that I have been working hard most of my life. Thank you.'

Then he sat down. And that was it.

Meeting in Oxford, England, 1991

In the summer of 1991, when I was a visiting fellow at the University of Buckingham, England, I chanced to hear that Ayya Mama was in Oxford, delivering a series of lectures. I rang him up and we arranged to meet for supper a few days later, on 21 May, along with Lalitha Periamma and Hem.

True to form, a few minutes after we met, the question of what I had been up to came up and I told him that I was completing some research on motivation and was writing a book on the subject. He began to ask me about my work and I was trying to explain my work to him even as we were walking from his accommodation to the restaurant, which was a mile away. He was getting increasingly irritated and kept questioning the soundness of the model that I had developed. My confidence was quite shaken and, by the time we sat at our table, I had started feeling quite helpless. Ayya Mama excused himself and left us for a few minutes.

Lalitha Periamma came to my rescue. She said, 'You have been drawing a model in the air with your hands and trying to explain to Chandra what you have been doing. Why don't you get a pad and sketch your model before he comes back and use it to continue your conversation? Chandra likes to see things in writing.' I did just that; and when Ayya Mama came back, I resumed the conversation with a sketch of my motivation model placed in front of him. After a few minutes, Ayya Mama said, 'Ah, now I understand what you have been talking about. Why did you not do it in the first place?'

After that, I had one of the most instructive conversations I have ever had on the subject of motivation. Let me recall two short snatches of that conversation:

Ayya Mama: I now understand. What you have developed is a general theory of motivation.

Me: Well, that would be putting it too, shall I say, pompously.

Ayya Mama: No, not at all. That is exactly what I understand your model to be. You are claiming it is universal and not restricted to any field of endeavour or culture or class of society. It is a general theory of motivation.

Me: After Einstein used that term, would it not be too much for me to claim that term?

Ayya Mama: Well, Einstein never claimed a copyright to that term. False modesty should not stop you from using that term if it indeed explains what you have come up with.

Despite Ayya Mama's urging, I copped out and used the term 'east-west model of motivation' rather than 'general theory of motivation' when I published my work. He was to recall this conversation the last time I saw him. During that same conversation, as we were walking back from the restaurant to their accommodation, I asked Ayya Mama to describe people he knew whose motivation to work was entirely intrinsic, with not a trace of external motivation. He kept talking of people who did not fit that profile.

I recall that part of the conversation well. Ayya Mama said, 'You know, there were two physicists, both Nobel laureates at Caltech, who were so competitive that when one left at the end of the day and saw the light on at the other's office, he would go back to his office and resume his work. I am not sure such an urge to compete is detrimental at all. I replied, 'Yes, I understand that, but I was hoping you would know of people who sustained very high levels of motivation without reference to what others were doing or saying ...'

When Ayya Mama continued to dodge around, Lalitha Periamma walked right between us, stopped Ayya Mama in his tracks and, like a schoolmarm talking to a mischievous child, said, 'Chandra, you are being naughty. Mahi is talking of people like Roger Penrose. You know them. Why don't you answer him properly?'

Ayya Mama chuckled and said, 'I was pushing Mahi hard to test how sure he was of his own model, without having to rely on more examples.' He then spoke of several people who were part of his circle of friends and colleagues, including some who were still in their thirties who fit the strawman model I had sketched perfectly.

Later that evening, when I returned to Buckingham, I heard the tragic news of the assassination of Rajiv Gandhi earlier that day. I immediately called Ayya Mama to give him the news. He was quite shattered. He had met Indira Gandhi a few times and admired her greatly. He was in deep shock that her son had also met with a similar, tragic end.

The Last Conversation

Soon after my book on motivation was published in 1993, I presented Ayya Mama with a copy when he was visiting Bangalore. A few days later, we travelled together from Bangalore to Bombay. At the airport, he said quite casually: 'I noted that you have not used the term, "general theory of motivation"' and smiled. That was the last time I saw him.

Thank you, Ayya Mama; for all the time you spared from your busy life and for the great conversations we had.

fourteen

My Stellar Uncle

Sudha Ramesh

> What a piece of work is a man! How noble in reason, how infinite in faculty ... In action how like an angel in apprehension how like a God!
>
> — Act 2, Scene 2, *Hamlet*

Anna, as I called my uncle, represents for me a noble human being whose profound understanding of music, literature and people left an indelible mark on me. He was the epitome of a Renaissance man. His life was dedicated to the pursuit of science; yet, in my interaction with him over a span of forty years, I encountered diverse facets of his personality. Rather than explore his science, I turn here to these aspects as I reminisce and write. I had a close relationship with Anna from the time I was a little girl in India in the 1950s, right until he went to the hospital in 1995. He was, in many ways, a long-distance mentor for me during my teenage years and was always genuinely involved with my life during my sojourn of over thirty years in the US, where I was a student and later a professional working for IBM. I spoke with him on the phone just before he went to the hospital in 1995 but little did I realize the finality of that conversation.

He was exceedingly fond of my mother Savitri (his sister) and stayed with my parents in Chennai on his several visits to India. Hence there was a natural affection and bonding between us. Anna became close to me during his visit to India in the early fifties. He played with me in our garden in Madras and taught me to play the swing – a physical activity of abandon that one hardly associates with Anna. The swing was in the garden of my parents' home, which was located in idyllic surroundings. He would make me sit on the swing and push it, and in his high-pitched voice, characteristic of him when he was excited, he would tell me to flex my feet on the upswing and bend my body backward, so that the swing propelled itself higher. 'I will now show you how to go even higher when you stand up on the swing. Don't be afraid,' he said once, and stood up on the swing and demonstrated how I should bend my knees and use my body weight to cause the swing to accelerate. He laughed and played with me and we had a splendid time. This indeed was a lesson in kinetic physics!

On that trip, he introduced me to the wondrous world of children's classics. My mother had already stirred my interest, but Anna with his gifts of *Alice in Wonderland*, *Pinocchio*, and *The Little Lame Prince* made me totally entranced by the world of books. Whenever I read Keats' 'On Chapman's Homer', I am reminded of this childhood experience: 'Then felt I like some watcher of the skies when a new planet swims into his ken.'

Anna had a vivid recollection of trivial incidents and, in moments of total relaxation, he would refer to them with an immediacy that made the incidents come alive. On the same visit that I have been referring to, he wanted to relate a joke to my parents and other members of the family who had gathered to meet him. He said to me: 'Why don't you go upstairs; I want to tell a bad joke to your parents. Good girls like you cannot listen to this joke.' I replied, 'Only a bad man like you could tell a bad joke.' He related this incident to me when I visited him in Chicago about twenty years later.

He loved discussing literature. He even discussed Kalidasa's *Megha Sandesam* and *Shakuntala* with me when I was reading these Sanskrit works as an undergraduate student in India. He enjoyed Anton Chekhov and when he talked about *The Cherry Orchard*, I could not help feeling that wistful memories of Chandra Vilas suffused him.

When I was reading Ibsen, I was excited by the play *A Doll's House* and the character Nora, who was striving to be a self-motivated human being in a society that was unsympathetic to the cause of women. Anna cut me short. He said, 'It is not *A Doll's House* but *A Doll House*. *A Doll's House* implies that Nora was a doll, and subverts the message of the play.' He pointed out that in his mother's (my grandmother's) translation of the book, the title is *A Doll House* and not *A Doll's House* as it is commonly called. Anna refers to this translation in his Nobel address.

Anna was enthralled by Shakespeare's use of language and memorized entire sections of his plays. He was especially fond of *Macbeth* and quoted and discussed passages like 'tomorrow and tomorrow' and marvelled at Shakespeare's delineation of Macbeth's overvaulting ambition. There was a line he loved from *Hamlet*: 'Would I were bound in a nutshell and count myself the king of infinite space.' When I got married, his gift, predictably, was a recording of select Shakespeare's plays. Towards the end of his life, he re-read *The Tempest* with great intensity and compared his life and worldview to that of Prospero's.

Anna enjoyed listening to Carnatic music and often attended the Music Academy concerts with my mother when he was in Chennai. He was an avid listener of Western classical music. On one occasion, he took me to attend a chamber music recital at a Harvard physicist's home in Cambridge, Massachusetts. He told the hostess: 'I didn't have time to pick up flowers for you this time, but I did bring you a really beautiful flower, my niece.' Anna was a charmer with his subtle compliments to women.

When I was fifteen, my mother bought me my first sari – white, with a burst of orange flowers, and Anna told me how beautiful it looked. He had an appreciation for elegance and beauty, not only in science, but in everyday things too. M.S. Subbulakshmi came to our house and sang the bhajan '*Hari Tum Haro*' for Anna. They had a mutual admiration for each other. I recollect how in Delhi University, they sat on the dais adjacent to each other along with Satyajit Ray and others who were being honoured by Indira Gandhi at the university. M.S. Subbulakshmi's convocation cap kept falling off, and Anna never tired of picking it up and handing it back to her with a gracious smile. Finally, with a twinkle in his eye, he exclaimed, 'You don't need it!' and cast it aside. I was teaching in Delhi University at that time and that evening, Anna and Satyajit Ray dropped me home in a swanky limousine. Young as I was, I was euphoric to be in such exalted company.

Anna dressed immaculately and conservatively. On one visit to Chennai, he wore a full suit with a crisp-white shirt and polished black shoes. The next day the coat had come off, and the subsequent day the tie had disappeared; on the third day, he was sporting just a shirt and ironed trousers. I recall remarking, 'Anna, you are shedding your clothes step by step.' He turned to my mother, said, 'Savitri, did you hear what Sudha said? As long as I don't shed them all, I am okay, I suppose,' and went into peals of laughter. He did have a very keen sense of humour beneath the veneer of high seriousness. He told me once: 'Do you know when I was in Presidency College, I wore a veshti, a shirt, tie, and an ill-fitting black coat and imagined myself to be the best dressed man in the world?'

Anna loved relating stories and, whenever I visited him in Chicago, stayed up and talked to me into the wee hours of the morning. He recounted that once, when he was walking in Princeton, he noticed Einstein heading towards him from the opposite direction. Anna crossed the street to the other side of the road so as not to disturb Einstein, who seemed lost in thought, and to not cause him the embarrassment of trying to place Anna. The story goes that having caught Anna's action, Einstein also crossed the street and held out his hand to Chandra.

Every time I visited Anna and Lalitha in Chicago, he would invite me to his office at the university. On one visit, he asked me for my comments on the photograph of a man on a ladder taken by Piero Borello, which was hanging in his office. I reacted by saying that it was a representation of life itself and the idea that even if a man were to scale the ladder, paradoxically, the goal remained beyond reach. I quoted from Tennyson's 'Ulysses': 'Yet all experience is an arch wherethrough/ Gleams that untravelled world whose margin fades/ Forever and forever when I move.' I also remembered Browning's 'Andrea del Sarto', 'Ah but a man's reach should far exceed his grasp or what's a heaven for?' He was delighted with my response.

Discipline and focus were Anna's key qualities. He often related the story of the Pandavas and Drona, where Arjuna alone displayed his unswerving concentration by focussing on the eyes of the parrot. Anna's focus on achieving great heights in science was formulated as he stood on the Marina Beach in Chennai, dreaming of Newton. Starting every morning at 6 a.m., he ruminated and worked relentlessly over scientific problems and would persist until they were solved. He continued in his quest by changing his field of work every few years and attempting problems that even much younger colleagues were hesitant to tackle.

When I was living in Cambridge, Massachusetts, I was faced with the practical problems of trying to complete my master's degree while coping with severe back pain, caring for a one-year-old child, and encouraging a husband enrolled in a rigorous MBA programme. On mentioning to Anna that I simply could not do it, he replied, 'Do not let other factors deter you from the goal. Surmount them.' Harsh advice, unexpected from a sensitive and understanding uncle, but I took it and completed my master's – realizing that discipline means persevering when disruptive forces attempt to derail our efforts.

On a few occasions, Anna had taught me trigonometry and analytic geometry when I was in school in India. He had complimented me on my discipline and ability not to get distracted by family get-togethers and celebrations, which were aplenty in our house when Anna was visiting. He challenged me by saying that studying on the last day before the exam would not alter my grades, and proved that he was right. He had urged me to go to Harvard to study math and physics. However, when I declined, he respected my decision and wrote a beautiful letter to me. During the course of my teenage years, he wrote several letters to me posing math problems, which I solved and sent back to him. He replied with comments and counter suggestions – an intellectual exchange that I thoroughly enjoyed.

He enjoyed Indian classical dance and attended my dance performances in India. The first performance he attended was in the early sixties. He loved a piece that I performed – a varnam – and asked my mother to arrange for me to perform it again at home. Later, in 1994, on his last but one visit to India, he attended my performance in a concert hall in Chennai. Once again, he loved the varnam and had me give a repeat performance at home. The varnam is the piece-de-resistance of a Bharatanatyam performance. I have my own theory as to why he loved the varnam. The item consists of a series of juxtaposed sequences of nritta (rhythmic sequences) and abhinaya (emotive passages). The item moves towards a crescendo with alternating fast-paced rhythmic sequences and mime. Perhaps he noticed a parallel – between the discipline, mastery and the focus needed by the dancer to perform this piece and the skill and the approach to his own work, where he moved from one grand question to another with consummate mastery.

Utter humility was a hallmark of his character. He asked me once how I managed to balance my professional work at IBM with classical dance, which seemed like diverse strains of activity. On another occasion, asking me to describe the job content of my work in software he said, 'It seems so complicated and difficult.' I was stunned by these responses from an uncle who had an intimidating intellect, held in high esteem by the scientific community.

He was visiting Columbia University when I was a student there, and said that I should come to the banquet hosted for him. I called the professor concerned to say that I would need a vegetarian meal, like my uncle. 'The whole dinner,' the organizer responded, 'is vegetarian in honour of your uncle.' I was stupefied.

When the Nobel Prize was announced in October of 1983, I was driving to work in IBM New York when I heard it on the CBS radio network. I ran up the stairs to my office not waiting for the elevator and called both my mother and Anna alternately and had difficulty reaching either. Finally when my mother heard me excitedly give her the news, she responded, 'Both *Indian Express* and *Hindu* [the two leading papers in India] have called and told me already.' Then, of course, I called Anna and said that I was delirious with joy. He replied, 'I am glad that someone young in the family is so happy.' Then he continued: 'It doesn't seem to make a difference to me. Perhaps it may have been different when I was younger.'

I called him again that evening after surfing every channel and seeing the news about the Nobel Prize broadcast everywhere. He said to me:

'Do you know what happened today? I went to fill gas at the self-serve local gas station and the owner told me: "Hey Prof. you can't do that no more; not after you gotten the Nobel Prize. I will fill it for you!"' This incident, related by Anna, was to downsize his superhuman achievements with his humility.

My mother wrote very often to my uncle, and they maintained a steady correspondence. He called me almost every other weekend. He would ask me if I would be home the following week and add that I should not be bound by the fact that he might call. Another time when I called him, he said he was just about to call me. We talked for a while and as soon as I hung up, he called back saying that he wanted to prove to me that he had indeed meant to call! He was extremely perceptive, and could find out from the tone of my voice if I was sick. My mother was the only other person who could do that. Anna was very supportive emotionally when my father passed away in 1990.

He was truly sensitive and genuinely caring. On one of his visits to India (1961–62), he put in Herculean efforts along with my mother to secure financial support from the Government of India for the widow of the great mathematician Ramanujan. She was living in abject penury. Later, Anna came to India for a symposium marking the birth centenary of Ramanujan. On the opening day of the symposium, Rajiv Gandhi presented the first copy of *The Lost Notebook* to Mrs Ramanujan. Anna spoke brilliantly on the occasion and I, along with other close family members, was privileged to be in the audience.

He was also invited to deliver a lecture as part of the 'Distinguished Lecture Series' in IBM Research Labs and I remember how the audience was struck not only by the content of the lecture but also by the style of delivery, which was so much like a great symphony.

Anna visited India in the beginning of 1994 and planned to come again in December. My mother was unwell at that time, and was looking forward to his trip with a lot of anticipation and eagerness. She had meticulously done up the room in which Anna was to stay with new sheets and curtains. She went to the hospital for a routine treatment for two days; but my next call to Anna was to inform him that she was no more. I broke down over the phone and told Anna that I have only him and no mother or father now. Hearing my words, he was shattered and could not speak. Though his trip to India was primarily meant to meet my ailing mother, he said he was coming to India anyway since he had promised her. On that last trip of his, he stayed in my mother's house as he usually did, and I and my sisters, Radha and Rajini did what we could to make his stay comfortable. During that trip, he recounted numerous incidents and conversations between him and my mother. He also was quite overwhelmed with the love and affection we showered upon him. He mentioned how a life with total dedication to science was not without any regrets. 'Thus unwatered life runs barren. My life is like distilled water,' he said.

I had several conversations with him after he returned to the US, in which he mentioned sometimes that he was feeling tired. Before his trip to the hospital on the last day, he had told me that he would call in a few days. I never heard from him.

Anna's was not a life just lived, but a life charged with intellect and humanity. In the pursuit of science, he had scaled not just the Kanchenjunga but the Everest, although he implied otherwise in his book *Truth and Beauty*. He had reached its summit and basked in the beautiful long stretches of snow and serenity stretching to infinity. The quest for beauty and truth in science and in life made him special; his deep humanity and knowledge of the arts made him so civilized and sophisticated a scientist and human being that he had few peers. What better tribute to his life than John Keats's words:

> Beauty is truth,
> Truth beauty – that is all
> Ye know on earth
> And all ye need to know.

fifteen

Resonating Stories[1]

Radha Sarma Hegde

In the summer of 1981, I accompanied my mother Savitri on a trip to Chicago to visit Ayya Mama whom she held in great awe and esteem. She had come from India to the United States to be with me and my sisters, Sudha and Rajini. However, it was the trip to Chicago that she awaited with great anticipation. Amma and I arrived a bit early, and in the distance in the crowded terminal at the O'Hare Airport, we saw Ayya Mama waiting in a brown coat, deeply engrossed in a book – a novel by Yasunari Kawabata, I distinctly recall. That image of Ayya Mama – lost in his own quiet world of introspection – is one that many of us carry. I remember the emotional intensity and silence of that quiet moment between a brother and sister meeting after a long time at the Chicago airport.

Amma and I spent a few days in Chicago with Ayya Mama and Lalitha Mami. Ayya Mama recounted many stories about their childhood with great animation. He talked about a college classmate from Presidency – the 'big bore' from whom he wanted to escape, Babuji the disciplinarian,

---

1 A version of this note was presented by the contributor in October 1995 when she attended a memorial held at the University of Chicago in Professor Chandrasekhar's honour.

and the fond and reverent memories of their mother. The conversation carried on into the small hours.

I recall our visit to Seminary Bookstore, his favourite haunt in Hyde Park. The highlight of the visit was a walk around the University of Chicago campus with Ayya Mama as guide and photographer. We paused as he spoke about the Henry Moore sculpture, *Nuclear Energy*. We walked by the photographs displayed at the Enrico Fermi Institute as he talked about his years in Chicago. Also memorable was a visit to the Chicago Art Institute to see an exhibition of the Vatican Collection. We wandered through the exhibits as he talked about something that engrossed him greatly – the later works of great composers and artists. His face would light up with excitement as he recounted stories in his exuberant, yet markedly professorial style. For Amma, meeting her older brother was always an event filled with admiration.

For over fifty years, Amma and Ayya Mama corresponded regularly. They maintained a closeness and an intense bond in spite of the cultural worlds that separated them. The times they met in India and in Chicago were few and far between. Amma passed away in December 1994, just a week before Ayya Mama was to visit Madras especially to be with her during her illness. After her death, I still remember the tremor of grief and disbelief in his voice which soon was replaced by a wrenching silence. Distraught as he was, he told us that he wanted to honour Savitri's last invitation to visit her in India. He knew that his ailing sister had prepared every detail in order to make his visit memorable. So Ayya Mama journeyed, in what was to be his last trip to India. He spent close to a week with Sudha, Rajini and me at a time of great sorrow. He recounted stories about growing up in Chandra Vilas and transported us to another time, another space – the shady side-street off Edward Elliot's road, lined with coconut trees in the 1920s.

'Your mother, when she was a little girl used to poke around in the garden. One day, she touched a soft, sticky thing.' He broke into peals of laughter as he recounted the story. 'It was a frog and do you know, I told her, now that she had touched a frog, she would *become* one. I really did upset her very much.' The past and present merged and blended in the childhood stories that Ayya Mama related with such joy and verve.

At other times during that visit to India, Ayya Mama would be lost in melancholic silence. With a great deal of hesitation, he asked us: 'Can I sit down at Savitri's desk?' We had heard countless stories from our mother about Ayya Mama's work ethic and his famous desk where he would work for hours, starting at the crack of dawn. We knew about the clutter-free desk in faraway Chicago which he dusted each night at the end of the day's work. And here he was asking to see our mother's desk, which incidentally was also a perfectly organized space. He sat at her desk where she too would work every morning amid a lot more interruption!

We showed him the letters that Amma had filed ever so carefully and dated by the decades – long, reflective letters that he had written to her over the years and across the cultural divide. Ayya Mama was overwhelmed by the way his letters had been preserved by his sister, starting from the forties down to the nineties. Here were letters and other reminiscences, even a detailed log of a 4000-mile car trip taken by Amma with Ayya Mama and Lalitha Mami in the fall of 1957 starting from Los Alamos covering Santa Fe, the Rio Grande Valley, Grand Canyon, Yellowstone National Park and Mount Rushmore and back to Williams Bay!

'It feels like a betrayal,' he said. Perhaps he felt it an encroachment to tread on the space of one who is no longer present. He told us that the most difficult thing was to carry on the day-to-day routine of living after the death of someone dear. I recall him saying with sadness: 'I have missed so much.' The fact of living between cultures, the loneliness that defines that migrant condition, and the meaning of returning 'home' surfaced repeatedly – almost as a motif – in his conversations. In a letter dated 16 February 1993, Amma wrote to him: 'The New Year opened with your long-awaited visit home. Much anticipated ... Yet these meetings somehow come like a flash and disappear like lightning. Sudha and I were so happy that you could find time to attend her Bharatanatyam recital, that I could listen to Mahler's music with you – a rare and rich experience for me.'

It seems that in one of his conversations, Ayya Mama had asked whether he had done justice to himself and to others by his single-minded dedication to science. In response, Amma wrote a poem which she called her dreamy answer to his question. I quote here only Amma's rendition of the question that Ayya Mama posed, because it captures not only their closeness but also the poignancy of the question itself:

> A lingering doubt besets the mind ...
> Does anyone hearken to my yearnings?
> Is my cry, a cry in the wilderness?
> Are the overtones of my voice heard on the other side?

It is with a sense of trepidation that I present these rather private exchanges between a brother and sister, and I do so only to reveal the intensity and depth that characterized their exchange, mediated mostly through letters. During that last visit, Ayya Mama asked if he could take back his letters to Amma for the Chicago archive, saying, 'I want a part of Savitri to be remembered through my letters.' At that time, with some hesitation again, he gave to Sudha, Rajini and me, another folder of letters that Amma had written to him during her terminal illness. 'I thought this is a facet of your mother you would like to know.' On the folder which contained Amma's letters, in his inimitable writing, were the words: 'From Savitri during her last illness.' The same handwriting and penmanship that all of us knew well.

When my sisters and I were growing up in Madras, Ayya Mama was the uncle who was far away. We cherished the books he sent to us – *Pinocchio*, *Grimm's* and *Andersen's Fairy Tales*, *Alice in Wonderland*, and many more. For my sister Sudha came books on science and mathematics and for Rajini and me, Louisa May Alcott and picture books on wildlife. Michelangelo's paintings and Herman Hesse's *The Glass Bead Game* for Amma. The beautiful penmanship of the inscriptions inside, in blue–black ink from a fountain pen, was always a source of wonder for us.

Stories abounded about the uncle, the scientist who was an icon, larger than life. We were constantly reminded about his daunting accomplishments by Amma. These included facts such as his having read all the plays of Shakespeare, all the novels of Dickens, Dostoevsky, Woolf, and others; and listened to all the music of Beethoven, Mahler, and more.

Tales about his childhood, his seriousness of purpose and academic intent were mythical. Details about the scholar who was beyond trivia, who knew the ferocious power of concentration, reverberated continually in our lives and in the lives of our cousins.

Over the years, Ayya Mama stepped out of the stories and became a real presence in our lives. The December 1994 visit left a deep impression on my sisters and me. We bonded over our shared pain and memories. He spoke eloquently about everything that mattered to him: living in the West, between worlds; about isolation and family; of Eliot and Chekhov, of mythical Indian heroes, of our grandmother, whom we had not met, and her literary pursuits.

The anecdotes continue to live. So too the emotions and respect we hold for Ayya Mama.

sixteen

He Noticed!

Nalini Easwar

Sitting down to write about my memories of Ayya Mama, I found myself totally lost. I did not know where or how to begin. Sorting through my memories, I realized that there has been a gradual evolution in my discovery of Ayya Mama and what he meant to me. Several specific personal incidents marked this evolution and so I decided to write about those.

In the early years, Ayya Mama was just a concept to me. He was that special person in the family who visited from a distant land and brought great excitement to everyone's lives. I recall Savitriakka's Chennai home buzzing during his visits. The earliest memories I recall are of people streaming in and out, groups gathering around him and listening carefully to catch every word he spoke in his soft, gentle voice. During his first visit I was unconcerned about all the excitement and played with my cousin Radha on the garden swing. Once, Ayya Mama remarked to us: 'I was watching you on the swing. I noticed that when you pushed on the swing with the right timing, you went really high.' I recall being absolutely thrilled that this special person had watched and complimented us on our swinging skills. I was awed that he had noticed.

His next visit was when I was in middle school. There was the same excitement, and this time my mother was all wrapped-up in planning and making arrangements since Ayya Mama was going to stay with us in Mumbai. We made room for him and Lalitha Mami in the only bedroom we had in our apartment. Amma made sure not to miss any detail; she kept coffee and snacks ready and flowing for the various visitors who came to meet him. One such visitor was a reporter from the national newspaper *The Times of India*. I was young enough to be unnoticed in the room when the reporter interviewed Ayya Mama. Their conversation wafted by me, until I suddenly heard the reporter ask him why he chose to stay in such a small apartment when he could have stayed at the Taj Hotel, or any other more spacious and luxurious place. I was absolutely embarrassed and hurt, and looked around to see where my mother was, hoping that she was far enough not to have heard the question. Thankfully, she was busy making coffee for the reporter. I sighed in relief and waited with keen impatience to hear Ayya Mama's reply, and was relieved to hear him say, 'Why, this is wonderful. If this is good for my sister, it is good for me too.' Suddenly, this special person in the family became a special person to me. This was the first personal connection I felt with him. I did not share this story with anybody at that time, definitely not my mother, lest she feel hurt by the reporter's assessment of our home.

Ayya Mama's next visit was when I was in college. By then, we had moved to a bigger flat. I was older, and a wide-eyed student discovering Ayya Mama's science and harbouring hopes of arranging for him to speak in my college. I was unsure if he would agree to such a request; but with my professors egging me on, I wrote to him. I did not hear from him until the day of his arrival. The usual entourage of cars packed with relatives went to Santa Cruz airport to receive him, and on the way back I carefully manoeuvred to seat myself in the car that he boarded. Sounds of animated conversation filled the car, but in my mind's silence I was rehearsing how I would broach the subject of my letter. Suddenly, Ayya Mama turned around and told me that he had got my letter but that he did not find the time to reply before leaving for India. He asked me, 'Nalini, do you want me to come and talk?' I said softly, 'My professors will be so happy ...' and let my voice trail. In a firmer voice he repeated, 'Do you want me to come?' I said, 'My friends and classmates are very excited and would be so happy ...' and left the sentence incomplete. He repeated yet again, 'Do *you* want me to come?' I said '*Yes*' and he said, 'Then I would love to come. I accept *your* invitation.' I was thrilled. The day of the lecture came. He started his talk with a verbatim account of our conversation in the car and just as he was finishing with 'She said *yes*, and that is why I am here,' he looked at me with a soft smile. I was red in the face with pleasure and embarrassment!

The next morning, Amma was all excited about the talk at my college and told Ayya Mama: 'Anna, Nalini likes physics a lot.' I felt petrified. What if he asked me about physics? This was the one situation I had tried not to get myself into, but here I was with no escape. He called me to the breakfast table, and asked me about the courses I was taking, the textbooks we used, and about the availability of these books. I must have muddled my way through the answers, but I clearly remember explaining how these were expensive 'foreign' books to which we had limited access since there was just one copy in the library. He nodded his head as though he had understood what I said, but went on to talk about pulsars and binary stars, and showed me how to set up a differential equation with the example of getting the density profile of the atmosphere. I realized that I need not have been so petrified after all. I held on to the papers on which he had worked these equations and continue to hold them as a treasured possession. When bidding goodbye to him at the airport, he asked if I would send him a written synopsis of his talk at my college – not an easy task for one who had sat through the entire talk recovering from his introductory remarks. This is also the point when I realized that this visit of his had taken on an even more personal angle for me: he had actually engaged in a conversation with me about physics at the breakfast table!

A month or so after his visit, a box addressed to me arrived from the US. He had sent me the three books that I had mentioned. Wow, I had my own copies and they had been sent by Ayya Mama! I was excited and eagerly opened the first page to see if he had penned a message for me, but alas, he had not. So I took a pen and inscribed in my handwriting: 'To Nalini, sent by Ayya Mama.'

After several years, I came to the US to pursue my graduate work. This enabled me to keep in touch with Ayya Mama and Lalitha Mami on birthdays and other special events. During one such call, he told me that he had read my paper published in the *American Journal of Physics* and started talking about its contents. A simple paper in a journal that focussed on pedagogy had not escaped him. I was, once again, awed that he had seen it and actually read it. He had noticed!

seventeen

A Rare Privilege

Radhika Ramnath

It is indeed daunting to try and write about someone so well known and about whose life and achievements, so much has been written. The reason I am attempting to do this at all is that in the fifteen years or so that I really got to know Peripa, there developed a very strong affection and rapport between us, which grew into one of the most treasured relationships of my life.

I should add here that while Peripa was of course a larger-than-life personality in the family, his nine siblings were fascinating characters in their own right. Like most children, I grew up assuming that all families are basically alike, and that mine was differentiated from the others only by virtue of the fact that it was 'mine'. It was during my teenage years that it slowly started dawning on me how wrong I was. And in the years since, this realization has just become stronger. Today I know that I have been privileged to belong to a family comprising of the most unusual individuals, men and women who have enriched the world around them in many different ways. Some of them became recognized figures in their fields. All of them were individuals with strong personalities and idiosyncrasies that made them unforgettable.

My grandfather Babuji was the patriarch of the family, and had pre-ordained that his four sons would go in for physics, chemistry, medicine and engineering – in that order! The daughters were mandated to learn the veena and the violin alternately, which they did. The three older sons went along with their father's wish even when that meant pursuing areas that were completely orthogonal to their personal interests and passions, and still did incredibly well and excelled in the areas they pursued! Peripa himself had wanted to pursue mathematics, but Babuji was against it because mathematics was 'too easy' for him, and hence would not prove challenging enough. Peripa once told me that though he was not happy with the imposition at that time, in hindsight, this was something he was thankful to Babuji for, since his foundation in both physics and mathematics became very strong. This proved extremely beneficial for him in the following decades.

Peripa left for Cambridge in 1930 at the age of nineteen. His first visit back home was in 1936, during which he and Lalitha Perima got married. After that, they came only after another fifteen years. When he left, he was close to his elder sisters and his brother Visvanathan – who were just 4 to 5 years apart in age – and also to Babuji's youngest brother Ramaswamy, whom he called by his nickname Ramudu. My father, Ramnath, who was the youngest in the family, was just four years old at the time, and so he really got to know his brother – and vice versa – only when he went for his Ph.D to Canada and met Peripa and Perima regularly.

Through the sixties and seventies Peripa and Perima visited India every few years. And every visit of theirs was reason enough for a family reunion, either in Madras or Bangalore: the two places they always visited. In Madras they would stay with my aunt Savitriakka and in Bangalore with my uncle Balanna. As I was still of a school-going age, I always accompanied my parents to these family get-togethers. When in India, Peripa usually wore a white veshti and shirt at home. His frame was slight, and he always spoke softly. But his personality and presence dominated any room that he was in, his very entry bringing with it an immediate and palpable change in the atmosphere. Wherever Peripa sat, there would be a sort of 'durbar', with everyone sitting around him. Most of the conversations would be between Peripa and his brothers, with the others listening intently.

I first met Peripa when I was just about a year old – or so I am told.

As I grew older, I too joined the congregation around him as I found the discussions fascinating. But I was shy and not unaffected by the awe surrounding him, and so never initiated any conversation and only answered questions that were directly asked of me – as briefly as I could. I saw to it that I was never alone in a room with him. However, since I was very close to my other uncles, aunts and cousins, I would often be talking and laughing with them, as well as playing Scrabble and various card games. Peripa seemed to have noticed this. One afternoon, when most people were taking a nap, Peripa came out to the verandah where I was reading and pulled up a chair next to me, saying that he finally had a chance to talk to me. I felt trapped! He asked a couple of questions which I answered briefly. Then he said, 'How is it you have so much to say to everyone here, except me?'

That stymied me even further, and I just stuttered in response. He went on to say that though I regularly sent cards, they were never accompanied by a note or letter. Fortunately, Daddy walked into the verandah at that point, sensed my discomfort even from a distance, and bailed me out by joining us. Clearly, my silent plea and its response had not gone unnoticed. Peripa later told my mother that he had observed a unique father–daughter relationship of friendship and trust between Daddy and me, which he found quite exceptional.

After that, I started talking a little to Peripa. I also attended the lectures he gave at various institutes. He would come back and ask us cousins whether we had any questions about his talk. Some of my older cousins would ask him about a few things, but I never did. He asked me why, and I remember telling him that I would not know where to start as I did not even understand terms like 'null dust' which seemed so basic in his lecture. The response seemed to please him, and he told me that many people would not know that, and went on to explain it to me in terms that I could easily understand.

I often find it easier to express myself in writing rather than verbally. So I finally did get down to writing a letter to Peripa, and explained to him why I found it difficult to talk to him, and then went on to tell him a little about my studies and news of the family. As soon as I finished, I went out and posted the letter before I lost my nerve. As I had expected,

I did lose my nerve soon after, but there was nothing I could do about it. Peripa responded with a wonderful letter and that started off a regular correspondence between us which continued till he passed away. They were long letters from both sides, and through these I lost my self-consciousness and could open up with him completely. This would, of course, not have been possible if he had not facilitated it. I often wrote to him of trivial things – scenes I had seen on the roads of Delhi, conversations or incidents that I had found amusing, anything that occurred to me. He seemed to enjoy my letters and felt very disappointed whenever one got lost in transit, which happened a few times. I still enjoy reading his letters – they bring him back to life and I feel I hear him speaking to me through those letters. He also started calling up every once in a while and our conversations would be a natural continuation of our correspondence.

But he was not always so forthcoming or welcoming, as many can vouch for. He would, at times, refuse to meet people, sometimes even relatives, causing much disappointment and even hurt. After one such refusal, he told me that he felt that at his age he owed it to himself to use whatever time was left to him in a way that pleased him and gave him most satisfaction, and not fritter it away.

***

Peripa would often compliment us, especially when we took care to get dressed for some occasion. The first time he did so, I was stunned that he had actually noticed what I was wearing, and that was one of the first incidents that made me start seeing him as an 'uncle'. On another occasion, when a cousin and I came back from a shopping spree in Bangalore, he wanted to see what we had bought. We sheepishly displayed our booty, including my 'big buy', a silver belt. He picked it up and looked at it carefully, and then said that had he known we liked those, he would have got some for us from some country (I forget which) where he had seen some beautiful hand-crafted ones. We were speechless. The thought of Peripa buying belts for us was beyond our combined imagination!

S. Chandrasekhar
5825 South Dorchester Avenue
Chicago, Illinois 60637

1990 Feb. 7

My dear Radhika,

It was a pleasure receiving your letter of New-Years day and to learn of of entrance of the Prime Ministers, the discredited and the discounted, of the 'idiot' of the bridegroom who mistook a fire for a festival and of the civilized monkey who closed the frig and left the housewife frigid!—

...

Yesterday, I sent to you by air mail one of the books you wanted: "Programming Pearls"; but the other book ('Computer program testing') is apparently out of print. Is there some other that you may wish in its place?

...

A few days ago, we had the opportunity to see Ibsen's 'Ghosts' — very well played. It reminded me of our talking about Ibsen and of your immediately buying a set of his plays. ...

We often went shopping en famille, for Perima to pick up gifts for friends in Chicago. During one such outing, Peripa mentioned that he had never travelled in an auto-rickshaw, and that it was something he wanted to do. Everyone remonstrated, but he was insistent. So he and I got into one while the others drove back in the cars. He found the ride exhilarating – noise, bumps and all! When we finally reached home, the fare amounted to eleven rupees. He offered a fifty-rupee note, but the driver did not have change. I started taking out the necessary amount from my wallet, but Peripa refused to let me do that and told the auto driver to keep the change. The driver and I looked equally astonished. I started protesting, but the driver immediately started the auto and took off at full speed, lest I deprive him of this completely unexpected windfall. When he had reached the safety of the end of the road, he turned and looked at us quizzically, his expression indicating that he seriously doubted our sanity.

In 1984, Peripa and Perima decided to visit us in Trivandrum. A similar plan on one of their earlier trips had not materialized and so they took pains to make sure that this time it did. That was a memorable trip. We went out on driving trips and visits to museums and beaches and there were many entertaining conversations and much laughter! The shared laughter and his wonderful sense of humour – which was a new facet of Peripa as far as I was concerned since I had mostly seen the serious side – broke the last barriers of restraint for me.

He gave a couple of lectures in Trivandrum, though he wasn't very keen to do so as his visit was short and he wanted to spend all his time with us. He asked me to decide if he should give the lectures that were being requested, and the justification for the decision. I did. He finally gave two lectures – one at the university and the other at the Vikram Sarabhai Space Centre, where Daddy worked. The university lecture remains memorable for more than one reason. The news of Prime Minister Indira Gandhi's assassination reached the dean when Peripa was just about halfway through his lecture. The message was conveyed to Peripa who wound up the lecture in the next couple of minutes, and we were escorted out since trouble was expected in the city as the news spread. The student bodies had got the news but had agreed to keep the area around the auditorium peaceful until Peripa finished his lecture.

Peripa had high personal regard for Indira Gandhi and was horrified at what had happened. The next couple of days were spent at home, riveted to the television screen, watching the scenes in Delhi and across the country, right until the funeral. Peripa had left India in 1930, well before India became independent. He had heard Nehru speak during his student days and was part of the overall environment that prevailed in the country at that time. But this was probably the first time after going to Cambridge that he was in India at such a momentous time in its history and could actually relate to it fully by being here with everyone else.

A couple of weeks later, we went to Bangalore to see them off. Peripa and Perima usually left for Chicago from Bangalore, and most of my aunts and uncles would make it to Bangalore a couple of days before they were scheduled to depart, and so there would be these huge gatherings at Balanna's house. The farewells were always quite emotional. Their flight was generally in the forenoon, and everyone would wake up early that morning and sit down together to have coffee. Each of Peripa's brothers and sisters would have a few minutes of quiet one-on-one conversation with him. Then we would all go to the airport, and after Peripa and Perima checked-in, they would join us in the waiting lounge, till the time came for them to board the aircraft. I remember once when Peripa and I had a long animated conversation in the lounge and he ended by saying, 'Isn't it amazing that two people so disparate in age and temperament share such a wonderful rapport?' I can never forget that.

* * *

Peripa was closely associated with many important phases of my life. While I was doing my master's at IIT Delhi, he would call me at the beginning of each semester and note down the names of books that I wanted but had not been able to get. He would then get his university bookshop to airmail them to me. My entire class benefited greatly from this.

When I was about to get married, Mummy wanted to follow the convention in her family that the wedding invitation goes out from the eldest member of the family. We were in a quandary as we felt that if we asked him, he may feel obliged to agree even if he did not really want it done that way. Right at that time, Savitriakka came to Delhi for a few days. She offered to talk to Peripa so that he could feel free to refuse without there being any awkwardness. It turned out that he said he would be very happy and feel honoured to have the invitations sent out in his and Perima's name, and so that was how it was. The card was a very simple one. When I met him a year later, Peripa told me that he had liked the card very much, and had kept it under the glass on his office table for a few weeks. An associate of his at the university, surprised to see a wedding invitation card with his and Perima's names on it, asked him in jest if he was planning on getting married again!

A month after our wedding, my husband Tilak was to leave for the US to take up a job there, while I wanted to wait and try to get accepted for a Ph.D programme before following him. Peripa called to offer to be a reference, both for the admission and the visa processes. Tilak's plans changed soon after and he decided to stay back in India. Being creatures of impulse, we decided to spend all the money we had received as wedding gifts on a month-long vacation in the US, during which we planned to spend some time with Peripa and Perima in Chicago. But that was easier said than done. First, we had to get US visas. Our first application was rejected by the US embassy as we fell into their 'red alert' category of 'recently married software / telecommunication professionals owning no property'. My immediate reaction was to change our plans and head for Europe instead. But the wisdom of more experienced family members prevailed, and after a couple of weeks we tried again, this time armed with several strong references and supporting documentation. We were called for an interview with a senior visa officer. I was also carrying a letter from Peripa dated a few months earlier in which he had discussed our planned visit. It came out clearly in his letter that this was just a personal holiday, and his stature ensured that his word was not doubted. But the visa officer got so interested in the letter that he read all three pages of it, despite my telling him that only that one page was relevant as far as any information related to our planned trip was concerned. At the end of it, the only question he had was why it was signed 'Peripa' and not

'Chandrasekhar'! He was obviously convinced that we had no intention to migrate, for he wished us a great journey, and offered us a ten–year, multi-entry visa though we had only requested for a one–year, single-entry one!

***

In the 1980s and early '90s, the frequency of Peripa and Perima's India visits increased to almost every other year. This meant many more occasions to meet. Once Daddy moved to Delhi, Peripa changed the schedule of his visits to India, landing in Delhi so that he could meet us, and then going to Madras and Bangalore. On the first day of their first such visit, our building had no running water for a whole day. They must have had enormous trouble lifting buckets of water, but they insisted on staying on and refused our offer of moving them to a hotel.

When they came to Delhi, we used to try and get the necessary permissions to receive them inside the airport and expedite their immigration process. Once we got this done through the police channel, and an officer accompanied us into the airport. Just when Peripa and Perima came past the immigration desk, the officer suddenly produced a garland of flowers from his bag and asked me to garland Peripa as he believed that was the appropriate way to receive a Nobel laureate. Since he had been very helpful, it was difficult to refuse and so I ended up doing just that, completely startling Peripa in the process! I could only explain the circumstances once we were in the car, and we had a good laugh over it.

The other occasion that stands out is the time when Peripa came alone, a week after my aunt Savitriakka had passed away. They were very close to each other, and Peripa was deeply affected when she was suffering from cancer. He had planned a trip on his own just to be with her. He was to land in Delhi and leave the next day for Madras to spend some time with her. About ten days before he was due to arrive, Savitriakka called me to check Peripa's flight schedule, and told me that she had got everything ready for him and was really looking forward to his visit. Just three days later, she suddenly passed away. Peripa was shattered. Had there been any indication that the end was so close, he would have come earlier. He then decided to come as planned as he wanted to stay in the room that Savitriakka had told him she had readied for his stay in her home.

When we went to receive him at the airport, we were shocked to see him come out of the plane in a wheelchair. He looked drawn, but all he said was that he was very tired. He was carrying only hand-baggage, and when he opened his briefcase for his passport, I saw that one of the few things it contained was a thick book titled *How We Die*. He told us later that he had been reading this in an effort to understand what Savitriakka was going through in those last few months. That was an extremely emotional visit for him, and he spent all his time with Savitriakka's daughters and others close to her, and refused to meet anyone else.

***

On most visits to India, Peripa would give a couple of lectures and the rest of his visit would be a private one spent with the family. A large family contingent always accompanied him to these lectures even though we understood very little of them, since these were the only occasions we got to hear him speak formally about his work. And we were always very conspicuous in an otherwise academic audience!

Many incidents and stories around these lectures come to mind. Organizing enough transport to get all of us to the venue of the lecture was always a challenge. The organizers would send a car with an escort for Peripa and Perima, and he would always offer that one other person could go with them in that car. No one was really keen to be the one as it was embarrassing to get out of the car in the midst of the reception committee and flashing cameras meant for them. Being the youngest one around, I was usually the one conscripted.

On one occasion, the lecture was at the Indian Institute of Science in Bangalore. As I was in their car, the director asked me to accompany Peripa and Perima for tea in his office before the lecture started. I could see then that the awe that surrounded Peripa was not limited to just the family. Prof. Rao, an eminent scientist in his own right, clearly felt the same. He ended up directing quite a large part of his conversation to me instead of talking to Peripa! I found it very odd, but found the same thing happening on other occasions also. Senior scientists and academics would typically come and ask one of the family members anything they wanted to know about Peripa – including using me to get them autographs!

While we were in Delhi, Peripa was conferred an honorary doctorate by the University of Roorkee. He asked my parents and me to accompany them to Roorkee so that we could spend some time together. We all enjoyed the drive, made livelier by a police check-post on the way with the request 'Please Beer With Us', followed soon after by a small liquor shop which bore the familiar legend: 'Chilled Bear'. Peripa loved it! The drive was enormously enjoyable for all of us. As his family, we were guests of honour at the convocation and seated in the very first row. After his return to Chicago, Peripa sent me a small booklet brought out on that occasion by the university, which had a photograph of us sitting there. His covering note said he was sending it as he thought I looked 'very regal' in that picture!

A few years later, he was invited by Dr Jayant Narlikar for the inauguration of the Inter-University Centre for Astronomy and Astrophysics (IUCAA) in Pune. Peripa and Perima had planned to land in Delhi, stay with us for a couple of days and then head to Pune. Peripa called to say that he would like Daddy, Mummy, Tilak and me to accompany them to Pune. At this point I had just changed jobs and was going through a busy time at work. So I explained to him that it would be difficult for me to get any time off. I had planned to go to Bangalore later, over a weekend, to spend some more time with them and to see them off. To my surprise, Peripa asked if my office would not reconsider allowing me the time off if I explained the circumstances and that he really wanted me to be there. I realized how much he wanted us to accompany him, and decided that I would do whatever it took to make it happen. I did, and we went along with him from Delhi to Pune. We all flew business class so that we could be together – this was quite an extravagance for us, and my first experience of luxury air travel.

The lecture at IUCAA was an outdoor one in the evening, and so it was more like a 'performance' with lights and big screens, and a diverse audience of several thousand! Peripa did not like that at all since he could not even see his audience, but the lecture that he delivered: 'The Series Paintings of Claude Monet and the Landscape of General Relativity' fascinated us.

A couple of weeks later, I went to Bangalore as planned. The day before they were to leave, Peripa called me into Balanna's study. When I went and sat next to him, he asked me what I would say if he wanted me to accept a gift from him without demur. He added, in his soft but strong voice, that he felt I should not object since, after all, he was my uncle and as such should have the right to give me anything that he wanted to. As he paused and waited for me to respond, I said, 'All I would say is "Thank You!"'

It took him a couple of seconds to realize what I had said, as he had been prepared for an argument. Then he laughed, and eyes twinkling, handed me a small brown paper packet. I did exactly as I had said I would. From the look and feel of the packet, it was obvious that it contained money; and it was his way of ensuring that we did not go out of pocket by having accompanied him to Pune. I brought the packet unopened to Delhi, and as I was unpacking, I brought it out and told Tilak the story behind it. He opened the packet and I heard him utter a shocked exclamation. I turned to see what had caused it. Being quite foolish in many ways, I had assumed that the packet contained hundred-rupee notes, as that was the common currency at the time. But the packet actually contained five-hundred-rupee notes. I was completely stunned, and was aghast that I had accepted it so casually from Peripa. Had it crossed my mind that the amount was anywhere close to what it actually was, I would definitely have protested. By this time Peripa was already halfway to Chicago, so there was nothing I could say to him. I went to the next best person in the circumstances. Daddy told me that he knew about it since Peripa had sounded him out on how he thought I would react. So this is how we ended up getting our first personal computer, a huge luxury for us at that time.

***

Lalitha Perima was Peripa's constant support and companion through all the years. She was a personality in her own right. She made him and his work the focus of her life, and gave up pursuing science or a career for herself, deciding instead to support him in every way she could. This is what she wanted to do. She created an environment which would help him focus on his work, which she considered very important. He could also discuss his work with her. When he was stressed, he would ask her to sing as that relaxed him. Both of them were fiercely independent and had strong likes and dislikes, mostly common. They shared a deep interest in literature and music, and often attended concerts. They also enjoyed detective movies. They led a very simple life. He helped in the housework – they often cooked together, but doing the dishes was totally his responsibility. Perima did not drive, so all the outside chores had to be done by both of them together or Peripa alone.

Perima and Peripa's world largely revolved around his work and themselves. They depended on each other for everything. We all worried to think what would happen if there came a time when she would have to fend for herself. This was Peripa's constant worry too, and he once said that he hoped he survived her as he did not know how she would manage alone. But she was to prove all of us wrong when such a time did indeed come. It was only after most of the family members much younger than her had passed away that she started looking upon her continuing good health and active mind as a bane and felt depressed. It was then that she said that there should be law of nature that ensures that an individual survives his or her spouse for a maximum of ten years. That in itself was difficult enough, but beyond that, it was untenable.

***

Our first visit to Chicago was in 1991, after we had succeeded in finally getting our US visas. We drove to Peripa's home in a rented car. As we were driving along Dorchester Avenue, I saw Peripa standing on the small terrace outside their apartment building, looking down the road. We stopped and I got out of the car and ran up the steps to greet him while Tilak parked the car. Peripa had come out just a few minutes earlier as he had thought it was about time for us to reach. As we waited for Tilak, a big, black-haired man wearing a courier company uniform shambled up. As he reached the top of the stairs, Tilak arrived at the bottom, and I said, 'There's Tilak!' Peripa turned and saw this other man, and walked up to him, holding out his hand to greet him! The poor man looked totally perplexed while Tilak and I looked on in amusement before jumping in to clear up the situation. After that I think Peripa was quite relieved to meet Tilak.

We went up to their apartment. It was large and beautifully kept, and had the most glorious view of the university as well as the sky at sunset. I was a little nervous as this was the first time I was going to stay in their home. But I need not have worried. It turned out to be a marvellous stay. Both Peripa and Perima had freed themselves of other commitments so that we could be together through those five days.

We went on a quick tour of downtown Chicago, including a visit to the Marshall Fields store. This was where Peripa had once seen a beautiful crystal apple on display, and immediately decided to buy it as he was working on Newton's *Principia*, and the apple was a very appropriate symbol. The shop assistant hesitated and asked him if he wanted to know the price, but he said it did not matter. She commented that he must really like it to buy it just like that. A few months later, when he was in the store again, the same girl saw him and came rushing over to tell him that they had got another similar piece if he would like to look at it!

For most of his stay in the US, Peripa drove a grey Ford town car, and he had an arrangement with the car dealer to automatically replace it every two years with an identical, new one. But during our visit their car was at the workshop for some repairs, and Peripa was using a rental car, which was unfamiliar and made the driving around a little stressful for him. On Sunday we drove down to Yerkes Observatory, a beautiful building. Peripa had a key to the main door. The place was deserted and he took us in, showing us his first office there. He said that it was a small office, and the furniture had been in bad shape, but he simply did not notice any of this, and did not realize that he was at the receiving end of subtle and not-so-subtle discrimination in many ways at that time. It was several years later, when he was around forty-two, that this realization dawned on him due to various events. The way he put it was that it was then that his 'age of innocence' ended.

As we walked around, a lone student who was working in the building came out to see who the visitors were. He was clearly shocked to see Peripa since he just stared at him in disbelief! Unperturbed, and perhaps used to such a reaction, Peripa asked him his name, introduced us, and we moved on. We went to see the telescope in the dome of the building. As Peripa was explaining it to us, something seemed to strike him, and he excused himself. He returned a few minutes later with the student in tow, who then gave us a live demonstration of how the telescope worked! This incident obviously left quite an impact on this boy as he wrote about it when Peripa died a few years later.

We then walked through the grounds, and went to house they had formerly occupied and were shown the sapling they had planted when they had lived there, which had grown into a massive tree. We walked by the lake, listening to their memories of their life there. Then we drove all the way back, stopping at their favourite restaurant on the way to have fried mushrooms and onion rings. There, Peripa was in a reflective and emotional mood, telling us about his mother, Amma – her being humiliated by some members of the extended family on her appearance, her focus on learning English and then translating Ibsen's *A Doll House* into Tamil, her aspirations for him ... We got back quite late at night, after what must have been a strenuous day for Peripa. As we were getting out of the car, he said thoughtfully that this may well turn out to be his last visit to Yerkes as he did not see himself being able to do it again.

Peripa took us on a tour of the University of Chicago campus, showing us the Moore sculpture, the bookstore, the various departments and his office. His office was somehow exactly as I had imagined it to be ... pictures of Ramanujan, Newton and Einstein on the walls, small Roman marble busts on the windowsill, a large table, a view of the campus from the windows ... and many books. What I found most amazing were the hand-written manuscripts of his various books – neatly bound reams of paper covered with complex equations and text in his impeccable handwriting, with nothing scratched out! They were books written in calligraphy. The university now has a Chandrasekhar room in which hangs a large portrait of him sitting at his table. There is also a special display containing his books, medals and some original manuscripts, as well as a Chandra archive which has many of his papers, personal belongings and letters, among other things. Peripa had a very distinctive style of writing papers, which was easily recognized throughout the scientific community; the long titles, his way of referencing, his language, were all his hallmarks. When he was the editor of the *Astrophysical Journal*, his colleagues and students famously wrote a spoof paper entitled 'On the Imperturbability of Elevator Operators' by 'S. Candlestickmaker' written in an imitation of his style, and submitted it to the journal for publication!

As we walked on the narrow, paved paths running through the university grounds, streams of students would part like the Red Sea as they neared us and recognized Peripa, go past us and join up again. We were able to keep walking as though the path was completely clear. Peripa did not even notice this happening since he was absorbed in talking to us.

We then went to The Oriental Institute Museum in the university campus. This was our only opportunity to visit the museum as we were leaving the next day, but it turned out that it was closed on Mondays. There was just a student volunteer on duty at the reception desk. Peripa asked him if it was possible to get the museum opened for a short while, and the student very politely said that it was not. He then asked if there was anyone else around, and was told that the director of the institute was in his office upstairs. Peripa seemed to know him and said that he would go and meet him. As he started going up the stairs, the student probably called the director to let him know that Peripa was on his way. The next thing we saw was the boy sprinting up the stairs, overtaking Peripa, and soon after, a gentleman coming down the stairs. He was obviously the director. He met Peripa halfway up the stairs and they greeted each other and came back together to where we waited, while the student opened the museum. What followed was the most fascinating personalized hour-long tour of the museum, with each room being lit up as we approached, and Peripa telling us about each piece, with the director pitching in at times. It was an unforgettable experience.

That evening, as we were sitting and chatting in the drawing room after dinner, I told Peripa that I wanted to see the Nobel Prize. He was very amused. But he went and got the medallion and the beautifully calligraphed citation, and patiently answered all our questions about the ceremony. He sounded us out on where we thought the medal should be kept after he was gone – with the family or the university. We felt that the university's Chandra archive would be the most appropriate place. He had also thought so, but was getting the view of family members to ensure that they agreed. That was the last evening before we left, and we stayed up, conversing till well past midnight.

Before we left the next morning, they brought out a visitors' book, which was traditionally signed by everyone who visited their home. It was a veritable list of the who's who of science! We went through the book reading the names of legends, and their remarks ... and by the end of it we felt like impostors trying to become a part of a group that we had no right to belong to.

***

I have mentioned several times that there were wonderful conversations and discussions whenever Peripa was in India, or when we were visiting them in Chicago. The conversations brought to life legends like Fermi, Dirac, Bohr, Bethe, Heisenberg, Penrose, Pauli, Ramanujan, Rutherford – names that had been institutionalized in our school textbooks – and revealed them as people of flesh and blood and eccentricities, and also gave insights into Peripa himself. I really wish that we had recorded at least some of those conversations so that I could remember more than what my star-struck brain does now. Let me relate the few that I do remember, at least in part.

Peripa often spoke of Ramanujan, of how Amma had told him about Ramanujan when he was a young boy; about Ramanujan's life, work and genius; about how Ramanujan's bust eventually got made. Being an Indian, people often asked him about Ramanujan. An oft-repeated question was whether he had known Ramanujan personally, to which his answer was: 'I am old, but not *quite* that old!'

Though all of us knew about the history with Eddington in Cambridge, I only heard Peripa talk about it himself when he was in his seventies. He said that looking back, he felt that in the long run, all that had happened in the 1930s had in fact turned out for the good in retrospect, since he believed that had it been otherwise and if his work had got recognition at that early stage, he might have become arrogant and may not have ended up pursuing science the way he did all his life. He also believed that his way of focussing on a particular subject that interested him for several years, publishing a book on it and moving on to the next, began after the experience at Cambridge.

A couple of incidents and stories from the time before they moved to Chicago ...

Peripa visited Russia in the 1930s and met many Russian physicists during his stay there, many of whom were imprisoned and died some years later during Stalin's regime and the Second World War. Peripa was presented a bust of Lenin as a gift after one of his lectures, which he had to leave in the room he was staying in since he could not take it back to England with him. It remained in that room for quite a while as someone who occupied it later told him that the bust was still there.

He had many stories to tell of the stimulating time he spent in Copenhagen at Niels Bohr's Institute, and the interactions with Bohr and his family as well as the other physicists there. During his time there, he sometimes baby-sat the Bohrs' young son Aage – who many years later won the Nobel Prize himself.

I asked him once if in his opinion the Nobel Prize had been given to people who may not be considered deserving of it. After thinking for a minute, he said that in the areas he was familiar with, he believed that everyone who had been recognized thus did deserve it – but not everyone who deserved it, got it. The fact that Mahatma Gandhi and Virginia Woolf had not received the Nobel Prize was evidence enough of that. Peripa felt that the Nobel Prize brought with it many side-effects which he did not appreciate. People who knew nothing about his work suddenly became very deferential and he started getting invitations to all sorts of events and gatherings. The only such 'effect' he smilingly accepted was from the owner of their self-help gas station who insisted on filling up the gas himself when they stopped there as usual the day after the announcement had been made.

Listening to him, I wondered how he evaluated people in domains different from his own. So I asked him how he would assess say, a physicist, a biologist, an economist and a dancer. He began by taking Einstein as an example of a physicist. Since he knew Einstein's work intimately, I immediately interrupted with: 'I don't want Einstein. Take some other example.'

He looked surprised for a moment, but then just laughed and the discussion went on. He, of course realized where it was heading and allowed that a recognition like the Nobel Prize would be something that people from a different domain would accept as signifying the very highest achievement. For some reason, what stood out for him in this entire discussion was my quick insistence on an example other than Einstein, and he repeated this to many in the family as something he had greatly appreciated and enjoyed.

Peripa had great regard for the noted Oxford mathematical physicist Sir Roger Penrose. When he got stuck in his thinking about a problem, he found that discussing it with Penrose for a couple of hours resulted in his looking at other ways of approaching it, which eventually led to the solution. He would go all the way to Oxford from Chicago for less than two days, meet Penrose for a few hours and return. He did this thrice and was successful each time!

We often discussed books. These conversations inspired me to read and enjoy Ibsen and Virginia Woolf. And he read and enjoyed *The Remains of the Day*, a book I had mentioned I had liked. Though I had read several of Shakespeare's plays more recently than he had, his ability to quote large parts verbatim just amazed me. Once I was talking about a book by John Von Neumann that I wanted to read but could not get hold of. When he went back to Chicago, he checked and found that the book was out of print. He told me on the phone that he had worked with Von Neumann many years ago and he would get in touch with the publishers to see if he could get a copy from them. Sure enough, a couple of weeks later, I received the book by airmail directly from the publishers!

Then there were some really funny stories ...

Travelling on a train in England on one occasion, his co-passengers in the compartment included two attractive young women who were friends and who sat across from each other, and a bearded man who sat across from Peripa. Throughout the journey, the women kept chatting with each other while the men sat silently. As the train passed through a long tunnel, it became completely dark in the compartment. Suddenly, one of the women screamed and said, 'How dare you?' This was followed by the resounding sound of a slap. Then there was an uneasy silence. When the train emerged into the sunlight, one of the women was glaring angrily at the bearded man who was holding a hand to his face and looking completely at a loss. Then the lady noticed that her friend's fur coat had fallen to the ground from the top berth. As it fell, it had brushed her face, and she had mistakenly thought that the gentleman sitting next to her was taking liberties! Confusion and apologies followed as realization dawned on all, and the poor misjudged gentleman left the compartment in embarrassment, leaving behind a red-faced woman and two very amused spectators!

Then there was the time when Peripa and Perima were in Europe and were invited by a scientist to his house for lunch. The food was excellent and Perima complimented the hostess calling her a 'born cook'. The compliment did not appear to go down well. It was a couple of days later that they came to know that their host had divorced his first wife and married his housekeeper just a few months earlier!

***

My second visit to Chicago was in August 1995. I was travelling on work to Europe and then Houston, and had managed to keep a few days in between to spend with Peripa and Perima in Chicago. While in Europe I happened to be going through a database of scientific journals and discovered that for several years running, the number of references made to Peripa's work was more than that of any other scientist in the world!

I reached Chicago on 1st August and left on the 7th. I can only say that my stay could not have been better. This time too, they had kept themselves free of other commitments so that we could be together without any interruption. Peripa's book on Newton's *Principia*, which had been his all-consuming focus for the last several years, had just been published and he had got an advance copy from the Oxford University Press. I had the unique privilege of Peripa taking me through the book, explaining different parts of it, telling me about his feelings of awe as he compared his proofs and Newton's, his experience as he went and looked at the original *Principia* at the Royal Society in London and when he got a replica of Newton's telescope made for himself (which he showed me). His eyes shone as he spoke. It was a truly magical experience.

Peripa's study was lined with books right up to the ceiling. There was also a large table and a bust of Ramanujan – the one he had bought personally so that the minimum number of four was met for the sculptor to make the busts. As he looked at the books, he said that he had no fear of death – his only regret was that the knowledge he had imbibed from all those books would be lost with him and wished there was some way to leave that behind.

I accompanied Peripa when he went grocery shopping. That was another interesting experience. Perima had drawn up a long list – and the items were listed in the order that they were arranged in the grocery shop! So Peripa could start at one end and keep picking up the listed items one after the other, without once having to retrace his steps! By the time we exited the last aisle and reached the cashier, everything on the list was ticked off. It seems that when the shop had been re-organized at one time, Perima had gone and meticulously noted down the changes and started organizing her lists according to the new layout thereafter!

We spent most of the time just conversing. One day, we went for a walk around the university, stopping again at the 57th Street bookshop. Another evening, we went to listen to the open-air concert at the university chapel, and our small group was the cynosure of all eyes. Then we went out for dinner with Peripa's young – and lovely! – Italian collaborator Valeria Ferrari. And Peripa actually thought that everyone at the restaurant was looking at us because the sari I was wearing was very beautiful!

One evening, Peripa played a particular stanza of Gustav Mahler's '*Song of the Earth*', that he said he resonated with. We listened in silence to the German rendering, followed by the English translation for my benefit.

> Whither I go? I go,
> I wander in the mountains,
> I seek rest for my lonely heart!
> I journey to the homeland,
> to my resting-place;
> I shall never again go seeking the far distance.
> My heart is still and awaits its hour!

I found it hard to speak after it ended. I did not know then that it would reverberate unendingly in my head in the coming weeks.

Over dinner one night, Peripa was talking about their plans for the next year. For their 60th wedding anniversary coming up in September 1996, they had already made plans to attend the opera based on Wagner's *Ring Cycle* as it was one of their favourites. They were also hoping to visit India soon, and planned on visiting only Delhi and Bangalore, omitting their traditional stop in Madras. I knew that this was because Savitriakka was not there any more. I told him what my aunt Vidyakka had said to me just a month earlier, that with Savitriakka's passing, not only had she lost a sister but also her connection to Peripa. Somehow she could never talk to Peripa easily, and relied on Savitriakka for all news of Peripa and Perima. Each time Savitriakka spoke to Peripa on the phone, she would call Vidyakka and give her an update, and Vidyakka really looked forward to these conversations. He listened in silence. The next day at breakfast he looked very pre-occupied. After a while, he asked me to repeat exactly what Vidyakka had said. He listened attentively, then nodded saying that is what he had understood. He then said that this would probably change their India plans and they would go to Madras too.

During this Chicago visit, I had a commitment to meet an aunt who also stayed close to the university. But this did not materialize as she was not at home when I called her, and I just left a message on her answering machine. As my visit drew to a close all too soon, Peripa asked whether I could cancel the next part of my itinerary and stay another day. I was to meet my sister-in-law in New Jersey for a day before heading for Houston.

I cannot forget him suggesting that I call her and leave a message that I could not make it, the way I had done with my aunt! I did think of changing to a later flight but that entailed an additional charge of a hundred dollars, which seemed too steep. On the night before I left, we were talking till very late, and continued even after Perima went to bed. Peripa suddenly said that he should have told me that he would take care of the additional amount so that I could have left in the evening instead of the morning, and deeply regretted not having suggested this earlier. Of course, by then it was too late to do anything ... but I was touched.

I signed the visitors' book this time too. As I got ready to leave for the airport, I hugged Perima, and then Peripa. As I stepped back, I saw tears in his eyes ... and mine had welled up too. We could hardly speak. At that point, I really wished I had changed my ticket and delayed my departure by a few hours. As the limo moved away, I looked back and saw both of them still standing together on the kerb. I leaned out and waved ... and saw that they remained standing there watching the limo till it was out of sight. I think he had known that we would not meet again.

***

I returned to Delhi on 16th August, and a few days later Daddy called up to say that Peripa had passed away. Having just met him, this came as a tremendous jolt. On hearing the details, it struck us that he had died as he had lived – strongly independent and on his own terms. He had felt unwell that morning and told Perima that he would drive himself to the university hospital. He added that in case it turned out to be serious, she knew what to do. As the doctor checked him, he was already having a heart attack and was immediately moved to the ICU. Perima was called in. He passed away four hours later. The only indication that he must have been in distress when he reached the hospital was the fact that his car was parked in the handicapped parking slot – something he would normally never do. As we sat there silently, awash with our memories, Daddy felt that it had been a perfect end ... having completed everything that he had wanted to do, and then going without a fuss and without being a burden on anyone – to the extent of driving himself to the hospital.

I got to know much later that Perima 'closed' the visitors' book after Peripa's death since she felt that that era had ended. It turned out that I was the last one to have written in that book. I will always be grateful for that wonderful week in August that I was privileged to spend with them.

When the Chandra Observatory was launched by the space shuttle Columbia in 1999, Perima was there to witness the launch. She had been asked to give a couple of Peripa's personal belongings to be carried on the shuttle to symbolically represent him. One of these was Peripa's pocket-watch, something that was very much a part of him since he always had it on his person and would refer to it during all his lectures to ensure he was keeping to time – he never wore a wristwatch. It was returned to Perima after Columbia returned to earth. Perima gave that pocket-watch to Daddy as a keepsake. Today, it is one of my most treasured possessions.

***

In July 2009, I had gone to Varanasi to watch the total solar eclipse. It was an unbelievable experience. Early morning, as we waited on the banks of the Ganga, with hundreds of thousands of people praying around us and taking a holy dip in the river on the adjacent ghats, the sky was still clouded over since it had rained the previous evening. Miraculously, the clouds blew away just half an hour before totality, giving us a magnificent view of the eclipse in a clear sky over the Ganga. The air filled with the sound of a collective gasp of wonder. An image for a lifetime.

Recently, I chanced upon Peripa's description of the total solar eclipse he had witnessed from the banks of the Pine River in Manitoba in June 1945, written in a letter to his brother Balakrishnan. His sense of awe and his description of the experience were almost completely identical to mine. I suddenly felt closely connected to him once again, across the years, through a shared sense of wonder.

Contributors

Ashok Dorairaja qualified as a chartered accountant and worked with Dunlop India for nearly twenty years, holding various positions in management and finance. Ashok now lives in the Netherlands having earlier lived and worked in India, the UAE, Indonesia, Germany, the UK and Romania. He is a turn-around manager and a corporate director with several organizations in the Netherlands and Romania.

Bharath Dorairaja is currently president of sales and marketing at Thinksoft. Earlier in his career, Bharath created India's first packaged software company, Sonata, in 1986. He has served as president, Cordys Asia, senior vice-president & director, Satyam Computer Services Limited, CEO operations, Baan Infosystems India Limited, and technical director, Sonata Software Limited.

Lalitha Chandrasekhar, Prof. Chandrasekhar's wife, received her BA honours degree in physics in 1930 from Presidency College, Madras and her licentiate in teaching degree in 1931. For a year, she taught at the National High School in Madras. She played the veena and the flute and shared a deep lifelong interest in music with her husband. She celebrated her 100th birthday on 15 October 2010 and continues to live in Chicago. In his Nobel autobiography, Prof. Chandrasekhar says, 'Lalitha's patient understanding, support, and encouragement have been the central facts of my life.'

Malathi Ramanathan, a Ph.D in history from Mumbai University, was a professor in the Department of History, University of Mumbai. She got 'The Teacher of the University' award for the year 1999–2000. Her publications include the book *Sister Subbalakshmi, Social Reformer and Educationist,* and research papers in journals like the *Political Weekly of India, China Report – A journal of East Asian Economic Studies* and *Proceedings of the Indian History Congress.*

Nalini Easwar is a professor of physics at Smith College, in Massachusetts, USA. She is on the executive board of the American Physical Society, a reviewer for the *American Journal of Physics* and serves on the Board of Counsellors at Smith College. Mentored by her, over forty women have gone on to building successful careers at leading laboratories and universities.

Radha Sarma Hegde is an associate professor in the Department of Media, Culture and Communication at New York University. Her research and scholarship is in the area of globalization and gender studies. Previously she taught at Rutgers University, New Jersey.

S. (Purasu) Balakrishnan (1914–1998), younger brother of Professor Chandrasekhar, was a man of two worlds – medicine and literature. He was a fellow of the Royal College of Physicians of Canada and a certified specialist of the American Board of Pediatrics. He retired as professor of paediatrics at Jawaharlal Institute of Postgraduate Medical Education and Research, Pondicherry. He was bilingual in letters and authored eleven books in Tamil and seven in English, and received recognition and awards in both languages. Among his books are a Tamil play titled *Krishnakumari* and in English, *The Gold Bangle and Other Stories* and *Bhagavad Gita and the Nuclear Policy*.

S. Ramanathan, a Ph.D in chemistry from the University of Mumbai, was a research associate at the Federal Institute of Technology in Zurich, Switzerland. During his professional career, he has occupied senior industrial positions in R&D and manufacturing in India and abroad. He is now an independent director on the board of a reputed company.

Shiv Visvanathan is a professor at the Dhirubhai Ambani Institute of Information and Communication Technology at Gandhinagar, India. Earlier, he taught at the Delhi School of Economics and was senior fellow, Center for Study of Developing Societies, Delhi. He is the author of *Organizing for Science* (Oxford University) and *A Carnival for Science* (Oxford University) and has edited *Foul Play: Chronicles of Corruption* (Banyan Books). Shiv has held visiting professorships at Smith, Stanford, Arizona, Goldsmith College, London and Maastricht. He is also a columnist for *Asian Age* and the *New Indian Express*.

Sudha Ramesh has held management positions in IT companies in the United States and India. In the US, she worked for IBM where she developed mathematical and reliability models. In India, she pioneered quality excellence models for the software company Polaris. Sudha is the recipient of many awards for her work in reliability engineering and software quality. She is also a classical Indian dancer and has performed across the world. She is now an independent software quality consultant.

Uma Parameswaran was born in Chennai, studied at Indiana University in the US and later emigrated to Canada. She is a retired professor of English and lives in Winnipeg, Canada. She is the author of several books including the award-winning *What was Always Hers* (short fiction) and *Writing the Diaspora: Essays on Culture and Identity*.

V. Chander graduated in commerce from Madras University, and after an initial stint in finance, his career was focussed on sales and marketing in several leading consumer companies. He is currently a director on the board of a real estate development company in Chennai.

V.H. Ram graduated from Presidency College, Madras after which he specialized in German and French at the University of Madras. He was awarded a Government of India scholarship to study Italian in Italy for two years. He worked with the Bureau of Indian Standards, New Delhi, from where he retired as a director. He has since lived in Chennai, doing freelance translation and editing.

V.S. Mahesh was vice-president (HR) for Taj group of hotels and corporate VP (HR) on the board of the Wipro group. He was on the faculty of the University of Buckingham, England where he was the founder director of the Centre for Service Management. His publications include the *Escorts Book of the Year* (1993), *Thresholds of Motivation: The Corporation as a Nursery for Human Development*. He is now a visiting professor at Cardiff and Buckingham and is a consultant to corporations in management of services and human resources.

Vasanti Ram has been a teacher throughout her professional life. She won a Fulbright scholarship for her graduate studies at the Indiana University, Bloomington, USA. After an MA in English, she started her career as a teacher in Bangalore, and then was a lecturer of English at the Janki Devi Memorial College, University of Delhi. After her retirement, she lives in Chennai with her husband V.H. Ram.

Vidya Shankar (1919–2010), younger sister of Professor Chandrasekhar, was an accomplished veena player and an acclaimed musicologist with a series of publications to her name including *Aesthetic and Scientific Values in Carnatic Music* and *Tyagaraja's Divyanama Keertanas*, the last one having released on her ninetieth birthday in December 2009. She was a recipient of the Sangeet Natak Academy Award. She taught at the Central College of Carnatic Music and at Kalakshetra in Chennai. Her lecture-demonstrations at the annual Music Academy gathering in Chennai spanned over fifty years.

Glossary

Akka: elder sister (Tamil)
Amma: mother (Tamil)
Anna: elder brother (Tamil)
Appa: father (Tamil)
Asamanjam: a dullard; layabout (Tamil)
Athai: paternal aunt, father's sister (Tamil)
Avvaiyar: ancient Tamil poet
Chitappa: paternal uncle, father's younger brother (Tamil)
Ekalavyan (or Eklavya): character in the Mahabharata
Ghat: steps leading down to a river bank
Gurukul: (guru: teacher; kul: extended family) traditional school in India, where students live in close proximity to the teacher
IUCAA: Inter-University Centre for Astronomy and Astrophysics
Kriti: type of musical composition typical to Carnatic music
Mama: maternal uncle, mother's brother (Tamil)
Mami: maternal aunt (Tamil)
Murukku: a south Indian savoury
Periamma, Perima: paternal aunt, father's elder brother's wife (Tamil)
Periappa, Peripa: paternal uncle, father's elder brother (Tamil)

Shashti Abtha Poorthi: 60th birthday, a milestone considered very significant in south India
Sloka: Sanskrit verse / poem
Thyagaraja: legendary 18th century composer of south Indian classical music
Upanayanam: a coming-of-age ritual (thread ceremony) for Brahmin boys
Vanaprasthashram: a later stage of life for a man given to spirituality
Veshti: traditional unstitched cloth (dhoti) worn by men in south India

Acknowledgements

I wish to acknowledge Sanjay Kumar, a true admirer of Chandra, who catalyzed the entire Chandra Vilas family into action – this book would not have happened without his persistence.

On behalf of Prof. Chandrasekhar's family, I extend our sincere gratitude to Dr Kalam for agreeing so readily to write the Foreword to the book. We are deeply honoured by his gesture.

– Radhika Ramnath

Copyright Acknowledgements

The publishers are grateful to the following institutions and organizations for permission to reprint lectures/articles from their publications or collections, in this book:

Bharatiya Vidya Bhavan & Jawaharlal Nehru Memorial Fund

- Astronomy in Science and in Human Culture (S. Chandrasekhar)
  Nehru Memorial Lecture, 1968

Current Science

- The Pursuit of Science: Its Motivations (S. Chandrasekhar)
  Inaugural Lecture - Golden Jubilee celebrations of the Indian Academy of Sciences, Bangalore, 6 February 1985. Published in *Current Science* 54, No. 4, 20 February 1985, pp. 161-69
- Newton and Michelangelo (S. Chandrasekhar)
  Current Science 67, No. 7, 10 October 1994, pp. 497-99

Imperial College Press

- My Everlasting Flame (Lalitha Chandrasekhar)
- Subrahmanyan Chandrasekhar: My Anna (S. Balakrishnan)

S. Chandrasekhar - The Man Behind the Legend, ed. Kameshwar Wali, Imperial College Press, 1997

Macmillan Publishers Ltd.

- Science and Scientific Attitudes (S. Chandrasekhar)
Nature 344, No 6264, 22 March 1990, pp. 285-86

Special Collections Research Center, University of Chicago Library

- Convocation address, Queen's University, Kingston, Ontario, 1991 (S. Chandrasekhar)
- Science in Pre- and Post-independence India (S. Chandrasekhar)

Vikas Publishing House

- Indira Gandhi: Some Recollections (S. Chandrasekhar)
Indira Gandhi: Statesmen, Scholars, Scientists, and Friends Remember, Vikas Publishing House, 1985

Vikram Sarabhai Space Centre

- Know About Black Holes (S. Chandrasekhar)
Talk given at Vikram Sarabhai Space Centre, Thiruvananthapuram, on 30 October 1984.
Published in the in-house journal *Countdown*, March 1985.

Heirs/Estate of Professor Subrahmanyan Chandrasekhar